PRAISE FOR JEREMY HUNT'S *ZERO*

'A real understanding of the NHS's many problems… essential reading for everybody involved in healthcare'

HENRY MARSH, AUTHOR OF *DO NO HARM*

'A thoughtful, serious and well-written book that tackles an immensely important subject'

RACHEL CLARKE, *OBSERVER*

'Humane and often persuasive…I expect that, if his suggestions were generally followed, thousands fewer would die unnecessarily'

CHARLES MOORE, *DAILY TELEGRAPH*

'A deeply moving personal account about what needs to change in the NHS – I wish I had read it when I started out as a doctor'

DAME CLARE GERADA

'A timely, salutary and occasionally contrarian intervention with an honesty and humanity that will rightly shape the NHS for years to come'

LORD SIMON STEVENS,
FORMER CHIEF EXECUTIVE NHS ENGLAND

'A compelling vision of what the NHS, and every other healthcare system in the world, can do to reduce avoidable harm'

CHRIS HOPSON,
FORMER CHIEF EXECUTIVE NHS PROVIDERS

'Readable, honest and sometimes unsettling… a powerful case for transparency and supporting a frontline workforce under huge pressure'

DAME CLARE MARX,
FORMER PRESIDENT OF THE ROYAL COLLEGE OF SURGEONS

CONTENTS

Foreword by Eric Schmidt   vii

Introduction   1

  1   Security Anchor   25
  2   Democracy Champion   53
  3   Tackling Mass Migration   83
  4   Climate and Energy Leader   103
  5   Free Trade Advocate   121
  6   Pandemic Prevention   139
  7   Human Rights Voice   159
  8   The Next Silicon Valley   177
  9   A Global Vocation   205

Letter to Sir Keir Starmer   227
Postscript   231

Notes   235
Image Credits   275
Index   277

FOREWORD

In 1976, when Henry Kissinger served as Secretary of State under Gerald Ford, he travelled to Arizona to deliver a speech entitled 'A Strong Foreign Policy for a Confident America'. The speech was concerned with what Henry perceived as growing pessimism among the American public about the US's role in the world. Public opinion on foreign policy, he remarked, is like a swinging pendulum: 'From over-involvement to a new isolationism; from enthusiasm to disillusionment; and back again.' Today, in the US and across the West – including, notably, in the UK – we find ourselves swinging toward an era of disillusionment.

A 2024 poll commissioned by Ipsos and King's College London is illustrative of this trend. Surveying nearly 24,000 people across 31 countries, respondents were asked to grade whether various countries use their influence for good or for bad in the world. Compared to when the survey was last conducted in 2019, people in most countries viewed US influence on the world stage more favourably. But there was one major exception: the US itself. Americans were much more wary of their country's global role than they were five years ago. The same sentiment was true for the UK. Compared to the rest of the world, the Brits viewed the UK more negatively than they did in 2019. Across many democracies, we are suffering from an epidemic of self-loathing.

Self-criticism, as Henry asserted in the Arizona speech, is inevitable in a democracy – and, I would add, often even productive. But if doubts obscure our collective ability to appreciate a national project – if we 'create an impression of impatience or uncertainty', as he put it – the consequences could be dire. Henry emigrated to the US in 1938 as a Jewish refugee fleeing Nazi persecution in Germany; thirteen of his relatives, including his grandmother and four of his father's sisters, were killed in the Holocaust. The collapse of German democracy forced Henry early in his life to reckon with the fact that democracies can be precious and fragile systems. They can be stripped away at a moment's notice if we forget why they are worth defending.

When I joined Henry on his last trip to China in 2023, we spoke at length about how his visits there had evolved since his first trip in 1971. Over time, he said, our Chinese counterparts had become more self-assured in their engagements. That's no surprise – since 1971, China's GDP has grown nearly 180-fold, from below $100 billion in 1971 to almost $18 trillion as of 2023. Yet it marked a glaring contrast to my conversations with leaders in the West and especially in the US, many of whom have grown more timid, more reticent, and more doubtful over the years. This is true even as America's share of global GDP has hardly declined since 1980. What struck me then, as it had struck me in all our conversations over the decades, was Henry's fundamental insight that power in international relations stems not just from objective capabilities, but from the perception of strength and the willingness to deploy it strategically.

This understanding – that national power is as much about psychology and self-perception as it is about GDP figures or military capabilities – is what makes *Can We Be Great Again?* so timely and profound. As I read Jeremy's careful and personal analysis of

Britain's position in the world order, I was repeatedly reminded of conversations with Henry about how nations can punch above their weight through strategic thinking and calculated diplomacy. Henry would have recognised in Jeremy's work the same clear-eyed realism that he himself brought to international relations, combined with an understanding that excessive pessimism can ultimately become a self-fulfilling prophecy.

The parallels between Britain's situation and America's current crisis of confidence are striking and instructive. Jeremy is unequivocal about Britain's potential for global leadership, even amid a changing world order – and rightly so. As he points out, Britain sits among the top ten most influential countries in the world, and that power can be put to good use. Just look at how the UK has carved its role around AI, the defining technology of our era. It is home to some of the world's most innovative AI research labs, and it has emerged as the global leader for AI safety, having established the first publicly-backed AI Safety Institute and hosted the inaugural global AI Safety Summit. Too often, our public discourse focuses on the threats posed by AI rather than our ability to shape its development in accordance with democratic values. This defensive mindset, this lack of confidence in our ability to lead, and the fixation on mere responses, is precisely what Jeremy identifies as the core challenge facing Britain – and, I would argue, facing America as well.

Despite remaining the world's leading superpower, with unmatched military capabilities, and the world's most dynamic and resilient economy, the US has become increasingly susceptible to a narrative of decline that threatens to reshape our global role. Just as Jeremy identifies a peculiarly British form of declinism, we in America have our own version – a creeping doubt about our ability to lead, innovate, and shape global outcomes. As Jeremy notes, over two thirds of the UK population believe their country is in decline. Similarly, according to Pew Research, 71% of Americans think the US will be less important in the world by 2050. It is remarkable that, in 2024, the American economy was crowned 'the envy of the world' by the *Economist*, outperforming every other developed nation along a number of metrics – and that same year, only around 20% of Americans were satisfied with the direction of the country in Gallup's monthly polls.

The depth of this pessimism, and its striking disconnect from objective measures of national strength and relative well-being, points to a deeper crisis of democratic governance itself. As Jeremy highlights, in 2023 a whopping 83% of Americans, 70% of Brits, 74% of French, and 63% of Germans believed that elected officials don't value what they think. When citizens lose faith in their governments, even world-leading GDP figures and technological achievements ring hollow. Democratic nations must undertake the hard work of rebuilding trust and reinvigorating confidence among their citizens.

If not, the epidemic of self-loathing will continue to fester in distinct ways on either side of the Atlantic. In Britain, as Jeremy astutely observes, it often takes the form of a reflexive self-deprecation about the country's diminished standing in the post-imperial era. In America, it appears as a growing isolationism, a belief that global leadership is too costly or too complex to maintain. Both forms of this crisis are dangerous, not just for our respective nations but for the global order that we helped create and sustain. The world Jeremy describes in these pages is one facing unprecedented challenges: from the rise of authoritarian powers to the existential threat of climate change, from the disruption of supply chains to the emergence of new technologies that will reshape humanity. These seismic shifts demand confident leadership from democratic nations.

Countries like Britain and America, with their deep democratic traditions, innovative capabilities, and extensive diplomatic networks, are uniquely positioned – likely the best positioned – to provide this leadership. But as Jeremy correctly identifies, this can only happen if they reject the temptation to retreat into nostalgic decline or defensive isolationism. The special relationship between our two countries was built not just on shared values and interests, but on a shared confidence in our ability to forge a better world. In the postwar period, this confidence helped build the most successful international order in human history – an order that, as Jeremy notes, has created more freedom and prosperity than any that preceded it. Today, as that order faces growing challenges from all directions – a revanchist Russia, an emboldened China, a turbulent Iran – the need for confident democratic leadership is greater than ever. *Can We Be Great Again?* invites us into that very conversation.

What makes this book particularly valuable is its combination of realism and optimism. Jeremy doesn't shy away from Britain's challenges or limitations, but he also recognises its enduring strengths and influence. This honest assessment is exactly what democratic nations need at this critical moment. In fact, in that same 1976 Arizona speech, Henry Kissinger maintained, 'The optimist is not one who pretends that challenges do not exist – that is escapism. The true optimist has faith in his nation; he believes that challenges are to be mastered – not avoided.' Democratic nations everywhere are facing grave challenges indeed. Now they must master them.

Eric Schmidt, January 2025

If you are just realistic, you become pedestrian […] you will fail. Therefore, you must be able to soar above the reality and say, 'This is also possible.'

LEE KUAN YEW

INTRODUCTION

On Friday, 14 October 2022, I woke up in a comfortable Brussels hotel.

Having tried – and failed – to become Conservative leader for the third time that summer, I was coming to terms with life on the back benches. I had published a book on the NHS and was touring rather enjoyable book festivals. After nearly a decade in the cabinet, I was also trying to be a better dad.

My wife, Lucia, doesn't like flying, so we were on a Eurostar weekend. The night before we had gone out for dinner in the old quarter of Brussels and tried some tasty moules frites with Belgian beer. The next morning, as Lucia was cleaning her teeth, I looked at my phone. A message from an unrecognised number jumped out at me: 'Please can you give me a call. Liz Truss here.'

My first reaction was disbelief. 'Darling,' I shouted out to Lucia, 'I can't believe how naive people think I am. Someone just tried to message me pretending to be Liz Truss. It's probably a radio show host trying a hoax call.' I ignored the message. We went downstairs for breakfast. I had French toast.

Then we went back to our room to get ready for some sightseeing. But on my phone were two more messages. One was from friend and former special adviser Christina Robinson asking if I knew that No. 10 was trying to get in touch. Another text from another unrecognised number asked me to call 'No 10 switch' as the No. 10 switchboard is known.

I was too suspicious to call back on the number given, but managed to find a different one for No. 10 in my contacts. Gingerly, I told the operator that it was probably a hoax, but I had received a message asking me to speak to the prime minister. 'No, it's not a hoax, she does want to speak to you,' the operator replied. 'But I'm afraid she's on the other line, can we call you back?' Within seconds the prime minister magically became available. I was put through.

Liz Truss and I had never been close politically. She had not supported any of my attempts to become leader, nor had I backed her in that summer's bitter leadership contest against Rishi Sunak. But on a personal level, relations had always been cordial. I respected her ballsiness and she was always fun company. When she became Foreign Secretary, she invited me in to pick my brains, a courtesy not always observed by others.

But this was a different and rather shorter conversation. She started by saying things were not sustainable. I cut to the chase: 'So how do you want me to help?' She replied with one word: 'Chancellor.'

Suddenly, the phone in my hand felt so hot that I wanted to drop it. Blimey, I thought, this was not what I was expecting. Unbelievable.

She was at pains to say that I was her first choice. She may have wondered if I had read press speculation that she would offer the job to Sajid Javid. I didn't care in the slightest. I thanked her and asked for half an hour to think about it. Then I put the phone down and leapt in the air. 'I don't believe it! She's offered me Chancellor,' I said to Lucia, who also leapt up and hugged me.

We thought about it in a bit of a daze. The Chancellor has the second most powerful job in government and lives in Downing Street. Being offered the post is an enormous honour. But after September's disastrous 'mini-budget', if ever there was a poisoned chalice it was this. I didn't have much confidence that Liz Truss would last. I could be the shortest-serving Chancellor in history.

On the other hand, as I had learnt from Theresa May, prime ministers in difficulty can survive a long time. Maybe, even in a short time, I could push through some good things for the NHS. It may seem a bit narrow to have been thinking about the NHS at that moment, but for the previous two years I had been chair of the Health and Social Care Select Committee, and health policy had been my focus. I had recently been campaigning to increase the number of doctors and nurses we train for the NHS as part of a new long-term workforce plan. The Treasury had blocked it. If nothing else, perhaps I could push that through?

Then there was the family. It would be an adventure for my kids, aged eight, ten and twelve, to live in one of the most famous addresses in the country, even briefly. But since the rather traumatising junior doctors' strike several years earlier, I had been promising Lucia that I would quit frontline politics. Despite that, I had agreed to be Foreign Secretary, and she had dropped everything (including her job) to support me. I even ran against Boris Johnson to be leader of the party and prime minister, again with her unstinting support. I felt like the political embodiment of St Augustine's prayer, 'Lord make me chaste – but not yet.' So I wondered how Lucia would feel about an even bigger challenge, not least one involving the upheaval of moving to Downing Street.

I needn't have worried. As always, when faced with my biggest challenges, she was all in.

There was one more person to consult. My brother Charlie had been battling cancer. The two of us had just run the London Marathon. Throughout the gruelling twenty-six miles, his right foot had been excruciatingly painful, but with enormous courage he managed to finish it. When I called him, he was thrilled. He said without hesitation that I should accept. We discussed what our late dad would have said. He had been an officer in the navy and had a strong sense of public duty. It wasn't hard to work out.

So after just twenty minutes I called Liz Truss back and accepted.

I had just embarked on the biggest challenge of my life. I had plenty of experience in government but none of my roles had been in an economics or business portfolio. As someone who likes to plan meticulously for all possibilities, I was in a no man's land. I had no idea how it would turn out. But even though I had been brought in to confront chaos and disfunction at the heart of the British state, I never lost my belief in the country. I explore and challenge the reasons why in this book.

We checked out of the hotel and got a taxi to Bruxelles-Midi station. In the train I was called by an official from the Cabinet Office for the standard pre-appointment checks. I had to move to the noisy corridor between carriages so as not to be overheard. The line cut out as we went through the Channel Tunnel, making the hurried process even more farcical.

When I got to my house in Pimlico, the press were already outside the door. An hour later I had changed into a suit and was on my way to Downing Street. After meeting the prime minister in the Cabinet Room, I walked out of No. 10. Media people told me I needed to head through the arch towards the Foreign Office, so journalists could get the pictures they wanted. Then I climbed into a car to travel the princely distance of around two hundred yards to my new office in His Majesty's Treasury.

Treasury officials are the most feared in Whitehall. Fearsomely smart and tough negotiators, they are the part of government whose job is to say no. I once met an African leader who said he called his finance minister 'Dr No', which rather summed it up. But face to face I found them quite different. They were clever, decent, eager to help and loved a good debate. They demonstrated an abundance of the most important quality needed in any civil servant: telling you exactly what they really think. As I sat round the large meeting room table in the Chancellor's office, I found they were surprisingly open to new ideas. It did not feel like a cult adhering to 'Treasury orthodoxy'.

But I also sensed fear. The previous Chancellor had taken the rap for a budget that had gone wrong. The Treasury was in the spotlight as an institution. The economy, for which it was responsible, was teetering on the brink. And their new boss was a complete novice. I decided to put them at their ease. 'Let me start by saying this,' I said. 'We are going to do whatever is right for the country. Even if it means I am a Ken Clarke Chancellor who makes the right decisions but ends up leaving a strong economy for his opponents to inherit.' Little did I know how painfully close to the truth my words would end up.

Our first challenge was a black hole.

A real black hole, not one fabricated to create a political narrative (Rachel Reeves, please note). And it was £72 billion. That equated to more than 2% of GDP – or around 10p on income tax.[1] Sorting it would require 'consolidation' – an economist's euphemism for tax rises and spending cuts. I would end up implementing one of the biggest public finance consolidations ever.

But tough decisions are something the Treasury just gets on with. A well-oiled machine has a tried-and-tested process to guide ministers into making unpalatable choices. Officials introduced me to what they called a 'scorecard'. It was a double-sided piece of A3 paper. On one side was a table detailing about £1 trillion of government spending. On the other side was another table with the equivalent £1 trillion in tax receipts – or actually less, which was why we had a black hole. Every number on the table was billions or millions. If it said '13,502' that was £13.5 billion. Tucked away at the bottom of the back page was the crucial number that really mattered – the gap between forecast tax receipts and forecast spending. For two years my life would revolve around getting that number down.

We also had fiscal rules designed to reassure the markets by limiting borrowing. A £72 billion black hole blew those rules out of the water. Indeed, it had spooked the markets so much that my predecessor had lost his job. I knew we would need radical and painful surgery. Tinkering over the odd hundred million would not cut it. Now I was in the hot seat, it came home to me why people really care about who the Chancellor is and what they do. Budget decisions affect the family finances of every household in the country. People's homes, holidays, childcare and nights out depend on what goes into a budget. You don't want to get the decisions wrong.

I had no idea how we were going to find the £72 billion. But somehow, even before I had a solution, I needed to reassure financial markets and the public that we would act responsibly. So even though the next day was a Saturday, I embarked on a painful set of media interviews. In the *Today* programme green room, I brushed past actress Miriam Margolyes. She went on air to say she had wished me luck but had really wanted to say 'F**k you, you bastard.'

INTRODUCTION

I got a grovelling apology from the BBC, although I later learnt they privately congratulated her. In the grander scheme of things, it was a tiny issue. But it showed how high emotions were running. People were scared.

Then, after the media, it was back to the Treasury for a long weekend's work. Lucia would have to deal with the kids – again.

At that stage we were working on the assumption that the markets needed a new set of plans to be announced in a matter of days. The prime minister had invited me and the family to lunch at Chequers to discuss this in more detail. I thought about what I should advise her. I also had to get my head round some extremely complex financial market issues. I had run a small business, but that was about as close as it got. Around me, however, I had a Treasury A-team of economists with double firsts. So I decided to follow a simple rule: if I didn't understand what they were saying, I would tell them. Luckily, they were always happy to explain – they needed the Chancellor to know what the hell he was doing.

Towards the end of that Saturday, I headed down to my family in Surrey. In the car I decided to call a few ex-Chancellors for their advice. I spoke to Philip Hammond, Sajid Javid and George Osborne. Saj told me I should worry about the high level of volatility in the markets, particularly when they opened on Monday morning. Robert Jenrick messaged me to say the same thing. Like me, they were worried by a mounting sense of chaos following a poorly received press conference the prime minister had given. She had announced a further U-turn – on the mini-budget's corporation tax cut – but the way the announcement came across meant it had backfired.

So I called James Bowler, the top official at the Treasury. His predecessor Tom Scholar had been unceremoniously sacked by my predecessor and James had only become permanent secretary a few days earlier. He looked and sounded like an archetypal mandarin. But if he was nervous about his new responsibilities, it didn't show. Right from the outset – and throughout our time working together – he gave me wise and thoughtful advice.

I asked him if we needed to announce anything first thing on Monday to avoid a market collapse. He said he didn't know but I was asking the right question. So we set up a conference call with the Treasury's chief economist (now deputy governor of the Bank of England) Clare Lombardelli, another phenomenally clever official. Together we concluded we needed to head off the risk of markets plummeting by making an announcement early on Monday. It would say quite simply that we were reversing nearly all the measures in Kwasi Kwarteng's mini-budget. But would the prime minister agree?

Back home, there was big excitement about going to Chequers for lunch. The children dressed up in their Sunday best for their first ever visit to the prime minister's historic country house. In the car my ten-year-old daughter Anna entertained our new team of police protection officers by mimicking different accents, one of her specialities. But I was only half paying attention as my mind raced with all the decisions we now faced. I prepared the arguments I would put to Liz Truss for making an announcement early on the Monday morning – particularly about the risk of market collapse.

On arrival I sat down privately with the prime minister. To her credit, she fully understood the risks we faced. She told me I had absolute freedom to do what was necessary – and she was as good as her word. We agreed that I would make a public statement the next morning and another in Parliament in the afternoon.

The next morning, I sat behind my brand-new Chancellor's desk with a Union flag behind me. I remember feeling absurdly prime ministerial as I announced the reversal of the mini-budget and that 'the United Kingdom will always pay its way'. The statement was well received by the markets. In the House of Commons the reception was more mixed, because the Conservatives were in shock and Labour was baying for blood.

Then on Tuesday came my first cabinet meeting as Chancellor. We still had that enormous black hole, so with five minutes to go I decided to ask every department for cuts, with plans to be delivered by the end of the week. I caught the prime minister for a minute beforehand and told her that was what I needed to do. Again, she did not demur.

I was the last to take my seat around the cabinet table. As I looked around, the hostility was palpable. Many were quite tribal in their allegiance, not just to the Conservative Party but to their wing of the party. I was not 'their kind' of Conservative and there was deep resentment that the mini-budget gamble had misfired. There was no possibility of placating them, so I didn't try. I said that every department would need to send me scenarios of 10% and 15% cuts in their budget. One let out an audible groan and attacked me for appointing four bankers as advisers. I replied that, of all times, now was a moment we needed to get advice from 'outside the blob'.

Back in the Treasury, meeting after meeting took place to bridge the £72 billion hole. After the mini-budget reversals we had got it down to £40 billion, but there was a long way to go to meet our fiscal rules. By the end of Wednesday that week, the scorecard still showed a £10 billion gap. We had raised every invisible tax, cut discretionary spending programmes, imposed painful future cuts on 'unprotected departments' – in other words anything except the NHS and schools. We managed to find more money for these two and a big increase for social care, which I had long worried about. I sent the team away and told them to find £4 billion more tax increases and £4 billion more spending cuts overnight. Nuts.

When I met Conservative backbenchers at the 1922 Committee later that day, I got a surprisingly supportive reception. Maybe they were rallying round in a crisis. Maybe they were grateful for my brutal honesty. More likely, I thought wistfully, it's because I had announced I didn't want to be prime minister. You're never more liked than when you are out of the race.

The next day I had a meeting with Liz Truss. It had been scheduled as a meeting with officials to discuss the Autumn Statement, but a message came through that she wanted to meet me alone. I knew something was up. We went into a boudoir she had created just off the Cabinet Room, where there was space for little more than a sofa and two armchairs.

'I don't think it's sustainable,' she told me for the second time in a week. 'Tiz [Thérèse Coffey] wants me to battle on, but I don't think I can.' She then outlined two options. The first was to trigger a four-week leadership contest. The second was to stay on with a 'unity cabinet' for six months and 'see where we've got to' in the summer.

I knew neither option would satisfy the markets and had thought carefully about what to say. 'Prime Minister,' I told her, 'since the moment you asked me to do this job you have been incredibly brave and acted in the national interest. You changed your Chancellor, reversed totemic policies and sat next to me in Parliament as I announced the changes. Now, if you are going, it's in the national interest that you do it quickly, because otherwise the markets will collapse. You need to make sure your successor is in place within a week. Then your legacy will be that you acted for the best for the country at a time of crisis.' She nodded. We stood up. I gave her an awkward hug. Whatever her mistakes, her decision at that moment was gutsy.

Then I went back to the Treasury to make sure there was no backtracking. I called Graham Brady, chairman of the 1922 Committee, which formally represents all Conservative MPs. I told him the prime minister was about to ask to see him. I asked him to back me up by telling her it really did need to be a quick one-week process if we were to avoid market meltdown. He agreed but said it was up to the party. I advised him not to announce anything until the party had agreed as well. I then called in party chairman Jake Berry for an emergency meeting. I asked two senior Treasury officials to explain to him the impact a prolonged leadership campaign would have on the markets. He was, it is fair to say, deeply suspicious. Part of him may have been wondering about my own motives, so I reiterated that I would not personally put my hat into the ring to be prime minister. He told me he was worried a leadership contest would provoke an election the party could not afford to fight. But he got the point on the markets and agreed to make a few calls to get the party board on side. At 2.30 p.m. the prime minister announced she was resigning, with her successor to be in place within a week.

By Friday lunch – in less than a week – we had turned a £72 billion deficit into a £10 billion surplus. I had, incidentally, rejected the idea of increasing employers' national insurance, even though it was one of the options presented to me – and easier politically than the income tax threshold freezes I extended. More than anything at that moment, I needed the economy to grow, and I knew that raising national insurance would damage investment and job creation. We were, however, helped at the last minute by some changed assumptions on GDP, which meant I was able to add back a small company R & D tax relief that had been pencilled in for a cut. But I still had no idea if I would be Chancellor when the package was announced.

In the event, I stayed for nearly two years. I didn't know Rishi Sunak well and he had no obligation to keep me on, but I had calmed the markets and he decided it was not a time for further changes.

They were the two most remarkable years of my professional life. I didn't get everything right. To my disappointment I left much unfinished business, particularly on reforming welfare, improving public sector productivity and getting taxes down further. But on the positive side of the ledger, the markets stabilised, inflation fell sharply, unemployment stayed low and we comfortably headed off what the Bank of England predicted would be the longest recession in a century.[2]

Nonetheless, the mini-budget – and the circumstances in which I had become Chancellor – were not our country's finest hour, to say the least. Nor has the page been turned under my successor, who has had her own issues when it comes to the confidence of the markets. What makes things worse is that our current economic travails have come after a series of other destabilising events: a once-in-a-century pandemic, the Partygate scandal, an energy crisis and hike in inflation, a messy Brexit process with a hung parliament, and austerity. Some of the pressures have been caused by 'black swan' events like the global financial crisis or Russia's full-scale invasion of Ukraine.

INTRODUCTION

But others have been self-inflicted – by parties of both colours. Whatever the rights or wrongs, my party was in charge during many of them. In the 2024 general election, we paid the price.

One consequence of so much upheaval has been a big decline in our national self-confidence. The number of people saying they are proud of Britain and its history has fallen from 86% to 64%.[3] Over two thirds of the UK population now think the country is in decline, markedly more than in our peers. Nearly one third of young people say they want to move abroad.[4] Many think we are finished as a serious player on the global stage.

The Brexit wars have played a part. Unreconciled Remainers feel unable to be positive about our future outside the EU. Brexiteers are disappointed that the benefits have been slower in coming than promised. I have always believed a successful Brexit is entirely possible – but by no means automatic. What we make of it depends on no one but ourselves. In the meantime, it has left many people feeling uncertain.

The political strategy of the incoming Labour government has also contributed. Like every new government, they set about blaming difficult decisions on their predecessors. But they went about the task with overblown relish, forgetting the real-world consequences of statements made by ministers. That was followed by some anti-business tax rises without any accompanying plan for growth. The result has been a vacuum, alongside a substantial decline in confidence among businesses, consumers and markets.

So should we just give up and go home?

Notwithstanding many mistakes made by governments, including the ones in which I served (and for which I was sometimes responsible), I always felt more positive about our prospects. As

Foreign Secretary, I would point out that we have Europe's biggest defence budget, its top universities and its most influential culture. As Chancellor I would cite figures showing that in the century of AI, we have the world's third largest technology ecosystem after the US and China; or that vaccines and treatments developed in the UK saved more lives in the pandemic than those from any other country; or that, in the age of clean energy, we have one of the largest renewables sectors in Europe and the world's largest wind farms. It was my job to present the UK in the best possible light – but I believed what I was saying.

Was I right?

That is the subject of this book.

Is there a path towards a more prosperous economy that enables us to shape the world as well as be shaped by it? Do we have the firepower to be a major world power alongside prosperity and decent public services at home? To paraphrase the MAGA movement in America, can we be great again?

Donald Trump was the most charismatic and enigmatic world leader I met in my time as Foreign Secretary. Our first encounter was just two days into my new job. It was at the now infamous NATO summit of 2018, when he nearly pulled America out of the alliance. Theresa May introduced me as her new Foreign Secretary, and Trump gripped me with one of his epic man-shakes. 'Heard great things about you,' he said to me. I was not convinced he had heard anything about me at all – but took the compliment.

I assumed he would not be interested in me, my being a mere Foreign Secretary. But in our meetings, he checked me out with his beady eyes, his mind clearly ticking over like the New York property developer he once was. 'Do I go in high or low? What does this guy want? What does he *not* want?' he seemed to be thinking.

A couple of days later we met again, this time at Chequers. The evening before I had done an interview on Fox News in which I had supported Trump's demand that NATO allies should pay more towards the cost of defending Europe. My media minder was worried that I was being too pro-American. 'Foreign Secretary,' he told me gingerly, 'you might want to remember that some British people watch Fox.' But some Americans do too – notably the president himself. And often the best way to reach Trump was to do an interview on his favourite TV station. It got our relationship off to a good start. He greeted me with a big smile at the entrance to Chequers: 'Great job on TV!' Then, in case it went to my head, he added, 'I said to my people I don't know who the hell that guy is but he's doing a great job.'

In a small way, I was about to see the 'special relationship' in action.

In the Great Hall at Chequers, the president and prime minister sat in the centre of a horseshoe of chairs. I sat alongside Theresa May. With us were the respective ambassadors and the president's national security adviser, John Bolton. Theresa was an excellent prime minister in impossible circumstances; but she was not known for her small talk. There were a few awkward silences. What should her new Foreign Secretary do? After a couple of lengthy ones, I sprung into action.

I remembered a meeting with the then Canadian foreign minister, Chrystia Freeland, at the NATO summit two days earlier. She had warned me that brave humanitarian civil defence workers in Syria, known as the White Helmets, were at risk of being butchered by President Assad if he recaptured the south of the country. So I chipped in: 'Mr President, if Assad wins, we need to think about what's going to happen to the White Helmets.'

Cue worried looks from the prime minister. The topic was not in her briefing. She did not like her Foreign Secretary flying solo.

'Are they good guys or bad guys?' Trump asked.

'Good guys,' I replied.

At this point I had firmly come to the end of my knowledge about the White Helmets. However, I was saved by the British ambassador to Washington, Sir Kim Darroch, who passed me a note. It explained that the only way to extract the White Helmets from Syria was through the land border with Israel. The issue was that the Israelis did not allow any Syrians across the border. I dutifully read the contents of the note out.

'The issue is that we cannot get them out without help from the Israelis.'

'Well if they're good guys we should get them out,' said the most powerful man in the world.

Bolton, unlike the president, was totally across the issue. He said he would square off the Israelis. Before the end of lunch he had done just that. Two weeks later, 422 people – 98 White Helmets and their families – were smuggled to safety across the border into Israel. This was the 'special relationship' in action. It was also, for me, a lesson about modern diplomacy that often gets lost among the cocktail parties: occasionally you can get things done that help real people in the real world… albeit with a bit of help from Theresa May's silences. The most treasured possession I have from my time as Foreign Secretary is not a lavish gift from a foreign government but a Syrian builder's helmet.

INTRODUCTION

Author meets President Trump at Chequers: shortly afterwards 98 White Helmets and their families were rescued from Syria

I also learnt from Trump the importance of communication. On another occasion, I asked General John Kelly, briefly his chief of staff, what time the president arrived for work in the Oval Office. 'Just before midday,' he said. 'What on earth is he doing before that?' I asked. Kelly replied he was in his private quarters in the White House, watching Fox and CNN and making comments on social media.

It's easy to take a potshot at the 'leader of the free world' for such an unconventional start to his working day. But think of it another way: he is the first president for a long time who arrives in his office knowing exactly what America is thinking – and with

17

America knowing exactly what he is thinking too. That focus on communication kept his base remarkably loyal, and led directly to his re-election.

Like every leader, Trump has failings, but negativity about Britain is not one of them. He thinks Brexit is a smart move and a 'great thing'.[5] In his first term, he championed a bilateral trade deal between the UK and the US. I was always sceptical that we would be willing to pay the price, particularly to open up our agricultural markets. But in every diplomatic interaction, a trade deal was top of his asks. His enthusiasm to help us make Brexit a success was palpable. The door was and is always open to a different kind of relationship to that intended for the EU or China.

Of course, we should not exaggerate our importance to his – or any – US administration. But how much we are listened to by a superpower depends partly on how much we believe in ourselves. And self-belief has to be based on reality.

So in researching and writing this book, I did something I could not do in office. I spent time looking at the evidence to see whether we can indeed aspire to be a 'great' country. My definition of a great country is one that is capable of shaping the world, and not just being shaped by it. In each chapter, I focus on a different global problem directly impacting on us in the UK. I look at European security following Russia's full-scale invasion of Ukraine and the threat to democratic values posed by the rise of China; I examine the challenge of global migration flows, which have become a huge issue on both sides of the Atlantic; I look at trade, and – given Trump's love of tariffs – ask how we should respond in a new era of mercantilism and protectionism; I also consider the danger to the planet posed by climate change and to our health posed by pandemics, the challenge of protecting human rights in an age of autocracies, and the risk of new technologies getting into the wrong hands.

In each case, I ask how we would want the problem to be addressed or solved, and what contribution – economic, military, scientific or political – Britain can realistically make to achieve that outcome. What influence do we have with friends and what leverage with foes? I then look at whether we have the resources to do so, given the pressures on the public purse, alongside any economic opportunities involved. In short, are we still an important country, and can we afford to be a force for good in the world?

If you polled people in the UK today, only a minority would say playing a more active role on the global stage was a priority. For them, being 'great' means better public services, higher wages and a higher standard of living. But all the issues I consider have a direct impact on everyone's lives – whether it's the taxes we pay to fund the defence budget, the prices in supermarkets, the cost of energy or our ability to avoid lockdowns in pandemics.

Nonetheless, this is not a book about how to address the entirety of the economic challenges we face (something I will come to in my next book). But I do look carefully at the economic implications of every issue. In particular, I look in detail at the UK's budding technology sector, which connects nearly all the issues. Becoming the world's next Silicon Valley would transform both our economic prospects and our ability to solve global challenges, which is why I spend a whole chapter looking at whether that is realistic.

Nor is this a book about me: the Conservatives gave the country too many Chancellors for them all to write autobiographies. But I do draw upon my own experiences. My time in office included four cabinet posts, including the largest spending department and two of the great offices of state, so where relevant I include 'inside the room' anecdotes. But I also include the stories of others, alongside key facts and figures.

I try – although it is not always easy – to maintain perspective. Absorbed as we are in our own problems, it is easy to forget others face equally grave challenges. American democracy is more polarised than ever. The German government has collapsed in the face of profound economic challenges. At the time of writing, France is on its third government in a year and was only able to muster a caretaker government for the Paris Olympics. Far-right parties have won elections in Italy, Austria, the Netherlands and many other European countries. It is not just the UK that has lost its bearings. Rather, we are part of a broader crisis of confidence facing the whole of Western democracy.

Likewise with our economic issues: our growth has stagnated since the global financial crisis. We are facing big challenges when it comes to productivity, worklessness and improving public services. But other countries have their own problems too. In terms of growth, the UK has not been at the bottom of the pack of large economies, but in the middle. We have the sixth largest economy in the world and are forecast to remain in that position for the next fifteen years, perhaps longer. As I demonstrate, our strengths in the fast-growing technology and service industries mean the UK has greater economic potential than many others – if we grasp the opportunity.

After looking at the evidence on each global issue in turn, my conclusion will surprise those used to a daily diet of declinism.

Despite not being a superpower, in every case the UK remains one of the top ten most influential countries on the planet. If you exclude autocracies, we are generally in the top five. Out of the 193 members of the UN, that's not bad going. And while there are costs to any global role, numerous examples from other countries show that helping to solve such issues can make us wealthier too. It is not all over for Britain – far from it. Unless we give up.

But a glorious future is not guaranteed. We now face a stark choice. If we are prepared to take long-term – and often difficult – decisions that strengthen our economy and buttress our influence, we can indeed remain a prosperous and influential player on the world stage. A no doubt bumpy but exciting ride awaits. But if we duck those decisions, irrelevance and possible bankruptcy await. The shadow of Denis Healey going cap in hand to the IMF in 1976 will start to loom larger.

This is not just about the choices made by our leaders. It is also about us. If we continue to wallow in the myth of inevitable decline, it will end up not being a myth. The post-war global order, largely set up by the UK and the US, has created more freedom, more scientific advancement and more prosperity than any that preceded it. Despite many imperfections, it is by far the most successful international order in the history of humanity. If the countries that helped build it are not willing to step up and defend it, who will? Given the extraordinary dangers in the world, every country with influence has an awesome responsibility to use it wisely. If I were French, German, Australian or American I would make the same argument: now is precisely the wrong moment to retreat into our shells. But to avoid that, we will need to rediscover our self-belief.

We also need to be honest with ourselves about the time and effort such an undertaking will involve. All four prime ministers I worked for understood the need for difficult choices. But inside Whitehall, trade-offs are often positioned as short-term, financial choices: do we fund an increase in defence spending or more doctors for the NHS? On a day-to-day basis, such decisions cannot be ducked, but they aren't the whole story either. A grand plan for a country needs to take account of the real sources of sustained prosperity: a safe and stable back yard, a culture of hard work, vibrant entrepreneurialism and innovation flowing from top-notch universities. The real trade-off is not between a strong economy or global influence but between the short and longer term. Smart leaders make sure the longer term gets a look-in. Sir Keir Starmer has promised he will do just that. Let's hope he does.

In 2014, Henry Kissinger published a book called *World Order*. It touches on many of the themes in this one. I met Henry for the first time in the summer of 2018, when I had been Foreign Secretary for only a month. It was in his apartment in New York, the day after I had given my first major speech in the role. He greeted me by saying that he had read the speech, 'but I am afraid I disagree with it'. From that moment, we became firm friends. He came to breakfast with me and my family in No. 11 to mark his hundredth birthday. It was just a few months before he died.

The speech Henry disliked was a hawkish attack on Western weakness in the face of Russian incursions into Georgia and Crimea. It was before Russia's full-scale invasion of Ukraine in 2022, so in some ways it was prescient. Henry was a strong supporter of freedom and democracy, but he also believed that ideas untethered to reality can cause chaos and tragedy. What outcome was I seeking with Russia? Would that be possible without dialogue? Likewise with China. I didn't always agree with Henry, but greatly respected his willingness to ask searching and difficult questions about what was actually possible in complex situations. He knew from bitter experience the cost of getting involved in a war with no exit.

He also strongly supported the alliance between the US and the UK. In many ways he was a natural Remainer but, to the surprise of many, refused to lend his name to those campaigning against Brexit. He told me he worried that the EU was diluting Britain's voice on the international stage. After the referendum, he said Britain should conduct itself on the international stage with 'supreme self-confidence'.

He was right. As the ultimate practitioner of realpolitik, he would have advised the clearest possible focus on our interests alongside hard-headed honesty about the limits of our influence. He understood the connection between political clout and economic strength. But he would never have allowed realism to turn into defeatism. I hope that when you read this book you will conclude, like me, that Britain's decline is neither inevitable nor desirable. The UK just has too much to offer the world. British ambition, ingenuity and pragmatism can make us a global force for good.

1
Security Anchor

Ramatu was just fifteen when ten men with guns broke into her house. She and her family were ordered outside, along with thirty or so of their neighbours. At gunpoint, the rebels then selected six of them, including children. Ramatu was one of them. They were marched up a hill and held face down on concrete slabs. Then the rebels started hacking off their hands or arms, sometimes one side, sometimes both. Ramatu lost her arm. 'And then they walked away,' she later told Human Rights Watch. 'I couldn't even bury my arm.'[1]

This was the bloody work of the Revolutionary United Front, or RUF, whose insurgency in Sierra Leone started in 1991. Their cruelty was notorious – not just amputations but torture, rape and kidnappings. What made their approach even more merciless was the extensive use of child soldiers. Children were 'recruited' by abduction. They were then brutalised, sometimes even forced to go back to their home and murder their own parents, to prevent them from returning home.[2] The weapons they used were funded through the sale of diamonds, which adorned the necks and arms of the wealthy and famous around the world. Most, but not all, were oblivious to the history of the gems, which became known as blood diamonds.

Over the next decade, the civil war in Sierra Leone cost an estimated 75,000 lives. Two million people were turfed out of their homes.[3] Many of the fatalities were civilians, and stories like Ramatu's were commonplace. What sustained the conflict was not ethnic or religious tensions. It was the demand for diamonds. The price was so high that human lives were cheap by comparison.

The Lomé Peace Agreement, signed in July 1999, was intended to be a turning point after years of failed peace talks and ceasefires. Under the deal the RUF agreed to surrender their forces in return for participating in a new unity government. The fragile peace lasted just six months.

As the rest of the world celebrated the new millennium, Sierra Leone slipped back into bloodshed. This time the insurgents had their sights on Freetown, the capital. Meanwhile the ineffective UN mission charged with implementing the peace agreement was losing control. Like the ill-fated UN mission to Rwanda six years earlier, an ignominious retreat loomed.

Then the British army arrived.[4]

The original purpose of Operation Palliser was straightforward: the evacuation of British and other non-combatants. Brigadier David Richards, commanding the British forces in Sierra Leone, decided to stretch the interpretation of his mandate to its limit. His orders were not to put down the rebellion, but simply to do what was necessary to evacuate civilians. But the wording of the mandate was vague, merely charging him to 'support the UN'. That gave him a chance to turn a Nelson-like blind eye to what UN bureaucrats and the British government had intended.

Brigadier David Richards in Sierra Leone

Having been a maverick for many years, what Richards did next should not have surprised his superiors: he made the momentous decision to commit British support to the government of Sierra Leone, promising the country's president that he would personally take command of the war effort and defeat the rebel forces. He knew the risks he was taking, both with the lives of his troops and with his own career. But having heard stories like Ramatu's, he was resolved. Under the cover of a less ambitious operation, he pressed ahead.

Within days most of the six hundred-strong battalion of 1 PARA had joined Richards in Freetown. In order to stave off the expected assault by the rebels, he needed more men. So he stitched together what he called an 'unholy alliance' of UN forces, the Sierra Leonean army and the Kamajor and West Side Boys militias. After some convincing, each group agreed to take part in the operation.

Then he decided to lure the RUF into a trap. A small group of twenty-seven men from the Pathfinder Platoon, or X Platoon, were deployed to a village called Lungi Lol north-east of the airport. They were to act as bait for the rebels, who he thought would not be able to resist attacking them. He was right. After just over a week of waiting, the RUF launched their attack. Hundreds of RUF fighters opened fire in the middle of the night and several hours of intense fighting ensued. It was the British army's first jungle battle for forty years.[5] What the Pathfinders had planned as a two-day mission turned into a sixteen-day ordeal. But in the end the insurgents retreated and the village was saved. For his bravery, Sergeant Steve Heaney was awarded the Military Cross, the UK's third highest military decoration.

After that, Operation Palliser made good progress. The British-supported 'unholy alliance' capitalised on the psychological setback suffered by the rebels and managed to capture RUF leader Foday Sankoh, after which the operation drew to a close. A British military training team of around two hundred people was sent to train and support the Sierra Leonean army through the transition.

But a couple of months later, a patrol of eleven soldiers from the Royal Irish Regiment arrived in the Occra Hills, territory controlled by the West Side Boys. Because the West Side Boys had been part of the 'unholy alliance', the patrol took a detour, to investigate a rumour that they were disarming. The visit, however, turned sour and the gang's leader Foday Kallay ordered the British soldiers to be seized. Outnumbered ten to one, the patrol surrendered.

Their weapons were confiscated, and then they were stripped and taken by canoe to the gang's base in Gberi Bana, fifty miles east of Freetown. They were held in huts made of bamboo and mud. Negotiations for their release started two days later, under the leadership of Lieutenant Colonel Simon Fordham. There was some early success, with the release of five hostages secured in exchange for a satellite phone. But on instructions from above, Fordham started planning a military operation in case the negotiations fell through. Special Forces were deployed to the area, where they set up reconnaissance near the West Side Boys' base. From there they gathered intelligence, watching safely from their position in the dense vegetation.

Things were grim for the captured soldiers. They were beaten and forced to take part in mock executions. But an opportunity arose when at one point Fordham was allowed to see some of the hostages. One of the men saluted and shook hands with him, secretly passing over a sketch of the village layout.

Two weeks later, the negotiations were going nowhere. Fordham became concerned that the captured patrol could be executed at any moment. He got permission to intervene, and on 10 September Operation Barras was launched. At dawn, Special Forces, supported by the Paras, flew in via helicopter. To distract the insurgents from the noise of the choppers, they fired flares. Two helicopters then circled, providing support fire. To prevent the West Side Boys from intervening in the rescue mission at Gberi Bana, the Paras attacked nearby Magbeni as a diversion. This required jumping into a deep swamp. Despite some of the men being wounded by mortar, they were victorious and managed to release civilians being held there. They also regained possession of the patrol's vehicles. Over at Gberi Bana, Special Forces fast-roped down from their helicopters and began looking for the hostages. Reconnaissance troops secured their position and drove the insurgents into the jungle.

All the hostages were safely rescued. The British suffered one fatality, but considering the risks of the mission the cost could have been far higher. In just ninety minutes they delivered a devastating blow to the West Side Boys. Morale among the rebel troops fell to rock bottom and within a couple of months they reluctantly agreed to a ceasefire. On 18 January 2002 President Ahmad Tejan Kabbah declared the civil war in Sierra Leone over. For the last twenty years, the country has been a beacon of stability in West Africa.

The geostrategic implications of the civil war were small. But the two operations showcased the effectiveness of British 'hard power'. They demonstrated the combination of technical skill, resourcefulness and controlled risk-taking for which the UK's armed forces are renowned. It showed the effectiveness of giving full operational independence to troops on the ground, especially with high-quality intelligence and after careful diplomatic groundwork. Many lives were saved, and a small country was given back control of its destiny. It was a textbook example of a successful military intervention, a big and welcome contrast to earlier Western impotence in Rwanda.

But what happened in Sierra Leone was a small-scale operation. It was followed – and indeed overshadowed – by much larger missions involving the British army in Afghanistan and Iraq. In those later conflicts the troops displayed the same courage and professionalism, but the absence of a coherent vision for how peace would work led to ignominious failure. A total of 457 British lives were lost in Afghanistan and 178 in Iraq.[6]

That severely dented British confidence. But the impact on the

US, which led both missions, was even more profound: hesitancy from Barack Obama and Joe Biden over being a 'global policeman' combined with more explicit isolationism from Donald Trump. Nor was the change simply a rejection of neoconservative policies associated with the likes of Donald Rumsfeld: Trump has repeatedly made clear that American commitment to security alliances such as NATO can no longer be taken for granted, at least on current terms. Anyone advocating the overseas deployment of troops – or 'foreign wars' – now has a much more difficult job.

That is a seismic change. NATO is often described as the most successful military alliance in history. It has deterred war and kept peace in Europe since the Second World War. American withdrawal from NATO would be a far bigger threat to peace in Europe than the war in Ukraine. US armed forces are so deeply integrated into the command structures upon which European defence depends that few believe that European forces would be credible on their own.

Trump has regularly complained about European countries free-riding when it comes to defence, so when I was Foreign Secretary, I asked to see the facts. I commissioned advice to find out the answer to what I thought would be a relatively straightforward question. What proportion of European defence was paid for by American taxpayers? No one had asked for the calculation before, and it turned out to be rather difficult to calculate. Defence spending by country is widely available, but not defence spending broken down by the regions where it is deployed. It is not easy, for example, to work out how much of the vast cost of America's nuclear arsenal should be considered as deterring war in Europe.

Initially, I was told it was not possible to give an answer to the question. But I refused to take no for an answer and sent officials back to try again. When they returned, I was taken aback. Foreign Office analysts said they estimated that between one third and one half of the cost of defending Europe is paid for by American taxpayers. The UK may spend more than other large European countries (2.3% of GDP compared to 2.1% in France and Germany) but none of us are spending anything like the 3.4% of GDP being spent by America.[7] Given that the US's GDP is much higher too, the difference in relative commitment is glaring.

Donald Trump has a point. And we should not be surprised, given the unequal commitments involved, that over 40% of Americans believe the US should stay out of world affairs.[8] When Vice President Vance said he didn't really care what happened to Ukraine, many outside America were shocked – but many US voters agreed with him.[9] US support for an indefinite conflict in Ukraine is over. The challenge now is to avoid an outcome that looks like victory for Putin.

Where does that leave Britain? Our armed forces remain a source of great national pride. But with multiple economic challenges, can we afford to increase defence spending in the way we need to if we are to undertake larger operations than Palliser? Trump has been crystal clear about his disdain for a NATO focused on European defence but largely funded by the US. A big increase in European defence spending is his price for staying in NATO – with an even bigger one necessary if he does not. Even if we find the money, and the recent commitment to spend 2.5% of GDP is a start, what about other European allies such as France and Germany? France has a bigger budget deficit than the UK[10] and Germany has a constitutional 'debt brake' preventing large increases in borrowing.[11]

In this chapter, I look at Britain's role at an extremely dangerous moment for European security. Anyone thinking that, since Brexit, the UK has become a minor and somewhat irrelevant power could not be more wrong – we are pivotal to what happens next. With a strategic approach to increased defence spending, we can reduce its cost to the economy by unlocking longer-term growth. And with effective diplomacy we can bring our European NATO allies with us in a way that keeps the US at the heart of the alliance.

But before I explain how, it is important to understand the nature of the threat we now face. Since the turn of the century, the international situation has deteriorated significantly.

In a corner of my office in Parliament is a photograph I will always treasure. It is of a meeting I had with Oleg Gordievsky, a KGB station head in London in the 1980s. He was perhaps the greatest hero of the Cold War era. At enormous personal risk, he fed information of critical significance to the West. At one point, he prevented a misunderstanding that could have led to nuclear war. He also helped Margaret Thatcher understand that Mikhail Gorbachev's reforming instincts were genuine, paving the way for a rapprochement that ultimately led to the fall of the Berlin Wall.

The work he undertook and his eventual extraction from the Soviet Union into Finland is an extraordinary story, told brilliantly in Ben Macintyre's *The Spy and the Traitor*. So when I was Foreign Secretary, I asked to meet Gordievsky. I wanted to thank him in person for his heroism.

The man I met did not disappoint. With quiet wisdom he explained to me that now, just as in the 1980s, the only language opponents of democracy understand is strength. He told me the West should be deeply suspicious of Putin and his motives.

What was most intriguing to me was Gordievsky's motives in taking such an enormous personal risk. Many of the KGB moles in the CIA, like Aldrich Ames, were bribed with money that allowed them to fund lavish lifestyles. But Gordievsky acted not for money but out of principle. He concluded that Soviet ideology was evil and that, ultimately, he believed in freedom. Other KGB officers may well have come to the same conclusion, but they did nothing about it. Soviet traitors were sometimes said to be hooked by their jaws and dipped into acid vats 'pour encourager les autres'. Gordievsky chose to take the risk of such a fate – and indeed was very nearly caught. His courage speaks to his character. But it also demonstrates the compelling power of freedom as an ideal.

Of late, it has become somewhat unfashionable to talk in such terms. Since the fall of the Berlin Wall in 1989, many assumed that democracy and open societies had won the argument and that we could move our focus to other pressing issues. Political scientist Francis Fukuyama even wrote a book in which he described this as 'the end of history'. Since the war in Ukraine, no one now talks in such complacent terms. Fukuyama himself says his argument was misconstrued.

My meeting with Gordievsky took place three years before Putin's full-scale invasion of Ukraine. But he had a message for me that proved prescient. Weakness – whether military, diplomatic or economic – is extremely dangerous because of the vacuum it creates. Peace comes through strength. That insight sits at the heart of any successful deterrence strategy: building military capability not because you want to use it, but to ensure you never will.

Unfortunately for Ukraine, the West was not listening.

Before he launched his full-scale invasion in February 2022, Putin will have carefully considered how the West would respond.

He made his intentions crystal clear in a long, rambling essay seven months earlier: 'I am confident,' he said, tellingly, 'that true sovereignty of Ukraine is possible only in partnership with Russia [...] we are one people.'[12] What he heard back were mixed signals at best. He decided he could get away with it.

Those mixed signals started as early as 2006, when Russian dissident Alexander Litvinenko was lethally poisoned with polonium by Russian agents in London; then, two years later, Russia invaded South Ossetia and Abkhazia in Georgia. Putin might have expected a strong reaction from democratic governments, but instead new administrations in both the UK and the US did not impose a single economic sanction and soon decided to 'reset' relations. They were repaid with Russia's annexation of Crimea in 2014 and multiple cyber-attacks intended to disrupt elections in the US, Germany, France and Ukraine. Just a few sanctions followed – at the same time as orders for ever more Russian oil and gas. Germany even signed up to building Nord Stream 2, to allow even more gas to flow.

There was a rather stronger reaction to the attempted murder of Sergei Skripal in Salisbury in 2018, as a result of which 153 Russian diplomats were expelled from countries around the world. But just weeks after the incident, President Trump congratulated Putin on his re-election, writing on Twitter that 'getting along with Russia (and others) is a good thing, not a bad thing.'[13]

Then, in 2021, came a final disastrous signal. The US, by then led by President Biden, withdrew ignominiously from Kabul in what must count as his most significant foreign policy error. In the biggest Western humiliation since Suez, the US and the UK unnecessarily abandoned Afghanistan to an enemy we had been fighting for nineteen years. If Putin had any lingering doubts about Western impotence, the fall of Kabul will have put his mind at rest. But just in case he had not got the message, the UK and the US went even further: both countries publicly ruled out a military response from NATO if Ukraine were further invaded.[14]

In fairness, our reaction was better after Russia's full-scale invasion started. Aggressive declassification of US and UK intelligence in the immediate build-up prevented Putin sowing a false narrative. Hundreds of billions of dollars of Russian assets were frozen, including nearly half the foreign currency assets of the Central Bank, reportedly nearly $300 billion.[15] The Nord Stream 2 pipeline was cancelled, even though it had already been completed. Britain cancelled 'golden' visas for oligarchs and seized their property in London. Over thirty countries introduced sanctions. But because Russia was able to continue selling its oil and gas to countries like India, its economy shrunk by less than anticipated and indeed is now larger than it was prior to the invasion.[16] In 2024 the World Bank even upgraded Russia to being a 'high income country'.

On the ground, Ukrainians have fought a braver campaign than anyone thought possible. With vital weaponry from the US, the UK and Europe, they have prevented Russia from taking more than 20% of Ukrainian territory.[17] But if Western powers had sent different signals in the first place, the war might never have happened.

Like the First World War, which also stretched over many years in a brutal stalemate, the impact of the Ukraine war has been global. China, having made non-interference in the affairs of other countries a cornerstone of its foreign policy, instead chose to support the Russian invasion with a 'no limits' partnership. It increased imports of Russian oil, made it easier for Russia to conduct financial transactions in renminbi rather than dollars and supplied critical components for weapons and drones.[18] Other countries such as India, South Africa and Brazil might have been expected to support Ukraine because of their own long histories fighting colonial oppression. Instead, they remained studiously neutral, quietly making the most of being able to buy oil and gas at lower prices. Any comfortable assumption that the world would unite against a return to 'might is right' has been shattered.

We are now sliding back to an era in which powerful countries feel at liberty to invade their smaller neighbours with impunity. If Ukraine is seen to lose, it will be the tip of an iceberg. Autocrats in every continent will calculate whether military force can resolve historic grievances and distract attention from domestic problems. The world will then divide into regional power blocks, as China and Russia (and possibly a Trump-led United States) would like, in which smaller countries have to play whatever tune is required by their larger neighbour. Democratic government, the rule of law and respect for individual rights would ultimately revert to being Western cultural traditions rather than rights aspired to by citizens in every corner of the globe.

That process has already started.

The number of conflicts between countries in 2023 was the highest in nearly eighty years. In terms of battle deaths, the three most violent years of recent times have been 2021, 2022 and 2023. In those three years almost 600,000 people have been killed, including more in Ukraine than in any war in Europe since the 1940s.[19] There was a slight decrease in the number of battle-related deaths in 2023, probably because of the end of the bloody Tigray war in Ethiopia.[20] Nevertheless, the rule of law, or what diplomats call the 'international rules-based order', has rarely needed such shoring up.

Number of Battle Deaths, 1989–2023

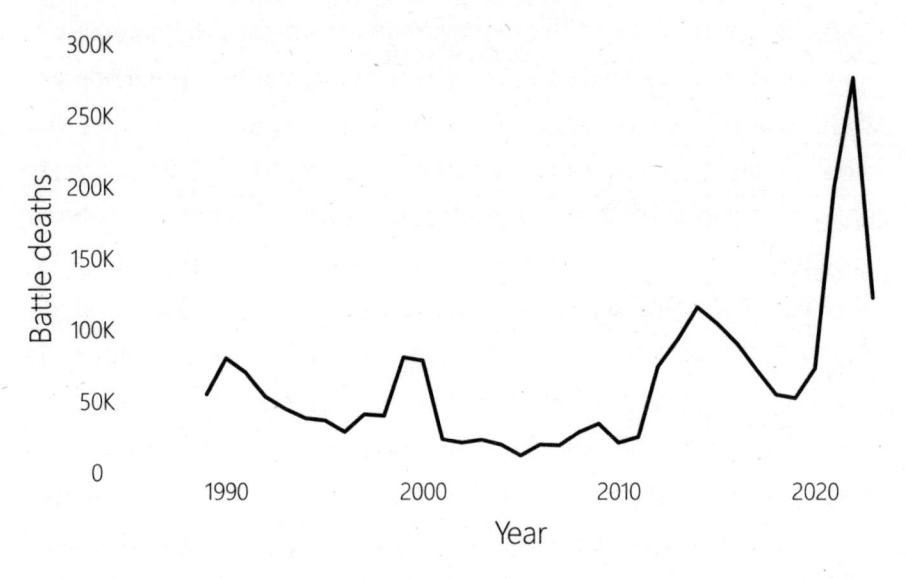

Source: Shawn Davies et al., 'Organized Violence 1989–2023, and the Prevalence of Organized Crime Groups', *Journal of Peace Research* 61, no. 4 (2024): 673–93, https://doi.org/10.1177/00223433241262912

Isolationism has never been an option for Britain, sitting as close as we do to the European continent. So if we are to heed Gordievsky's warning, what is the right approach? Peace does indeed come through strength – that is the point of NATO, which was always set up to prevent rather than prosecute war. But NATO is dependent on the US, so our first objective should be to re-secure American commitment to the alliance. On that most critical of issues, the UK is far from being a bystander.

Britain remains a formidable defence power. For many years, it has spent more on defence than any other European country – or indeed any other NATO country bar the US. That changed, probably

Global Defence Budgets, 2024

Country	Overall Rank	Defence Spending 2024 (current USD billion)
US	1	968
China	2	235
Russia	3	120
Germany	4	86
UK	5	81
India	6	74
Saudi Arabia	7	72
France	8	64
Japan	9	53
South Korea	10	44

Source: 'International Comparisons of Defence Expenditure and Military Personnel', *The Military Balance* 125, no. 1 (2025): 520–25, https://doi.org/10.1080/04597222.2025.2445483

temporarily, in 2024, when the UK was for the first time outspent by Germany.[21] Nonetheless, Britain is considered the pre-eminent European defence power: according to Professor Peter Robertson of the University of Western Australia, at 'military purchasing power parity' – which accounts for differing cost levels between countries not accounted for in the table above – the UK is the eighth biggest spender on defence globally. That puts us in a similar position to France, although well behind the US, China, India and Russia.[22] Outputs matter more than inputs, so in 2019 the Henry Jackson Society went further and ranked the military capabilities of the G20 countries. They looked at defence spending, global reach, nuclear capability, force projection and military-industrial base. On that basis, the UK's military might was ranked third greatest globally, slightly ahead of China and France.[23] If these scores were recalculated today, China's recent increases in defence spending would surely mean that it has overtaken the UK. But Britain would still sit alongside France as having the best-equipped and most battle-ready forces in Europe, among the most formidable of any democracy after the US.

The UK armed forces generally score well in terms of how up to date much of their equipment is – such as the Starstreak missiles the army has been supplying to Ukraine for short-range air defence. In the case of the RAF, we have Storm Shadow missiles and the Lockheed Martin F-35B Lightning II planes, some of the most lethal and technically advanced fighter jets in service. The Royal Navy has two relatively new aircraft carriers, and its *Astute*-class submarines are considered by many to be some of the best attack subs. Those capabilities are given strong support by two of the most highly rated special forces units in the world, the SAS and SBS. They in turn are backed up by the UK's three intelligence services, MI5, MI6 and GCHQ, also considered top notch.

Britain also rates highly on less tangible factors that also matter in any assessment of military capability. These include levels of discipline, quality of training, technological capability and battle-readiness. As Russia has found out to its cost in Ukraine, such intangibles can matter more than sheer numbers. Iraq and Afghanistan may not have ended how we would have hoped, but in neither conflict were British or American troops defeated on the battlefield. Both conflicts have given the army a high degree of combat-readiness and a good understanding of counterterrorism. That professionalism is recognised by more than a hundred countries who turn to the UK to train their own military.[24]

But having a strong military is of no use if you aren't prepared to use it. And perhaps the biggest reason the UK remains a leading defence power is that we have shown we are indeed prepared to use the capabilities we have. Sierra Leone, Bosnia, Kosovo, Afghanistan and Iraq have all shown us to be one of the few countries around the globe able to get parliamentary authority to project force in defence of democratic values. Prime ministers can use what is called the 'royal prerogative' to enter a military conflict without prior parliamentary approval and have shown themselves willing to do so. They are usually (but not always) able to win votes they need to in Parliament. That sets us apart more than we sometimes realise.

That willingness to project force has been amply demonstrated in the Ukraine war. Even though there have formally been no British 'boots on the ground', the UK supplied NLAW anti-tank missiles even before the full invasion. It was the first country to confirm it would supply main battle tanks, the Challenger 2s.[25] It was the first to supply cruise missiles and the first to conclude a long-term security agreement.[26] Perhaps even more significantly, its vocal and visible support for Ukraine has had a major impact on galvanising other allies. My last act as Chancellor was to persuade my G7 finance minister colleagues to support a $50-billion facility for Ukraine secured on Russian sovereign assets, an agreement supported by my successor. Walking through Kyiv, it is impossible not to be moved by the sight of street vendors selling the Ukrainian flag intertwined with the Union Jack.

But everything has to be paid for, as all Chancellors understand. British taxpayers fund the armed forces generously, giving them a higher proportion of the country's GDP than many similar (i.e. G7/

G20) countries. That money is then, by definition, not available to fund other public services – such as the NHS – even though they are a higher priority for many voters. That can be tricky politically, because as Chancellor you are expected to produce budgets that are 'popular', especially ahead of an election. What makes it a bigger challenge still is that even current levels of funding are not sufficient for what we expect the armed forces to deliver. We may have the foundations of a superb military but the changing international situation means it now urgently needs an upgrade. That will be expensive.

The first area that needs looking at is size. Personnel numbers are never the definitive metric for military strength – no one considers North Korea a match for the US, even though their active personnel numbers are similar. But even in an age of technology, size does matter – and thirty-four countries now have more military personnel than the UK. At around 70,000 troops and just one deployable division at most, our army has now fallen to its smallest since the pre-Napoleonic era.[27] Indeed it is already smaller than the armies of major NATO allies, such as France[28] and Italy[29] – and is only just bigger than Germany's army.[30] Furthermore, its ability to move quickly and safely has been undermined by procurement problems, with the much-needed upgrade to Warrior armoured fighting vehicles and the new Ajax armoured personnel carriers delayed. As a result, the UK is reported to be halving its presence in Estonia – even though the latter is a NATO member sitting right on the frontline with Russia.

When it comes to the Royal Navy, there are equally serious issues. The two new carriers are extremely impressive, but we appear to have bet the farm on them. Because they were so expensive, they will only have twelve planes each, not the thirty-six they are designed for.[31]

And these will only have a limited range, because the navy has no mid-air refuelling capability. The new carriers also lack anti-missile self-defence capability, even though they will soon need to be able to deal with attacks from the now technologically feasible long-range anti-ship missiles. This is particularly risky, because their size and prestige makes them prime targets. As a result, they need substantial protection from other ships. The result is that after assigning two destroyers and two frigates to protect each of them,[32] the navy is left with only nine warships[33] – of whom many could be undergoing maintenance. A navy that only has a quarter of the warships it had during the Falklands War feels very underpowered.[34]

The RAF too has vulnerabilities. Its total number of fighter jets is declining, down from 210 manned combat aircraft in 2007 to just 172 in 2024, with around a fifth out of service,[35] and our anti-missile defences cannot counter the precision missile attacks which have had a devastating impact in Ukraine. That conflict has also led to a dwindling of our munition stocks to worryingly low levels, something I had to address with emergency funding in my 2024 budget.

These weaknesses across our services lead to real concerns about the UK's ability to operate independently of our allies. We generally try to make a virtue of this by saying our approach is 'allied by design'.[36] It is, of course, sensible to develop interoperability with other partners through alliances such as NATO and AUKUS, but the independent projection of power is vital, not least given that allies are not always predictable. Many worry the UK lacks such capability, at least beyond smaller conflicts.

But perhaps the biggest challenge is new technology. Tanks have proved far less useful than predicted to either side in Ukraine, because they are held at bay by hundreds of inexpensive drones continuously in the air. The Russian Black Sea fleet has been holed up in Novorossiysk, far away from Ukraine, after spectacular attacks on ships such as the *Moskva*. Russia's MiG and Sukhoi jet fighters can be downed relatively easily by high-tech surface-to-air missiles. Autonomous drones, crewless seaborne missiles, cyber and, increasingly, space capabilities are transforming the way modern battles are fought. Much of this is driven by cost: an F-35 jet costs around $100 million, compared to $250,000 or less for a munition drone, and an aircraft carrier costs up to $13 billion, compared to just $7.5 million for a Saildrone Surveyor.[37]

The UK has impressive technological capabilities, particularly when it comes to high-end military drone manufacturing. But the respected defence think tank RUSI fears that the UK is being left behind. 'Basic areas of the national security and defence landscape are out of date and risk going backwards in terms of the curve of technological advancements,' it says. 'There is a cognitive dissonance between officials who live in a world of cloud, AI, biometrics, data analytics and augmented reality, yet return to their Whitehall desk to deliver programmes that are not able to fully embrace the latest technologies.'[38]

Some might ask whether such deficiencies matter if you have a nuclear deterrent. Our Trident programme, due to be replaced by the new *Dreadnought* submarines, is a vital part of the UK's defence capability. Unlike the French nuclear deterrent it is fully committed to NATO, meaning that if US commitment weakened, it would become Europe's nuclear umbrella. It is also extremely expensive, taking up nearly one fifth of the UK defence budget.[39] But while nuclear weapons have so far prevented *nuclear* war between similarly armed opponents, they may not prevent *any* war. Either side may gamble that, provided their home territory is not threatened, the other will not escalate a conflict to nuclear. And they may still be willing to risk conventional war or use tactical nuclear weapons on third party territory, as Russia has threatened to do in Ukraine. Nuclear deterrence would then have worked in the opposite way to that intended: deterring us from defending a free country, but not deterring an aggressor from invading it.

Tackling such issues will be expensive. But if we want NATO to continue as the cornerstone of European security, we don't have a choice. Trump has made it clear he expects European allies to spend up to 5% of GDP on defence, far more than the current 2% of GDP benchmark (which nearly one third of members are still not doing[40]). He has publicly questioned whether the US would come to the defence of a European ally not spending their fair share. He may well settle for something closer to the 3.4% of GDP spent by the US – but that would represent a near-doubling of defence spending by European NATO countries.

Securing US commitment to NATO was the main reason why, as Chancellor, I fought hard to increase defence spending. With Rishi Sunak's support, we announced a commitment to spend 2.5% of our GDP on defence by 2030. Sir Keir Starmer initially cancelled the plan and then wisely accepted it, even bringing the increase forward to 2027 (funded by a painful reduction to the aid budget). That was the right decision, but can only be the first step.

The sleeper train slowly rumbled across the Polish–Ukrainian border in the middle of the night. I was on an undercover visit to Kyiv, by far the riskiest trip I made as Chancellor. I had a small team with me. For security reasons, no one in the media had been told.

Mobile phones and computers were left in Poland in case GPS signals were tracked. With its basic facilities, the train reminded me of backpacking through China in the 1980s. But I was intrigued to see that previous occupants had included presidents Biden and Macron, as well as Boris Johnson. I wondered if, like us, they had stopped at the last McDonald's in Poland to fill up with comfort food before the overnight journey.

My mission was simple: after nearly two years of pressing the case for more defence spending in Whitehall, I had finally got agreement to increase it to 2.5% of GDP by 2030. It was a significant increase – £75 billion more over six years.[41] Now, after Rishi Sunak announced the new policy in Poland, I was to travel on to Ukraine and brief President Volodymyr Zelensky on what it meant for the war against Russia.

Author with President Zelensky in Kyiv in April 2024 to discuss increased UK defence spending

In Kyiv it was raining. We were ushered into armoured cars to take us to the embassy, where I was given a military briefing. The professionalism of the army officers was inspiring, but the news was bad. Ukraine was, as their finance minister Serhiy Marchenko told me later that day, on the brink. Russian troops were massing north of Kharkiv, Ukraine's second biggest city, and could attack within the month.

Then it was off to meet the president. In my books Zelensky is probably the bravest man on the planet. He has survived reportedly dozens of assassination attempts,[42] one by his own security guards, who were arrested just in time. In person, he was calm, softly spoken and – like every strong leader I have met – crystal clear about what he needs. How do you survive as a hunted man for two years, and still manage to pop up in Washington, London, Paris and Berlin, I wondered.

As I walked through the presidential palace, I noted sandbags piled up in the vast corridors with their high ceilings. Then we were ushered in. After handshakes and photos, we got down to business. I told him about our 2.5% defence commitment and its implications for Ukraine: if matched by other European countries it would mean an extra $172 billion spent on European defence, much of which would find its way to Ukraine. He listened carefully, asked searching questions and spoke honestly about the military challenges he faced. As we left, I mentioned that our family had a Ukrainian nanny and it happened to be her birthday. He wrote her a birthday message in Ukrainian which she translated for me the next day: 'I hope you can come back to your homeland if we win.' I noted the 'if'.

After meetings with the prime minister and finance minister, I headed back out of Ukraine on the overnight train. I had a chilli vodka nightcap with my team before turning in, which one of them, a Royal Navy officer seconded to the Treasury, had handily brought with her. When we arrived in Poland we dashed back to the same McDonald's for breakfast. The woman serving us looked startled and asked me, in English, 'Are you a celebrity?' She had lived in Britain for nineteen years and couldn't quite put a name to the face. The strange triviality of politics rather grated with the plight of a country fighting for its survival.

Finding the resources needed to prevent further wars or invasions in Europe will be the most difficult decision facing finance ministers across the continent in the next decade. For the UK, an increase in defence spending from that currently planned to the US level of 3.4% of GDP would cost nearly £30 billion a year at today's prices.[43] If that happened in one go (which it would not in practice) it would amount to around four pence in the pound on income tax.[44] So is there a way to turn the money we are going to have to spend anyway into economic benefits that help to pay for it? The answer is yes.

The short-term financial pressures created by such a substantial increase cannot be ducked. But if a staged expansion of defence spending happens as part of an economic plan – and not just a military one – it could be transformative. Because much of the new investment will be in technology, there is a golden opportunity to strengthen Britain's place as a European tech hub. Indeed, that is exactly how Silicon Valley got off the ground in the 1950s. Not just the US, but Israel and Taiwan also show how smart defence investment can nurture a thriving civilian technology sector, generating huge wealth for the economy. I look at the broader opportunity for our tech sector in a later chapter, but when it comes to defence, why not use a necessary increase in spending to help turn the UK into the world's next Silicon Valley? It would then be part of the solution to our economic challenges rather than simply making them worse.

To do so we would need to make big changes. In particular, we would need to overhaul our approach to defence procurement so that additional funding flows to university spin-outs as much as to the big contractors. The US has done this successfully by setting up organisations like DARPA and the Defense Innovation Unit. The DIU spends around $1 billion every year backing tech start-ups which are developing innovations that help the US armed forces. The prospect of defence contracts means those seed investments then attract a wall of private equity backing. What worked in the original Silicon Valley continues to do so today – and could easily do so in the UK. It is an argument I will return to later, because any international engagement by Britain should be positive rather than negative for our economy.

In the end, though, this is less about creating wealth than preventing war. For all the talk of decline, the UK has more influence on the future of European security than any other country on the continent. An even bigger strategic imperative than avoiding a Russian 'win' in Ukraine is the preservation of the NATO alliance with the US at its heart. I judged it the single most important foreign policy objective when I was Foreign Secretary – and if it was true in 2019, it is doubly so today.

It is also something we can make happen. As Europe's leading defence power, a decision to raise defence spending to 3% or more of GDP would have a significant knock-on impact. When, at the 2014 NATO summit in Newport, David Cameron led the charge to secure a commitment from all NATO members to spend 2% of GDP on defence within a decade,[45] the UK was one of just three member countries to meet the target. Now twenty-three out of thirty-two NATO countries meet it.[46] Because of the UK's credibility on defence issues, others follow our lead. The result is that nearly $400 billion is being spent on European defence every year.[47]

Likewise this time. When Trump demands that European NATO countries spend more on defence, other European countries will watch carefully how Britain reacts. However browbeaten and down in the dumps we may feel as a country, we should not underestimate the defining influence the UK has on this most critical of issues. If we bite the bullet, there is every chance others will too. The result will be a reinvigorated NATO with an infinitely better chance of deterring potential aggressors and avoiding war. And although it is primarily a security issue, when it comes to securing economic growth, the most important thing we can do is prevent conflict.

I remembered that visit to Ukraine when we lost the general election just a few months later. It was such a tight race in my own seat that I only held on by 891 votes. When the result was announced, I gave a short speech, which concluded with a mention of Ukraine:

'Finally, a message to [...] my children, who I sincerely hope are asleep now. This may seem like a tough day for our family as we move out of Downing Street, but it isn't. We are incredibly lucky to live in a country where decisions like this are made not by bombs or bullets but by thousands of ordinary citizens peacefully placing crosses in boxes on bits of paper. Brave Ukrainians are dying every day to defend their right to do what we did yesterday, so we must never take it for granted. Don't be sad – this is the magic of democracy.'

If we believe in the magic of democracy, the last thing we should do is reduce our commitment to defend it. With a dangerous autocrat on our doorstep, our strategic objective must be a stronger NATO that is better at deterring aggression than it has been of late. That is a lesson which extends beyond Europe to democracies such as Australia, Japan and South Korea. Like us, they need to decide whether to invest individually or collectively as part of a US-led umbrella. It doesn't take long to work out which will be taken more seriously by our opponents.

Author meeting Oleg Gordievksy in 2019

Peace does not come for free, but the alternative is infinitely more expensive. And money alone won't solve the problem. We need to rediscover self-belief in Britain and in other democracies whose way of life is at risk. The security threats we face today are grave, but no more so than previously with the Soviet Union or Nazi Germany. Between them, the large and wealthy democracies account for half the world's military strength and half the world's GDP. When we operate individually, we can be picked off. But when we work together – generally with the UK near the front of the pack – our shared commitment to freedom and democracy can become an unbreakable bond. That is greatly underestimated by our opponents. Whatever the strains the western alliance is under at the moment, we should not underestimate that inner strength ourselves.

In March 2025 Oleg Gordievsky passed away. Unlike most of us, he knew what it meant to risk your life for an ideal. He believed, as we saw, that peace comes through strength. This time we must listen.

2

Democracy Champion

It was my first visit to China as Foreign Secretary. I had only been in the job for a month and was a little nervous.

At the first formal meeting, I sat in the centre of a long table, flanked by my advisors. Opposite me was my counterpart, Foreign Minister Wang Yi, surrounded by his staff. At the head of the table were the two national flags fanned out side by side. At the other end, a bank of TV cameras was there to record the opening remarks. I had come prepared. Not only did I have my Foreign Office script, but I also had some ideas of my own to break the ice. I was going to mention that my wife was Chinese, and that Wang and I both spoke Japanese (he was formerly Chinese ambassador to Tokyo).

But when I opened my mouth, the two icebreakers muddled into one. 'I am delighted to be here, partly because my wife is Japanese,' I blurted out. I realised immediately I had made a terrible faux pas. But perhaps the media had already left? I anxiously edged my head round to check if they were still at the end of the table. A barrage of camera flashes told me I had no such luck.

'I don't think it will be the main story from the meeting,' my Foreign Office media adviser told me somewhat optimistically. I was more worried about my wife's reaction than the public one. She was going to be front page news. I desperately wanted to speak to her before the media onslaught. But it was 3 a.m. in London, so she didn't answer her phone. When I finally got through several hours later, she cheerily greeted me with 'konnichiwa'. Relieved, I remembered that her sense of humour was one of the main reasons I fell for her all those years ago.

Politicians dread the way unexpected banana skins can intrude into matters of state. But at that moment there was no time to fret, because straight away I had to wrestle with a much less trivial issue: how to broach our concerns about the erosion of democratic rights

Author with Chinese Foreign Minister Wang Yi. Moments earlier I had made a terrible gaffe.

in Hong Kong. The meeting was two years before the major crackdown of 2020, but even then there were plenty of warning signs.[1]

I knew any discussions on human rights issues would be prickly. By contrast, there was always great willingness to engage on business and trade issues. The calculation from my perspective was whether there was any point in bringing up more difficult issues when the Chinese government neither cared what we thought nor even recognised our right to discuss them. Was a certain loss of political capital worth a far from certain gain?

I felt it was. Chinese citizens, after all, cannot talk to their rulers about such matters. But as a visiting member of a foreign government, you have access at the highest levels that ordinary citizens can only dream of. I used to imagine myself meeting a dissident after I had left government. I wondered what I would say if I was asked whether I had 'done something' when I could. I also believed, perhaps idealistically, that if we were going to forge a constructive relationship with a major power like China, we needed to discuss areas of disagreement openly rather than gloss over them. So I made sure that they were on the list to discuss.

But just as it was my default position to raise such concerns, it was China's to shut them down. Every time I raised them, I got a formulaic response. The Chinese assumed we were just going through the motions, putting a tick in a box so we could tell a domestic audience we had 'tried'. They didn't think we actually cared about their replies. Sometimes they were right, but not always.

So we went through predictable and rather ritual exchanges. Tellingly, though, Wang did ask me not to raise awkward issues publicly in our joint press conference. His seemingly innocuous request was another part of China's approach: acquiesce to meaningless discussions in private but close down debate in public. That way inconvenient issues gradually get shut out of the narrative and lose their salience. I did, however, agree to his request. I knew that if I didn't bring such issues up at the press conference, they would be raised anyway by British journalists. Having a press you can't control can serve a useful diplomatic purpose.

The press pack did precisely as I expected, not that it really made any difference. We then moved on to a formal lunch hosted by the foreign ministry. It was another curious occasion, at least from a Western point of view. Although twenty people sat round a table, the only two who spoke were Wang and I. We both had interpreters, so every point took twice as long to make. The result was an awkward dialogue, neither formal nor informal. It was somewhat more free-flowing than the earlier meeting, because we had both got through the main issues we wanted to raise earlier. But with so many eyes and ears hanging on every word, there was no chance for the chemistry-building that is also important in diplomacy.

Perhaps that was the intention. Most foreign ministers exchange mobile numbers to allow the easy exchange of messages without the rigmarole of official channels. Wang was the only one I met who did not. When I asked him for his number, he looked rather astonished and told me he didn't have a mobile phone. I felt like a barbarian kept at the gate.

But then something happened that made me realise that raising awkward issues was not totally pointless. The next item in my programme was described – with no detail attached – as a 'meeting at British ambassador's residence'. It was an unusual event that had been arranged by ambassador Dame Barbara Woodward. She is a smart, principled and highly capable diplomat who is now the UK's ambassador to the UN. For reasons that soon became clear she wanted the purpose of the meeting to be secret. Hence the mysterious diary entry.

I was about to spend time with some very brave people.

Barbara had arranged for me to meet Wang Qiaoling, a human rights lawyer, and Li Wenzu, Wang Yu and Xu Yan – three women whose husbands had been detained for representing political dissidents in the Chinese legal system. Li Wenzu told me it was three years since she had last seen her husband, Wang Quanzhang. Wang was a human rights lawyer and co-founder of the campaigning organisation Chinese Urgent Action Working Group. He had represented Falun Gong practitioners, political campaigners and victims of land seizure, among others. That work had put a target on his back and three years earlier he had been detained by police in Shandong province.[2] His detention was part of a wider crackdown on human rights activists called 'the 709 crackdown', named as such because it began on 9 July 2015.

For the first six months, Wang's fate was largely unknown. In January 2016, it came to light that he had been officially arrested for 'subversion of state power'. For nearly three years he remained in pre-trial detention in Tianjin, not able to see his wife, their young son, or even his lawyer.[3] Li and Wang Qiaoling had marched a hundred kilometres from Beijing to Tianjin, home of the No. 2 Detention Centre where they believed he was being held.[4] But despite their exertions, they had no idea if he was actually inside. They didn't even know if he was alive.

When I heard their stories, I felt humbled by their courage. There was something awe-inspiring about people who just weren't prepared to accept unfair and untrammelled state power. For them, simply coming to the British embassy was an act of bravery – and something that would probably not be possible today. Would I be as brave?

There was, however, something I could do from my ivory tower. The next meeting in the schedule was with someone even more important than the foreign minister. I set off to meet the Chinese premier, Li Keqiang.

Li was second only to President Xi Jinping in seniority. For someone so important, he always came across as a modest and thoughtful man. He listened intently and courteously to the points I made. His replies were considered. With leaders like this, you began to understand why China embarked on its phenomenally successful reform programme. It was time to make the most of my privileged access, so I made my earlier secret meeting public. I raised Wang Quanzhang's case and those of the other human rights lawyers. Without rancour, he said he would look into the issue. His officials looked rather less relaxed and furiously took notes. I didn't expect anything to change, but at least the Chinese authorities knew that the world outside cared about what happened to these courageous political prisoners.

On other occasions I was heard out less politely. Three years earlier, in 2016, I had been invited to China to meet Deputy Premier Liu Yandong, the most senior woman in the country. I was Health Secretary, and responsible for the British side of something called the 'People to People's Dialogue' with China, an annual meeting designed to promote cultural links. The setting for a private dinner the night before was lavish: a banquet on an island in the middle of an ornamental lake in Beijing's historic Forbidden City. Liu was generous with her hospitality. Although she often stuck to formulaic responses, she too was unfailingly polite. She sometimes had a slight twinkle in her eye which revealed, I suspected, a rather warm person underneath. But as we settled into a magnificent eleven-course banquet, I knew there would be less warmth ahead. I had decided that I would raise the case of Liu Xiaobo, a prominent human rights defender who had been imprisoned for six years for campaigning for multi-party democracy. To China's fury, he was awarded the Nobel Peace Prize while in prison.

As usual, we had interpreters doing consecutive translation, so progress in the discussions was frustratingly slow. I found myself unable to get onto the topic of Liu Xiaobo until we reached the eighth course. When I did, the conviviality vanished. The warm night air suddenly began to feel oppressive as the Chinese education minister launched into a tirade. I was obviously a young and inexperienced minister, he said. I should realise that if I insisted on raising such issues we would soon find Chinese students going to the US or Australia rather than the UK. He hoped I would have the 'wisdom' not to raise those issues in public the next day. I was told later that he said even stronger things which the interpreter didn't feel she could translate. Deputy Premier Liu remained gracious and unfazed throughout the exchanges. Was she a little uncomfortable or was it part of a good cop, bad cop routine? I never found out.

Liu Xiaobo died of cancer two years later, still in prison. But Wang Quanzhang's story ended more positively. He was one of the last of more than two hundred people detained during the '709 crackdown' to be given a trial. It happened a few months after I raised his case.[5] He was convicted of 'subversion' and sentenced to four years and six months in prison. He was finally released in April 2020, having served much of his sentence before his trial. He was met by his wife in the apartment they shared with their son, who had transformed from a toddler into an excitable six-year-old. 'Daddy, we're having dumplings for tea,' he shouted before his father scooped him up for a hug.[6] Freedom of a sort – although he is still under constant surveillance and facing daily harassment.[7]

China's strategy never changed: politeness in private but 'wolf warrior' aggression from its diplomats if challenged in public. I experienced the latter in July 2019, when I told a BBC interviewer there would be consequences if people lost their freedoms in Hong Kong, not least because it would be a breach of the Sino-British Joint Declaration of 1984. The result was instant, confected fury. My face was plastered over newspapers in China as public enemy number one. If it was meant to intimidate me, it didn't work, because I wasn't even aware that it had happened. I was right in the middle of the 2019 Conservative Party leadership contest and had other things on my mind. But Chinese friends later told me to avoid travelling to the country.

Over the decade in which I was having exchanges with Chinese government officials, the tone gradually hardened. Initially, as long as there was no intention to humiliate, your counterpart would listen attentively. Sometimes they would hint at some understanding or agreement. 'Be patient with us, because China is at a different stage of its development,' they would say. Or perhaps, 'We want Chinese people to have social and political rights too. But for the moment we are prioritising economic ones.' But after Xi became leader, that started to change. Any suggestion that China was on the same path as developed countries was replaced with a belief that China was on a different – and superior – path. Xi then told Biden that democracy and human rights are now one of four 'red lines' on which China will allow no challenge.[8] Its spectacular growth, alongside Western countries' domestic travails, has given Chinese leaders – and many Chinese citizens – a striking new self-confidence, which extends well beyond economic policy. As Xi told Biden, 'Democracies cannot be sustained in the twenty-first century. Autocracies will run the world [...] Things are changing so rapidly. Democracies require a consensus, and it takes time, and you don't have the time.'[9]

The result is that once again the world finds itself in a struggle between democracy and autocracy. But whereas in the last century the outcome depended on military might, this time it is more likely to be decided by economic might. That struggle has been put into sharp focus by America's re-election of a president with long-standing and vocal concerns about the rise of China. For Trump, though, the issue is not so much about values as about strength, especially economic strength. As he put it to me when we first met at Chequers, how on earth have they managed to become a superpower without a shot being fired? Hence his utter determination to make sure China does not get even more rich and powerful on the back of access to US markets. An economic cold war has started.

Medium-sized countries like Britain may think we are too insignificant to do anything except pick a side. But as with the security issues discussed in the previous chapter, we are far more than a passive observer. British institutions, such as its universities, the media and the judiciary, have enormous global reach. They live and breathe the benefits of open societies in a way that is widely noticed and frequently influential. They also make a lot of money for Britain's economy.

What role can and should Britain play in the debate between autocracy and democracy? What are the costs and opportunities of leaning into an issue that will define this century? To answer that it is important to examine the link between economic and political strength.

In the middle of this century, China is likely to become the world's biggest economy. The International Monetary Fund (IMF) and World Bank say that at purchasing power parity, which accounts for different cost levels, the Chinese economy is already larger than that of the US.[10] Assuming it goes on to overtake the American economy in dollar terms, a seismic milestone will have been passed: for the first time in our lifetimes, the largest economy in the world will not be a democracy. It will become much harder to argue, as we have done for many years, that our system is not just morally superior but economically more productive.

But getting there is proving harder for China than it hoped. It has major difficulties with its property sector, which accounts for around 30% of GDP.[11] Tensions with the US, under both Trump and Biden, have seen foreign investment fall to a thirty-year low.[12] Its tech sector has been hit hard by a political crackdown in which leading figures such as Jack Ma have been silenced or disappeared[13] although recently the government seems to have relented somewhat on this approach. China also faces severe demographic challenges: its working age population will fall by 25% by the middle of the century,[14] partly because of the now abandoned one-child policy.[15]

Growth, which was regularly above 8%, has fallen to below 5%[16] – and all that before the tariffs imposed by Trump on exports to its biggest overseas market. Some forecasters now doubt whether

China's economy will ever overtake that of the US. Others think it may only do so temporarily, not least because of its less transparent markets and weaker property rights, which deter investors. The Centre for Economics and Business Research (CEBR), was forecasting only a few years ago that the 'overtake year' would by in 2028. Now it thinks it will be in the mid 2050s.[17]

But the iron determination of China's leaders to match US levels of prosperity should not be underestimated. The Communist Party has a formidable track record in using autocratic tools to unlock economic growth in ways unimaginable for democracies: instead of elections, local mayors throughout the country are accountable for growth targets, upon which their prospects depend. Planning permission for new developments is granted at speeds inconceivable in systems with stronger property rights. Criticism of the party may be banned but scientific freedom is not: Chinese universities are generating formidable numbers of new patents in areas such as AI. The result is that, since the turn of the century, China has become the world's largest lender[18] – often to developing countries – and has been able to fund the world's largest military.[19] Notwithstanding its current economic challenges, China – unlike the Soviet Union – will not be bankrupted by the West.

A key part of China's plan is to use its economic transformation to make the case for autocracy to non-aligned countries. Its wolf warrior diplomats are quick to capitalise on the current sense of disillusion inside many democracies. They get a particularly good hearing in newer democracies in Africa, where there is widespread frustration with corruption, weak government and economic stagnation. In South Africa, a recent survey of young people showed less than half preferred democracy as a form of government. In an Africa-wide survey, a majority said they would accept a military takeover if their government behaved corruptly.[20] In reality military dictatorships are more corrupt because there is no free press to expose wrongdoing – but the fact that such an obvious point is not registering demonstrates how badly the argument is being lost. The result, according to the recent World Values Survey, is a disturbing rise in global support for the idea of having a 'strong leader who does not have to bother with parliament and elections'.[21]

Advanced economies are not immune from the disenchantment – indeed President Trump has capitalised on it to make one of the most extraordinary comebacks in American political history. But growing self-doubt, sometimes self-loathing, in the oldest democracies has made China's job easier. According to Pew Research, 83% of Americans, 70% of Brits, 74% of French and 63% of Germans believe that elected officials do not care about what they think. The same survey found that 66% of Americans, 59% of Britons, 73% of French and 42% of Germans were unsatisfied with how democracy was working in their country.[22] In 1986, 40% of British citizens trusted the government to put the needs of the nation first most of the time. By 2023 that had fallen to just 14%.[23]

Some – but not all – of that self-doubt has been fuelled by disinformation and fake news. In several European countries, hostility against migrants has been stirred up by Russia on social media to foment social unrest.[24] A false claim, also originating from Russia, suggested that Kamala Harris had paralysed a thirteen-year-old girl and covered it up.[25] Ken McCallum, the head of MI5, describes it as a 'sustained mission to generate mayhem on British and European streets'.[26] Tim Davie, the current director general of the BBC, has talked about 'an all-out assault on truth worldwide', pointing out that Russian media is now broadcasting in Lebanon on a radio frequency that used to be occupied by BBC Arabic.[27] William Hague has written about a 'colossal effort' to degenerate our societies in which 'we first stop believing each other and then stop believing in ourselves'.[28]

That crisis of confidence will ultimately only be fixed when we demonstrate to our own populations that democracies are properly capable of delivering effective government – including better economic growth. But in the meantime, we should not allow self-doubt to cloud the reality that liberal democracies remain a vastly superior way to unleash human potential than China's surveillance state. The people of South Korea need no persuading: when their president tried to introduce martial law in 2024, thousands marched on the parliament to protest. Instead of leading an army state, the president found himself impeached. Like the Ukrainians, having tasted democracy relatively recently, South Koreans will not give it up without a fight. In both instances, the case is made stronger by the presence of a brutal autocracy next door.

But until we start to make the case for liberal democracy more effectively, the overall picture will continue to slide in the wrong direction. After the fall of the Berlin Wall in 1989 the number of countries considered democratic by the think tank Freedom House rose sharply. Now it is falling. Indeed, the number of countries classified as 'free' has gradually declined over the last decade, with only one fifth of the world's population now living fully in freedom. Nearly double that live in countries classified as 'not free' – with those in the middle increasingly heading in the wrong direction.[29] According to another think tank in 2023, 46% of countries have seen a decline in the rule of law, with just 24% seeing an improvement.[30]

Countries/Territories Deemed 'Not Free', 2013–25

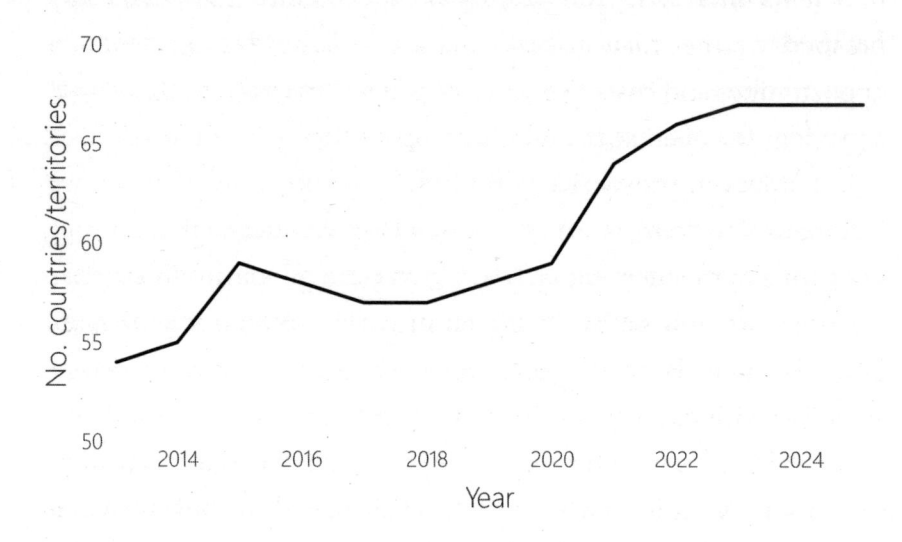

Source: 'Freedom in the World 2013–2025 Raw Data', Freedom House, 2025, https://freedomhouse.org/report/freedom-world[31]

Britain has always been one of the world's greatest defenders of democracy. Alongside the US, the UK played a pivotal role in seeing off fascism in Europe and Asia in the Second World War. It led Europe in facing down the Soviet Union in the Cold War. It relinquished its empire more peacefully and with more attention to democratic principles than had ever happened previously. Britain has also been a strong voice in defending the post-1945 international order that we played a key role in setting up. It is also a more lonely voice following the election of President Trump who has little interest in values diplomacy.

Of course, we are not a superpower – but nor have we been relegated from the Premier League. Given what is now at stake, we have a grave responsibility to exercise the influence we have wisely.

But can we afford to? As we saw in the previous chapter, investing in defence in a smart way, as part of an economic plan, can create prosperity rather than just cost money. This chapter considers the opportunities and costs to the UK of playing our part in winning the argument for open societies. Once again, doing so can help rather than hinder our prosperity.

One way to do so, at very low cost, is through our diplomatic network, one of the most extensive in the world. Alongside France, the UK has more embassies in more countries than anyone other than the US and China.[32] British diplomacy is a proven and effective vehicle for engaging with countries 'in play' when it comes to the great debate between democracy and autocracy. But it can also play a constructive role in something even more fundamental, namely helping the world to avoid the economic and human catastrophe of war.

If, after careful consideration, two opponents choose to engage in military conflict, little can be done. But most wars don't start that way. They often happen because of flawed calculations or misunderstandings about an opponent's likely response – as happened in Ukraine. In the Cold War one of the biggest diplomatic achievements was to avoid misunderstandings that could have led to a nuclear war, most famously during the Cuban missile crisis. We need the same approach in the new cold war with China that we have now entered. Neither side wants war. Neither side realistically thinks a military victory over the other is possible. Uncomfortable though it is, we are going to need to find a pragmatic way to coexist with China.

Typically, in the West such debates divide between 'hawks' and 'doves'. Hawks tend to believe that only the language of strength will prevail. Doves tend to stress the need for understanding and engagement. Hawks point to appeasement in the 1930s as an example of what happens when democracies are weak in the face of aggression. Doves point to the First World War as an unintended tragedy that could have been avoided with more effective diplomacy. In the case of China we need insights from both sides. The end point should be a combination of strength and engagement: strength, because ultimately it is the only language autocratic regimes understand; engagement, to avoid the risk of dangerously crossed wires. Both matter but neither is sufficient without the other.

A key starting point for engagement is to reduce misunderstandings. When it comes to Taiwan, Hong Kong, Tibet and Xinjiang we often fail to appreciate China's unshakeable conviction that its rise has come after unifying a historically divided country. For the Chinese leadership, that makes territorial issues non-negotiable. At the same time, they seriously underestimate Western commitment to freedom and the rule of law. They assume our leaders merely pay lip service to such values, and only really care about winning elections. Sometimes, of course, they are right. But they frequently forget that many foundational moments in Western history have been defined by a willingness, whatever the cost, to fight for our values.

The biggest potential flashpoint is Taiwan. We see it as a plucky democracy. China considers it unfinished business in the country's essential and inevitable reunification. The Chinese armed forces have been asked to ensure they have the technical ability to secure Taiwan by force by 2027, but neither side wants an invasion. Doing so might, of course, become a more attractive option if Putin is seen to win in Ukraine. But it would still be a hugely risky enterprise, given the current weakness of the Chinese economy and the difficulty in predicting the response of a US president who is effective in exploiting his own unpredictability.

Sensible engagement on this and other issues will mean making sure there is enough dialogue to avoid misunderstandings. It will also mean building space for cooperation and trust in areas where we need to work with China. Little progress will be possible on climate change, gene editing, AI or restricting the spread of dangerous weapons without at least some support from the world's second largest economy.

But alongside engagement, there needs to be strength. That means stronger military alliances with friendly democracies like Japan, South Korea and Australia. It means confronting our dependence on Chinese technology, including potential vulnerabilities arising from the use of electric vehicles and consumer appliances. It also means stepping up our advocacy for open societies in swing regions of the world, such as Africa and South America.

Some may say that ultimately this is a superpower issue, in which medium-sized democracies like the UK have only a bit part. A straightforward look at the facts shows why this is not the case: China's 17% share of global GDP may eclipse that of the US in the next few decades, but, taken together, the leading democracies account for 52% of global GDP.[33] If – admittedly a big if – we resolve the current extreme pressure on the Western alliance by taking a pragmatic approach to tensions on defence spending and trade imbalances, we can still muster formidable economic firepower between us.

After the United States, few of those allies match the UK in terms of military prowess or global influence. Our diplomatic experience, honed over many years, can play a constructive role in fostering the sometimes awkward compromises that are needed. Our strong relations with similar-sized economies such as Germany, Canada, Australia and Japan make us a key second-tier player. Many in those countries are coming to similar conclusions, including former Australian prime minister (and Chinese-speaker) Kevin Rudd, who has written a thoughtful book about how to head off what he calls an 'avoidable war' with China.[34]

Perhaps the biggest cause for concern, when it comes to winning the wider argument for democratic values, has been the election of an American president with a totally different agenda. He is determined to extract the US from expensive foreign commitments in a way that borders on isolationism. He also regularly suggests he would prefer a global order in which powerful countries operate unchecked in their own spheres of interest.

Before rushing to criticise this new approach, we should acknowledge the failings in American and European democracies that have led to the election of leaders so opposed to the benign internationalism of previous decades. As in other countries, the creaky plumbing of UK democracy has made it harder to deliver effective government, leading to the widespread disaffection discussed earlier.

In the UK, over-centralisation of power in Whitehall is the biggest culprit, making the NHS over-bureaucratic and local government toothless. Judicial reviews and occasionally judicial overreach make building infrastructure and welfare reform too hard. In the US, polarisation of the political system means that Democrats and Republicans often cannot agree on the basic facts necessary for a reasoned debate. In continental Europe, a failure to deal with mass migration has led to the rise of once pariah far-right parties. On both sides of the Atlantic, politics can be frustratingly short-term when it comes to the most entrenched problems.

Perhaps surprisingly, British democracy remains in good health by international standards, as the tables overleaf show. It continues to score well in global rankings of corruption, doing better than most of the world including the US and much of Europe (although behind the Nordic countries.)[35] That reputation is one of the foundations for the global reach of English law, which still governs many international commercial contracts. The UK scores highly for internet freedom[36] and its media remains one of the freest globally, ranked fourth in the G20.[37]

That gives the UK credibility when it comes to any contribution we choose to make towards winning any global battle for hearts and minds. We also have other assets. The influence of our universities, our media and our culture gives us a major role through what is often called 'soft power'. The extent of that influence has made the UK what David Cameron termed a 'soft power superpower'.[38] And among those assets, one sector in particular brings billions of pounds into the economy every year – Britain's universities.

For many years, British universities have been educating large numbers of overseas students. Often, they have returned home to become leaders in their own countries. One such person was Bill Clinton, who travelled to the UK on the SS *United States*, arriving in Southampton in October 1968 as a 22-year-old graduate of Georgetown University. When he finally arrived, late at night, it was raining and everything was shut except for a food truck on the high street selling bad coffee. Nonetheless, he went on to fall for the University of Oxford's Brideshead charms and engaged in earnest political debates with eclectic new friends late into the nights.[39]

Corruption Perception Index, G20 countries

Country	G20 Rank	Overall Rank	Score
Australia	1	10	77
Canada	2	15	75
Germany	2	15	75
Japan	4	20	71
UK	4	20	71
France	6	25	67
US	7	28	65
South Korea	8	30	64
Saudi Arabia	9	38	59
Italy	10	52	54
China	11	76	43
South Africa	12	82	41
India	13	96	38
Argentina	14	99	37
Indonesia	14	99	37
Brazil	16	107	34
Türkiye	16	107	34
Mexico	18	140	26
Russia	19	154	22

Source: 'Corruption Perceptions Index 2024', Transparency International, 2025, https://images.transparencycdn.org/images/Report-CPI-2024-English.pdf

Internet Freedom

Country	Overall Rank	Total
Iceland	1	94
Estonia	2	92
Canada	3	86
Chile	3	86
Costa Rica	5	85
Netherlands	6	83
Taiwan	7	79
Japan	8	78
UK	8	78
Germany	10	77

Source: Allie Funk et al., 'Freedom on the Net 2024', Freedom House, 2024, https://freedomhouse.org/sites/default/files/2024-10/FREEDOM-ON-THE-NET-2024-DIGITAL-BOOKLET.pdf

Press Freedom

Country	G20 Rank	Overall Rank	Score
Germany	1	10	83.84
Canada	2	14	81.70
France	3	21	78.65
UK	4	23	77.51
South Africa	5	38	73.73
Australia	6	39	73.42
Italy	7	46	69.80
US	8	55	66.59
South Korea	9	62	64.87
Argentina	10	66	63.13
Japan	11	70	62.12
Brazil	12	82	58.59
Indonesia	13	111	51.15
Mexico	14	121	49.01
Turkey	15	158	31.60
India	16	159	31.28
Russia	17	162	29.86
Saudi Arabia	18	166	27.14
China	19	172	23.36

Source: 'World Press Freedom Index 2024', RSF, 2024, https://rsf.org/en/index

Clinton was a Rhodes scholar. Since the Rhodes scheme started in 1902, it has brought over 8,000 overseas students to the UK, often selected for their leadership skills.[40] Another scheme, the Chevening scholarships run by the Foreign Office, has brought in more students earmarked as future leaders. Partly because of this, of the 193 countries in the UN no fewer than 58 have a head of state or government who studied in Britain, the second highest after the US.[41] Current UK-educated leaders include the presidents of Ireland

and Singapore, the emperor of Japan and king of Jordan. They also include many inspiring leaders in other fields, such as Summia Tora, the first Rhodes scholar to come from Afghanistan who went on to found a remarkable organisation assisting Afghans fleeing persecution.[42]

But it isn't just leaders. Britain is now the second most popular study destination in the world for all overseas students.[43] In 2022–23 they numbered a staggering 750,000 and contributed over £40 billion to the UK economy.[44] That number will decline following recently introduced visa restrictions on family members, but it remains a formidable contributor to Britain's trade surplus in services. It also represents a key element of Britain's soft power, generating enormous goodwill towards the UK at one of the most formative moments in people's lives. A British education was often an easy point of first connection with the foreign leaders or dignitaries I met as Foreign Secretary. As Bill Clinton said: 'I love this country and feel deeply indebted to it. It gave me two of the best years of my life.'[45]

UK universities are currently in financial difficulty. And they don't get everything right when it comes to the protection of free speech. Two former Conservative Home Secretaries, Amber Rudd and Suella Braverman, have recently had events cancelled at Oxford and Cambridge after being targeted by protesters. Philosopher Kathleen Stock was notoriously hounded from her job at the University of Sussex after 'questioning the idea that gender identity is more "socially significant" than biological sex'.[46] In one survey, 43% of students said they felt nervous about expressing their own views.[47] That is indefensible. Thankfully, the new Labour government has reversed an early decision not to implement a free speech law.

Number of Inbound International Students, 2023

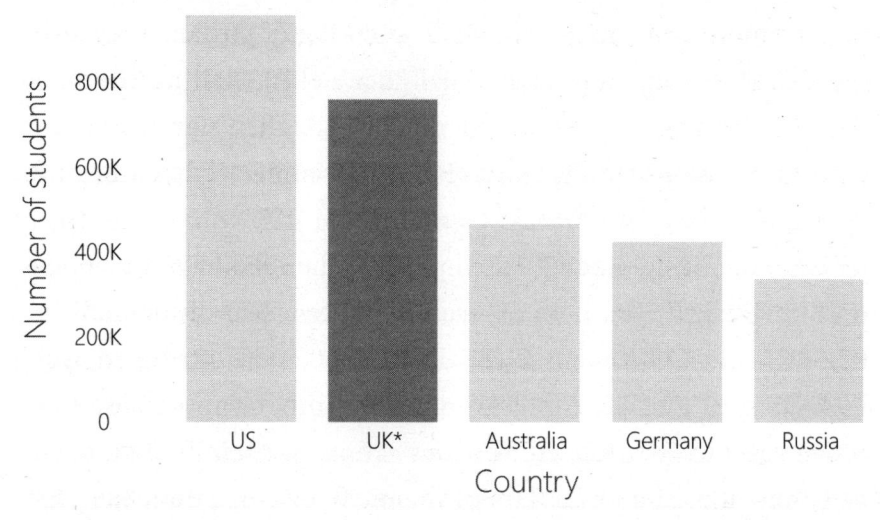

Bar chart showing number of students by country:
- US: ~830K
- UK*: ~750K
- Australia: ~450K
- Germany: ~400K
- Russia: ~340K

Source: UNESCO Institute for Statistics, 'Total inbound internationally mobile students, both sexes (number)', https://databrowser.uis.unesco.org/view#indicatorPaths=UIS-EducationOPRI:0:26637; Luke Perrott, 'Higher Education Student Statistics: UK, 2022/23 – Where Students Come from and Go to Study', HESA, 8 August 2024, https://www.hesa.ac.uk/news/08-08-2024/sb269-higher-education-student-statistics/location

Note: *As of writing, because the UK had not yet reported figures to UNESCO for 2023, the UK's figure is the 2022–23 equivalent from HESA.

World Leader Alumni by Country

Country	Overall Rank	No. of heads of state/ heads of government
US	1	70
UK	2	58
France	3	28
Russia	4	10
Australia	5	7
Belgium	5	7
Spain	5	7
Germany	8	6
Italy	8	6
Switzerland	8	6
Netherlands	11	5

Source: Nick Hillman, 'HEPI Soft-Power Index 2024', HEPI, 10 October 2024, https://www.hepi.ac.uk/2024/10/10/the-us-pulls-further-away-in-the-latest-soft-power-index-while-the-uk-stands-still-and-france-slips-back/[48]

But important though they are, such issues are not unique to the UK. And they haven't stopped its academic institutions from wielding enormous global influence. Three of the world's top ten universities are British and its higher education sector has more top-fifty universities than France, Germany and Italy combined. When it comes to universities with the most international outlook – measured partly by the number of research papers co-authored internationally – the UK has no fewer than thirty of the world's top fifty institutions.[49] Outside the US, no higher education sector is more respected. Provided UK universities overcome their current financial difficulties and protect the academic freedom upon which they are built, they have formidable potential to project the virtues of open societies.

Another way the UK can help win the argument for democratic values is through its media.

Like every politician, I have had my battles with the media, which I was responsible for as Culture Secretary. I had to adjudicate on Rupert Murdoch's proposed takeover of Sky, one of the thorniest issues I ever dealt with. But despite countless tricky interviews, I have always welcomed the right of the media to scrutinise everything done by me and my colleagues. The British media probably does that more robustly than any other democracy, with its unique combination of tabloids, broadsheets, popular and highbrow journalism.

Or so, at least, thought many of the fellow ministers I met on my travels. They often privately expressed relief that they did not have to deal with a media like ours in their own countries. I was even told by FIFA that fear of the UK media was one of the reasons they chose Russia instead of England for the 2018 World Cup. Bribery of key officials is a more likely explanation – bribery that was ironically exposed by a British newspaper, the *Sunday Times*.

Good journalism, combined with global use of English, makes the UK media a potent force internationally: 5% of the world's population speak English as a first language and a further 15% can communicate in it, placing it head and shoulders above any other second language.[50] That creates 1.5 billion potential consumers of British media output across the globe. As a result, many global media businesses are based in London – and, for better or worse, the world is remarkably well informed about what is happening in the UK. In some ways that makes us a world champion at washing our dirty linen in public. But a willingness to be open about your flaws is surely part of being a confident democracy.

In a time when liberal values are under challenge, the global reach of the UK media is also a responsibility. The BBC, despite much criticism at home, is one of the world's most trusted news broadcasters.[51] It reaches just under 450 million people every week, less than the large social media platforms but ahead of other major international broadcasters.[52] Like others, I feel extreme frustration when the BBC gets things wrong, but to its credit, it thinks harder about what impartiality should mean – and cares about it more – than any of its major competitors. In an age of fake news, that matters. Aung San Suu Kyi praised the BBC World Service for sustaining her through her years of confinement in Myanmar. Now she is back under house arrest, one hopes it is still doing so.[53]

Nonetheless, the BBC could do more. Cuts to certain services, such as its BBC Arabic radio service, are short-sighted, given what is happening in Lebanon and Gaza. When I was Foreign Secretary, I had several discussions with the BBC's then director general, Tony Hall, about how we could double its global reach to one billion people every week, a level that would make it the world's dominant news broadcaster. Neither of us was around for long enough to see 'Project One Billion' come to fruition, but I know it is of interest to his successor, Tim Davie. Someone will get to that level of reach one day. For the sake of democracy, I hope it is the BBC and not Russia Today.

There is one more British creation that can have great influence in this century's unfolding battle of ideas, namely our culture. Thanks to its extraordinary creativity and the power of the English language, UK popular culture has become one of our most successful exports. Britain, for example, is the world's largest exporter of TV formats including quiz shows like *The Weakest Link*,[54] comedy gameshows like *Taskmaster*,[55] dating shows like *Love Island*[56] and cooking competitions like *MasterChef*.[57] After years of sustained expansion, we now have by far the biggest film and TV sector in Europe. Even many films that might be considered 'all-American', such as *Barbie* and *Oppenheimer*, are made wholly or partly in the UK.

When it comes to music, many of the bestselling artists of all time are British, including the Beatles, the Rolling Stones, Pink Floyd, Led Zeppelin and Elton John.[58] London's West End continues to boom, with Andrew Lloyd Webber's *The Phantom of the Opera* now having been performed in 195 cities in 46 territories.[59] Our cultural reach extends to sport, where the Premier League is broadcast in 189 countries,[60] more popular than any other European league or America's NBA or NFL. The UK also exports more books than any other country,[61] with British authors dominating the top ten bestselling books of all time. Perhaps the best example of the reach of British culture is the monarchy: the weddings of Prince William in 2011 and Prince Harry in 2018 are estimated to have been viewed by as many as two billion people worldwide.[62] Queen Elizabeth II's funeral is thought to have been seen by even more.[63]

As a result, the UK's creative industries as a whole account for around 6% of national GDP and employ more than two million people.[64] With the advent of streaming, the film and TV sectors have now become a high-profile subset of Britain's burgeoning technology industry. The UK has Europe's largest production facilities and featured in seven of the top ten highest-grossing blockbusters of 2023 – including *Barbie* and *Oppenheimer*, as discussed. Netflix alone has spent $6 billion on original UK productions since 2020.[65] Studio space in Britain has nearly doubled over the period.[66]

There is only a limited extent to which that cultural penetration can or should be harnessed to promote a particular set of values. But, indirectly, it can often be an excellent advertisement for the advantages of living in an open society. How many UK authors or musicians would have been able to create their art without artistic freedom? British films and TV programmes often have storylines which showcase a free press, an independent judiciary, and corrupt politicians being held to account. As a result, many citizens in less free countries know pretty well how society works in advanced economies. Far from turning their backs on supposedly failing systems, they choose to invest their money in them, send their children to study in them, and even move there.

Global Soft Power Index 2025

Country	Rank	Score
US	1	79.5
China	2	72.8
UK	3	72.4
Japan	4	71.5
Germany	5	70.1
France	6	68.5
Canada	7	65.2
Switzerland	8	64.9
Italy	9	62.4
UAE	10	60.4

Source: 'Global Soft Power Index 2025' (Brand Finance, 2025), https://brandirectory.com/softpower

It is not easy to quantify the extent of any country's soft power. One organisation, however, has tried to do just that. The Brand Finance Global Soft Power Index has been published in different iterations for the last five years, and always ranks the UK right near the top. Its latest version, published in 2025, examines perceptions of all 193 UN members, and the UK was ranked as having the third highest level of soft power globally, sitting just after the US and China.[67]

In a century which will once again decide if the world moves towards autocracy or freedom, such soft power shows that Britain is far from irrelevant. It matters for our economy too, because what is good for democratic values is also good for business. Our universities, film and TV industries and other arts and media have flourished because of their global reach. They generate enormous inward investment and make a major contribution to exports, one reason that I backed the creative industries with generous new tax credits.[68]

But boosting our national soft power doesn't just support key sectors of the economy: at little cost, it helps to win an argument with which we have always been associated. The history of Britain and its empire is not without its blemishes. Nonetheless from Magna Carta to the Bill of Rights, from the Great Reform Act to the Suffragettes and from two world wars to the Cold War our national story is closely linked to the progress of democracy. Even the British empire, for all its failings, left behind more democratic institutions than any other empire in history.[69] They too have formed part of the long tail of British influence.

Without the full-throated support we are used to from the world's most powerful democracy, championing democratic values will be harder. But for a country like Britain, that surely makes it more – not less – important. At the same time, we should be brutally honest that, right now, we are not the ones on the frontline when it comes to the struggle for freedom. Ukrainian soldiers, Russian opposition leaders, Chinese lawyers, Iranian schoolgirls and Hong Kong's democracy campaigners are courageously taking risks that put to shame the often feeble efforts we make. Yet as one of the oldest defenders of democracy, it is to us those campaigners look. The least we can do is make sure we support them with the tools we have. With Britain's unique combination of hard and soft power, the question for us is not about capability but about willingness. We have much to bring to the table – if we choose to.

3
Tackling Mass Migration

Yafet was born in 2002 in Eritrea, one of the most repressive countries on the planet.[1] With an unforgiving climate, it sits across the Red Sea from Saudi Arabia and Yemen. Politically, the country has languished under authoritarian rule since it gained independence from Ethiopia in 1993, remaining a one-party state with no freedom of religion, assembly or press. Military service is compulsory, and draft dodgers are severely punished. Those who try to flee the country are routinely arrested, imprisoned and tortured.[2]

When Yafet was two years old, the authorities discovered that his father had plans to quit his job working for the police and make his way to Sudan. He was arrested and detained. After being briefly released in 2006, he was rearrested. His family never saw him again.

Yafet's mother was terrified for their safety. So she decided to do what her husband had originally planned, and fled westward across the border to Sudan with her son and his aunt. There, they were happy for a few years. But when Yafet was just nine, his mother died, leaving him in the care of his aunt.

Their new home was not particularly stable either. When Yafet was sixteen, in 2018, his best friend started attending anti-government demonstrations. At the time there was widespread dissatisfaction with the Sudanese government over inflation, austerity and corruption. A year later police and paramilitaries were sent in to disperse a sit-in in front of the army headquarters in Khartoum. His friend was killed. It was the last day of Ramadan; around 120 protesters lost their lives, bodies were dumped into the Nile, and 900 more were wounded over the days that followed. The incident became known as the Khartoum massacre.[3]

Enraged by what had happened, Yafet started joining demonstrations too – making him a target for the security forces. They warned him not to take part, because he was not Sudanese. Perhaps unwisely, he ignored them. He ended up being run down by a car, breaking his hand and severing a nerve. He was left with permanent scars and lasting pain.

His aunt persuaded him he wasn't safe, so in 2021, aged nineteen, he fled Sudan. Thus began a long and tortuous journey through Europe. The final leg was a small boat across the English Channel.

First, he travelled through Chad to Libya. From there he set off in a small plastic dinghy towards Sicily, on what has become the world's deadliest migration route.[4] That year the UN refugee agency, UNHCR, estimated that around 1,100 refugees and migrants departing from Libya ended up missing or dead at sea – around 3% of the total.[5] It was a risk Yafet and many others were prepared to take.

Fortunately for Yafet, his group were picked up by a ship while still in African waters and taken to Sicily. His first choice was to settle there, but he still needed medical treatment for his arm.

Because nothing was available in his camp he decided to head to Rome. When he arrived, there was no accommodation, so he slept on the streets. Unfortunately, he could not get medical care there either.

His aunt sent him a message saying that he might have better luck in France or Britain. So after borrowing twenty euros from a friend, Yafet arranged to be smuggled to France via lorry. Having already decided to continue through to the UK, he then had to choose how. Was it underneath a lorry, where he risked being crushed to death if he fell off? Or should he take his chances in a boat and risk drowning in the notoriously choppy Channel? Given his injury, Yafet decided he stood a better chance in a boat.

He was told the journey would cost him €500. His aunt sent him the money. It was so much for her that he later found out she struggled to buy food as a result. But then the smugglers nearly scuppered his journey by upping the price at the last minute to €1,500. Because he couldn't get any more money, they relented but told him he would only be allowed one attempt.

He and his group waited for their boat in a wood near the French coast. After three days of waiting, with no food or water, the boat finally arrived. They then had to carry it for an hour to somewhere on the shoreline where there were no police. Then, finally, they set off.

The group used iPhones to check their position at sea. After a while they realised they were headed the wrong way. Getting lost in one of the world's busiest shipping lanes could have spelt disaster, but eventually Yafet's boat was found by a French ship which sent them in the right direction for Dover.

After arriving in the UK, Yafet applied for asylum. He was put on a waiting list for surgery on his hand. He eventually ended up in a hotel used for migrants in the West Midlands, where he spent his time learning English at a local college and playing football. Some anti-immigration riots outside his hotel in August 2024 were moved on without incident. At the time of writing, he is thought to be still in limbo, waiting for the outcome of his asylum claim.

Yafet is one of 150,000 people who have crossed the Channel in small boats since 2018.[6] Poverty and persecution in countries like Eritrea and Sudan remain a big reason why so many want to travel – but paradoxically, it is increased prosperity that makes them able to do so. The World Bank defines extreme poverty as an income of less than $2.15 a day[7] – far too little to be able to afford the often extortionate fees charged by people smugglers. But whereas in the 1960s half the world's population lived in extreme poverty, today it is less than 10%. Countries previously considered poor, such as Kenya and Tanzania, are now classified as 'lower middle income', firmly on a growth path that is raising living standards.[8] Much of Africa and nearly all of Asia has 'got' capitalism and is embracing it with gusto. The number of people able to migrate has expanded dramatically.

Unsurprisingly, that is what they are doing. Between 1970 and 2020 the number of people not living in their country of birth rose from 84 million to 281 million.[9] The number of people officially registered by the UN as refugees has nearly trebled to 32 million over the last decade, more than the population of Australia.[10] The number seeking asylum has increased sixfold.[11]

Those global trends have led to a dramatic increase in the number of people coming to the UK. Jobs, benefits and the NHS make it an attractive destination. A decade ago, less than a thousand crossed the Channel in a small boat every year. Today, when the weather is good, the same number can cross in a single day.[12] In 2024, more than 35,000 people made the journey.[13] That has been made possible by people-smuggling gangs, who have built up a business estimated to be worth $10 billion globally.[14] Only arms trading and drug trafficking make criminal enterprises more money.

The trade is plied ruthlessly, with little or no concern for human life. Since 2020, more than 160 people have died trying to cross the Channel. Around 4,000 have drowned trying to cross the Mediterranean.[15] Not all have been accidents, and not all are the responsibility of the gangs. The Greek coastguard, in particular, has been accused of deliberately sinking vessels or sending them back out to sea.[16] Some of the horrors of people-smuggling came to the world's attention in 2015, when images emerged of a drowned two-year-old Syrian boy lying face down on a Turkish beach. He was called Alan Kurdi, and he died trying to reach the Greek island of Kos. His five-year-old brother Galip and mother Rehan drowned with him.[17] The family were trying to join Alan's aunt in Canada.[18]

Then there is the domestic impact. Massive migration flows have had a seismic impact on the politics of established democracies. My own parliamentary constituency in Surrey is a rural area. Compared to many areas, it has low numbers of foreign-born citizens. Nonetheless, concern about migration – legal and illegal – was so widespread when I knocked on doors in the 2024 general election, that it nearly cost me my seat. In an area with high housing costs, many worried that immigration was contributing to housing shortages. Others believed it was taking them longer to get a GP appointment or NHS operation as a result. There was palpable anger at the £8 million a day it costs to house asylum seekers in hotels.[19]

Partly on the back of such concerns, four million people voted for Reform UK in that election. Across Europe, wherever there were elections it was the same story. In Germany, the AfD saw huge gains. In France, Marine Le Pen's National Rally deprived President Macron of a parliamentary majority. And later in the year, Trump won in the US on a promise to implement the 'largest deportation operation in American history'.[20]

Supporters of such policies are no longer fringe. They are using their votes to insist they are listened to by political elites who have often written off their concerns as racist. Unless politicians find a way to address the massive global increase in migration flows, that anger will continue to rise. Yafet's and Alan Kurdi's stories are heart-rending, but sympathy ebbs rapidly when people's sense of fairness is offended.

Inside the UK, the focus by successive governments has been on practical measures to stop the flow of small boats. That includes the last government's Rwanda scheme which the new government will surely regret cancelling. It includes repeated attempts to disrupt or dismantle people-smuggling operations. But there has been little debate about tackling the root cause of the problem, namely the combination of enough wealth to make travel possible but not enough of it to close the disparity with richer countries. All advanced economies have been affected by these changes and many feel powerless to prevent it. In fact, for a number of reasons, the UK can play a decisive role in finding a solution. With its long-standing commitment to international development, Britain has much experience of the challenges involved in reducing the disparity in wealth between richer and poorer countries. We also, for better or worse, played a major role in setting up the flawed international legal frameworks that have turned people-smuggling into such a huge industry. Could we now be the country that learns from what went wrong and unlocks a solution?

The pattern for most of the last few decades has been a declining gap between developed and developing nations. But since 2019 that gap has started growing again. According to the International Labour Organization, the purchasing power of someone on average earnings in India is currently 35% that of someone in the UK. In Ethiopia it is 10% of UK levels.[21] Although absolute wealth is often increasing, relative wealth is not. If the gap between developed and developing countries was narrowing, there would be hope. There might be a logic to avoiding the risk and upheaval of being smuggled over a border. If that gap is widening, the calculation changes.

In the very poorest countries, the gap has been widening for much longer. In such countries, despite large aid budgets, the battle against extreme poverty and destitution is also failing. Progress in tackling infectious diseases, getting children into schools and reducing child mortality has all but ground to a halt.[22] The situation is particularly dire in countries recovering from major wars, such as Afghanistan and Syria. But other low-income countries have also been stuck for many years including Mali, Malawi, the Central African Republic and the Democratic Republic of Congo. Such places, often described as 'fragile states', do not have the basic tools necessary for economic development, including basic security, transparent government, a functioning private sector and an effective legal system to secure property rights.

At the same time, something else has happened that makes finding a solution harder. The previously close relationship between advanced economies and developing ones has started to fracture. Many of the latter remained disappointingly neutral after the invasion of Ukraine. Some blamed Western double standards over humanitarian losses in Gaza. Others remembered the absence of any major US-led initiative to help them secure access to vaccines during the pandemic.[23] But the biggest reason is that they now have a choice.

Since the launch of the Belt and Road Initiative in 2013, China's aid to Africa has surpassed that of both the UK and the US. Unlike Western aid, it comes with no strings attached regarding governance or human rights. Because it is often a loan, there are sometimes concerns about debt traps, but many African governments still welcome the fact that it tends to be focused on economic growth rather than poverty reduction. Fifty-three out of fifty-four African countries attended the 2024 Forum on China–Africa Cooperation summit hosted by President Xi.[24] Their leaders may speak English, play cricket and hold parliamentary elections, but they feel absolutely no obligation to side with their former coloniser.

France has felt this chill every bit as much as Britain and the US. Once a dominant force in Francophone Africa, it had the indignity of seeing its ambassador and peacekeeping troops expelled from Niger after a coup in July 2023.[25] Again, Niger knew it had a choice – in this case, to get help with internal security from the Russian Wagner Group and its successors.[26] Their no-questions-asked approach includes summary executions, something French forces rightly could not match. Russia has also been very effective at spreading pro-Russian and anti-French propaganda in Africa.[27] As a result of rising anti-French sentiment, France is now in the process of withdrawing its military presence from all Francophone countries except Djibouti.[28] It is a major setback for Western influence in a very volatile part of the world.

Most developing countries have no desire to swap dependency on the West with dependency on Russia or China. But they are looking for a different kind of support to what we have generally offered. Richer and more confident, they want a partnership of equals rather than paternalistic support from a former colonial power. They also know we have been having difficulties of our own. Before you tell us how to run ourselves, they say, why not hold a mirror up? Trust has fractured just at the moment when advanced economies need strong partnerships to tackle global migration flows, fight climate change and counter autocratic influence.

Britain is not an economic or military giant. But it does have deeper connections with many developing countries than nearly any other advanced economy. We have a shared history and ongoing relationships sustained by institutions such as the Commonwealth. Because of the growing influence of UK-based diasporas, our cultural ties with many of them are actually getting stronger. What is the best way to use the influence we have?

The law is a good place to start. One of the reasons illegal migration is so difficult to tackle is the web of international treaties and conventions to which the UK is a signatory, and which it often even helped formulate. A good example is the European Convention on Human Rights (ECHR), which only exists because of a rather unlikely British establishment figure from the last century called David Maxwell Fyfe.[29] Maxwell Fyfe was a Conservative MP who was from a family he described as 'always poor, but perfectly self-contained and happy'. His teacher parents were well read, and their intellectual curiosity was clearly imprinted onto Maxwell Fyfe, who became a barrister and then, in 1935, MP for Liverpool West Derby. His busy double life led the *Daily Telegraph* to dub him 'KC by day, MP by night', a moniker that my friend the current Conservative MP Sir Geoffrey Cox might recognise.

In 1942, Maxwell Fyfe added further jobs to the list: Solicitor General in Churchill's wartime administration, Attorney General in the caretaker government, then Home Secretary and finally Lord Chancellor until 1962. Given his reactionary views on homosexuality, which he never recanted, he was not the most obvious creator of what has become modern human rights law. Nonetheless, he had a profound influence on putting in place the legal structures under which we now operate.

It started with a particular challenge. After the Second World War the victorious allies needed to find a way to deal with the Nazi war criminals. In previous conflicts, the approach would have been quite straightforward: a show trial followed by summary executions. But given that the arbitrary exercise of power was precisely what the war was trying to end, the momentous decision was taken to put in place a legal framework against which the defendants would be tried in as fair a way as possible.

So in 1943, Britain and its allies established the UN War Crimes Commission and started collecting evidence of offences 'against the laws and usages of war'.[30] As Solicitor General during this period, Maxwell Fyfe was deeply involved in such decisions from the outset.

That became very important when deciding what to do with war criminals after the conclusion of the war. Instead of summary executions, Maxwell Fyfe and Robert Jackson, the US's chief prosecutor at Nuremberg, decided to give all those accused a hearing, with clear charges and evidence, as well as a chance to respond. Maxwell Fyfe wrote that he considered it 'a deplorable beginning to a world in which everyone was looking for the rule of law if we irresponsibly cast it overboard in our first difficult sea'. He also believed that only the public deployment of 'impregnable evidence of guilt' would prevent Nazi war criminals from becoming martyrs.

He then chaired the International Conference on Military Trials, which was held in London. After finding compromises on many issues such as the scope and location of the court, the Charter of the International Military Tribunal was born. It sought to codify the new rules governing international crimes, of which there were to be four: war crimes, crimes against humanity, genocide, and the crime of aggression or waging a manifestly illegal war.

On his first visit to Nuremberg, where the trials would be held, Maxwell Fyfe saw banks of rubble at the roadside, discarded machine-gun cartridges and shattered housing. But the Palace of Justice and nearby prison were still standing and could be used for the trial. The plan went ahead.

Then Churchill was unexpectedly defeated in the 1945 general election. As Conservative Solicitor General, Maxwell Fyfe thought his work at Nuremberg would end. But the new Labour Attorney General, Hartley Shawcross, magnanimously offered him a chance to continue his work as deputy chief prosecutor. Shawcross took the lead role and delivered immensely powerful opening and closing speeches for the prosecution. But the heavy lifting was left to Maxwell Fyfe.

His most famous moment during the trials was the cross-examination of Hermann Goering, someone he described as

British Prosecuting Counsel at Nuremberg with Maxwell Fyfe front left and Shawcross front centre

'[w]ithout question [...] the most formidable witness I have ever cross-examined'.[31] Unlike Robert Jackson, who had unsuccessfully cross-examined Goering before him, Maxwell Fyfe was undeterred by his cunning. He managed to make the Nazi leader look both devious and duplicitous in a way that helped to secure his conviction. But the seminal success of the Nuremberg process was broader than ensuring Goering faced justice: it established firmly what the 'rule of law' actually meant. Unlike in previous post-war trials, proper evidence was required, the accused were given a chance to defend their case and the highest standards of justice were upheld.

The next step for Maxwell Fyfe was to codify and enshrine such principles in the laws of the new nations emerging in war-ravaged Europe. Thus was born the ECHR. It was and remains a legally enforceable list of basic personal rights that all signatories were required to acknowledge alongside a 'minimum standard of democratic conduct'.[32]

It also includes implicit protections for irregular migrants and asylum seekers, something of great relevance to today's migration flows. Those rights were included in order to make sure that Jews could escape if there was another Holocaust.[33] The UK was one of the first to sign and ratify the new treaty, extending the application of the convention to many of its Commonwealth territories. Little did Maxwell Fyfe know that a creation conceived with such noble motives would one day contribute to industrial-scale people-smuggling.

As a European country that wrote much of the international law underpinning the treatment of migrants, the UK is probably in the strongest position to make it fit for purpose in the modern era. Like others, the UK has made it illegal to arrive as a migrant in a small boat or from a safe third country. But the ECHR and the 1951 Refugee Convention both make it extremely difficult to enforce any law that mandates the deportation of irregular arrivals such as those arriving on small boats. Both need reform in a way that is true to their original objectives, while recognising how much the world has changed.

The Refugee Convention, for example, gives people the right to come to the UK on extremely broad terms, with no stipulation that an asylum seeker must make a claim in the first safe country they reach.[34] But if the convention makes it too easy to enter, the ECHR makes it too difficult to deport people, sometimes including drug dealers, rapists and murderers. Some of our own laws, including the Human Rights Act, make the process still harder.

Threatening to leave the ECHR may be a necessary catalyst for reforming an institution that can only change with the unanimous support of its forty-six signatories. But a far better solution would be for a country that helped set up the convention to lead efforts to reform it. He won't thank me for saying so, but there is no one better suited for that task than our prime minister. Sir Keir Starmer has a background as a human rights lawyer who has supported and defended the rights enshrined in both the ECHR and the Refugee Convention over many years. His credentials for reforming them both are impeccable. Now is the moment to use that credibility and experience to negotiate the changes needed not just by the UK but by many other countries. It may seem like a formidable challenge, but consider it from a different perspective: no European leader, given their domestic politics, would want to be seen obstructing reform. If Britain took the lead, others would be more than likely to follow.

Such changes could involve making it easier to reject claims made by those who enter a country irregularly. It could involve reforming elements of the ECHR, such as the right of individual petition, so that it cannot be used to frustrate a deportation order. New legal frameworks should of course be balanced with better access to safe and legal routes for genuine refugees. But public support for generosity towards those in need requires confidence that elected governments can actually decide who is allowed to enter the country. Reforming outdated international legal frameworks is a vital first step to making that happen.

*

On their own, such reforms will make a big difference. But their impact may be temporary, if we do not also tackle the root causes of the issue. That means a better plan to tackle the poverty that makes people want to leave home in the first place – an area in which, despite recent cuts to the aid budget, the UK has enormous experience.

I saw that for myself when I was elected to Parliament in 2005. I had been involved in setting up a charity for AIDS orphans in Kenya. Tackling grinding poverty was close to my heart and I even talked about it in my maiden speech. As an opposition backbench MP, I asked to join the International Development Select Committee, so that I could campaign for better access to HIV drugs in Africa. I had Labour's Secretary of State for International Development, Hilary Benn, in my sights. But he didn't make it very easy for me to criticise government policy: just two months later he and Tony Blair hosted an international event that was to transform the lives of millions of people living with HIV.

That event was the Gleneagles summit of the world's most powerful countries, the G8 (now the G7, without Russia). Blair, then at the height of his powers, oversaw proceedings. With full support from US president George W. Bush, he announced a plan to get antiretroviral drugs free of charge to everyone who needed them. It wasn't just a vague plan either: there was funding to deliver it and a target date five years later. I added what little value I could by urging Benn to set up intermediate targets to make sure the programme stayed on track, something he agreed to do.

The results have been spectacular. Today around four fifths of those who need antiretroviral drugs in Africa receive them. AIDS-related deaths have come down by two thirds and new HIV infections have more than halved.[35] The vast majority of those receiving treatment have a viral load that is low enough to allow their immune systems to work with minimal impact on life expectancy. The summit also unveiled a $50-billion fund to help cancel debt for the very poorest countries.[36] A few years later, Britain became the first major country to fulfil its commitment to spend 0.7% of its GDP on development.[37]

That commitment was abandoned after the pandemic, and then reduced further to fund an increase in defence spending. But we should not forget the positive impact our aid has had: in the second half of the last decade, the UK provided immunisations for 74 million children, saving an estimated 1.4 million lives; it got clean water and sanitation to 62 million people, and access to family planning for around 25 million women and girls each year; it helped 15 million children get a decent education; and provided humanitarian assistance to 33 million people.[38] Britain also played a big role in setting up the UN's Millennium Development Goals and their successor, the Sustainable Development Goals. It currently ranks seventh globally for its commitment to international development, although both the US and the UK are likely to drop down the rankings substantially following recent cuts.[39]

Other big European aid donors include France, Germany, the Netherlands and Norway. In Asia, Japan has shown sustained commitment and now gives more overall than the UK.[40] While USAID is being dismantled – to what extent still unclear at time of writing – the UK remains (at least for now) in the top ten countries in terms of its commitment to development. Experts score the UK highly for the size of its aid programme, expertise on development finance and focus on security.

Given its credibility and influence, the UK has the opportunity to tackle uncontrolled migration flows with an ambitious refashioning of the relationship between developed and developing countries. We need their help to stop people-smuggling, and they want to see the gap between rich and poor countries once again shrinking. A win-win should be possible.

One way to do this would be for the UK to champion something akin to a new Marshall Plan for North Africa. It would be funded from the combined aid budgets of European countries and modelled on the original Marshall Plan, which successfully laid the foundations for post-war European growth. Because there remain conflict zones in North Africa – unlike post-war Europe – it could not be identical. But as with the original plan, in return for aid there would be obligations. One would be to make sure that the funds really are used to foster economic growth. The most important – from our perspective – would be a cast-iron commitment to stop people-smuggling gangs using their countries as a bridgehead to cross the Mediterranean.

At the same time, we need a more modern partnership with emerging and influential middle-income countries such as South Africa, Nigeria and Kenya. When I visited Nigeria as Foreign Secretary, I was taken to UN World Food Programme warehouses doing vital work tackling hunger and destitution. But the government ministers I met in Abuja weren't really interested. What they wanted to talk about were the tech clusters they were trying to nurture in the capital city. They hoped Britain – and particularly the City of London – could help finance them. They understand capitalism, are making big strides forward – and want any help we can offer. It isn't that they don't want to tackle poverty, but that, more than immediate poverty relief, they want the economic growth to be able to deal with it themselves in the longer run. Even though China has often been better at speaking the language of growth to such countries, the strong institutions and free markets of an advanced economy are a more reliable path to prosperity. We need to be better at making that case.

A change of approach with the poorest countries is also needed. Experts like Sir Paul Collier of the University of Oxford argue that we should be more honest about the failures of current aid programmes, which have sometimes left recipient countries poorer. While humanitarian aid saves lives, sustained aid can create a dependency that hinders development. Collier points to the economic success of Somaliland after it realised that the fact that it was not recognised as an independent country meant it would not get any aid. Neighbouring Somalia had no such issue, but has fared much worse economically, despite access to large aid budgets.[41] Aid dependency is likely one of the reasons it has a GDP per head 25% lower than Somaliland.[42]

What such countries need most is help creating vibrant private sectors that allow them to generate their own wealth. Again, the UK has much experience in doing just that. Under Clement Attlee, Britain set up one of the first attempts to do that by establishing the Colonial Development Corporation, now called British International Investment (BII).[43] It is still one of the very best development finance institutions, and a big focus of the 2023 white paper published by the then Foreign Office minister, Andrew Mitchell.[44] Investment from BII should be supported by British help with setting up independent courts, less corrupt police forces, effective parliamentary democracy and a free press – all of which reduce corruption, protect property rights and stimulate investment.

Changing the legal framework for migration, refocussing development aid and refashioning the relationship with developing countries is an ambitious set of objectives. But we will need ambition if we really are to address the porous borders that are destabilising advanced democracies. And Britain's history, experience and influence give us an opportunity to play a decisive role. Not doing so is a choice – but means ignoring a solution to one of the top concerns for many voters.

The economic benefits would also be significant. We would reduce and possibly eliminate the cost of housing and processing illegal asylum seekers, now exceeding £10 billion a year[45] – equivalent to more than 1p on income tax.[46] But, more importantly, by demonstrating that we are able to control illegal migration, we would unlock a more rational debate about the levels of migration we actually need.

That is because our economy has always thrived on openness to global talent. If we are going to be Europe's Silicon Valley, we will need to attract ambitious tech entrepreneurs from all over the continent to set up their businesses here. If we want to be a global centre for new medicine discovery, we will need the best scientists, wherever they come from. Our universities remain among the most respected in the world – partly based on their ability to attract the best PhD students. Our financial services sector has become the world's second largest off the back of talent attracted to London. When overall immigration levels are too high – fuelled by Channel boat crossings – the social consensus for the openness from which Britain has benefited for many years starts to fray.

It is therefore essential to address the issue head on. In doing so, we will not just reduce pressure on the public purse and improve relations with emerging powers. We can make possible a more balanced consensus in which controlled migration continues to support key sectors of our economy without undermining social stability. In doing so, we would be demonstrating once again that using our influence abroad can help resolve key challenges at home. Just as a smart approach to European security could help unlock a booming technology sector and a smart approach to promoting democracy supports key British industries, so tackling the challenge of international migration flows will make us both more secure and more prosperous.

4
Climate and Energy Leader

James Lovelock was puzzled. He looked out of the window of his Wiltshire cottage and stared at the unseasonal haze. Why, he wondered, could he only see a few hundred yards ahead in the middle of summer? It looked like smog. It smelt like smog. But at that time of year and in the countryside? Friends at the Met Office told him it couldn't possibly be smog. They suggested the local farm could be causing it. But Lovelock had a hunch something else was going on.[1]

And he was just the person to investigate.

He could already boast an impressive and varied career as a chemist, a medic and an inventor. He had worked on everything from cryogenics to the NASA space programme. His experience had taught him to ponder and think out of the box. And his hunch this time was that the cause of the haze might just be chlorofluorocarbons (CFCs), a compound used widely in aerosols and refrigerators. The next time it happened, Lovelock put one of his inventions to use. It was a device originally designed to measure wind speed and direction, but it could also do something else, namely record minute particles in the air from things such as cigarette smoke. He had adapted it to detect CFCs.

Just as he suspected, his machine confirmed that CFCs were three times more abundant during the 'haze'. On a trip to the west of Ireland he was able to demonstrate that smog there had blown all the way from cars in southern France and Italy. He noted that even the air coming from the Atlantic carried CFCs.

A friend of Lovelock's suggested he apply for a grant from the Natural Environment Research Council (NERC) to travel to Antarctica on one of their vessels. There, he would be able to take measurements to see whether CFCs were building up in the atmosphere across the globe. But after being peer-reviewed by other academics, his proposal was rejected as being too off the wall. One senior chemist argued that his premise was bogus: it was 'common knowledge' that CFCs were exceedingly difficult to measure in parts-per-million, let alone the parts-per-trillion he was proposing.

To their credit, the civil servants at NERC disagreed. While they couldn't give him a grant, they did at least facilitate his travelling for his research. So in 1971, Lovelock made all of the required equipment for just a few hundred pounds and set off for the Antarctic, not by plane but on a research ship, the RRS *Shackleton*. He took measurements as he went. And when he got there, he was able to confirm for the first time the presence of CFCs as far south as Antarctica.

What did this mean for the environment? Three years after Lovelock's trip, chemists F. Sherwood Rowland and Mario Molina suggested that CFCs were likely to be depleting the planet's ozone layer – the section of the earth's atmosphere that absorbs most of the sun's UV rays and sits just above the height at which planes fly. Lovelock wondered if he could prove the hypothesis.

He requested that the Met Office take his equipment up in a Lockheed C-130 Hercules. Again, he hit a bureaucratic brick wall. But in a stroke of luck, the SAS offered to take Lovelock on a test flight planned for the following week. Just as Rowland and Molina had hypothesised, Lovelock's flight found that readings of CFCs started to fall off as the plane entered the stratosphere, and began to be broken down by the intensity of the UV rays. The problem was that when the CFCs were broken down, they released chlorine atoms, which then reacted with the ozone molecules. According to Rowland, one chlorine atom can cause around 100,000 ozone

James Lovelock

molecules to be destroyed.[2] Lovelock's trip confirmed that the worst-case scenario many feared was indeed happening: the ozone layer was shrinking. But the article he then wrote for *Nature* was never quoted – or indeed seen – by Rowland and Molina, something Lovelock attributed to polarisation within the scientific community.[3]

In the race to discover the impact of CFCs, the baton then went to another Brit, Joe Farman, and his colleagues at the British Antarctic Survey. Farman had collected atmospheric data from Halley Bay in Antarctica since the late 1950s. In 1982, the data showed an unexpected 40% decrease in ozone levels. It was such a big drop that Farman thought it must be an error. NASA's scientists hadn't reported any anomalies in their satellite readings, so he concluded that the reading was caused by a machine malfunction, perhaps caused by extreme cold. He ordered a replacement machine.[4]

But when Farman and his team took their next measurements the following year using the new machine, the numbers didn't change. In fact, a closer examination of historical data on file showed that ozone levels above Halley Bay had been declining since 1977. The team took their next measurements a thousand miles north-west to see whether the decline was localised, and found levels had also gone down at the new location.[5] The scientific hypothesis linking ozone depletion to CFCs had finally been confirmed.

This shocked political leaders into action. In 1987, the Montreal Protocol was signed. Despite geopolitical tensions, the UK, the US, China and Russia all agreed to phase out the use of CFCs. Today, 197 parties have ratified the treaty – it was the first UN treaty to ever get universal ratification.[6]

CFC emissions are not the biggest direct driver of climate change – that is carbon dioxide. But they do have a warming effect, accounting for perhaps 10–20% of man-made warming.[7] By depleting the ozone layer, they also create a serious health risk because of the increase in UV radiation on the ground. Lovelock's discovery and the global effort to outlaw CFCs that followed was the first key step in demonstrating how man was damaging the planet. It also showed that we could stop it. British science was at the heart of that pivotal moment.

James Lovelock turned ninety-nine in 2018. That year, NASA announced that for the first time the hole in the ozone layer was beginning to shrink. It was the best birthday present he could have hoped for. By around 2066, the levels of ozone in the Antarctic are predicted to be back to their 1980 levels.[8] The UN Environment Programme says the Montreal Protocol's 2016 amendment calling for the reduction in emissions of hydrofluorocarbons (HFCs) represents the 'single largest contribution the world has made towards keeping the global temperature rise "well below" 2 degrees C'.[9]

But it will not be enough.

The 22nd of July 2024 saw the hottest ever average global temperature recorded. The following day it went even higher. In the previous twelve months, temperatures exceeded the previous global record on fifty-seven separate days.[10] Just weeks earlier, another milestone had been passed: average global temperatures had remained above the 1.5°C threshold for an entire year.[11] One study estimates they will be 2°C higher than the pre-industrial threshold by the end of the next decade[12] – despite the Paris Agreement commitment to keep it 'well below' that level.[13] The director of the EU's Copernicus Climate Change Service described rising temperatures as 'truly uncharted territory'.[14] During that year, there were wildfires in Russia and heat warnings for thirty million people in the US. Global average sea levels also hit a new high.[15]

Among other risks is a threat to the food chain on which we all depend. CO_2 increases the acidity of the oceans, which imperils the plankton that provide food for fish, turtles and shrimps right at the start of the food chain. According to the Natural History Museum, plankton shells are now 76% thinner than samples taken by the HMS *Challenger* expedition in 1872.[16] If they become extinct, there will be a knock-on effect for other species – and ultimately all species. That could be very dangerous indeed.

Projections now suggest that, on current trends, global temperatures will rise by nearly 3°C by the end of the century.[17] Such a rise will almost certainly generate more heatwaves, droughts and storm surges and increase sea levels. As well as the threat to many animal species, it could lead to more food and water shortages, mass migration and an associated rise in poverty and conflict. Increased coastal erosion and flooding could leave several island nations and low-lying coastal cities uninhabitable.[18]

An even bigger risk is that we then pass a tipping point from which there is no going back. If temperatures rise above a certain level, the Arctic permafrost will start to thaw. It stores billions of tonnes of CO_2 and methane, and if that is released into the atmosphere, temperatures will rise further, creating a feedback loop in which yet more thawing leads to ever higher temperatures. Each 1°C increase in average global temperatures could release up to 175 billion tonnes of CO_2.[19]

The oceans absorb about half of all CO_2 and are becoming more acidic as a result. That in turn is creating another feedback loop: as the acidity reduces biodiversity, it reduces the ability of the oceans to sequester CO_2. That means more of it remains in the atmosphere, leading to further temperature rises. No one knows the exact levels at which these feedback loops become unstoppable.

These are no longer theoretical risks, particularly in Africa. Despite only accounting for around 3% of global emissions,[20] the continent is being disproportionately affected. Desertification is a major issue for countries such as Burkina Faso, Djibouti, Eritrea, Ethiopia, Mali, Mauritania, Niger, Nigeria, Senegal, Sudan and Chad.[21] Madagascar has already been the victim of what was dubbed the first ever 'climate change famine'.[22] Zambia has seen the Zambezi river, which supplies much of its electricity through hydroelectric power, severely depleted following an El Niño-induced drought,[23] which has also depleted the Victoria Falls, threatening tourism in both Zambia and neighbouring Zimbabwe. Nearly seventy million people in southern Africa have felt the effects of a drought which has caused large-scale crop loss.[24]

Climate sceptics tend not to dispute the statistics about rising temperatures. Instead, they challenge the hypothesis that climate change is man-made. But even if that's the case, higher temperatures are causing real-world effects that few dispute. Warmer seas have seen the area covered by hard coral fall by 13.5% in a decade.[25] Glaciers are retreating worldwide, with Greenland reported to have lost a trillion tonnes of ice since 1985.[26] Scientists overwhelmingly believe that man is responsible, with the consensus level now at 99% in peer-reviewed academic literature.[27] That consensus could of course be wrong, as it has been in the past. But even if our scientists are a new generation of flat-earthers, we should still do what we can to limit temperature rises and the damage they are causing.

For that reason, the IPCC, an independent panel of scientists set up by the UN to monitor climate change, continues to stress the importance of limiting global temperature rises not to 2°C but to 1.5°C. That 0.5°C difference has a significant real-world impact: ignore it and more than one third of the global population will experience extreme heat events every five years. Instead of losing two thirds of coral reefs, we lose nearly all of them.[28]

But international cooperation to restrict such temperature rises has hit big roadblocks. The biggest challenge came when Trump withdrew America from the 2015 Paris Agreement, which he has now done for the second time. His energy secretary has said publicly that 'there is no climate crisis, and we're not in the midst of an energy transition either'.[29]

Nonetheless, during Trump's first term, progress continued without the US. It is likely to do so this time as well, not least because a number of major countries have gone in the opposite direction. Russia talks about working 'with' the Paris Agreement and making it more efficient. China has urged the US to continue its support for energy transition (although it continues to increase its own use of coal[30]). Even Saudi Arabia has said it wants to be 'part of the train'.[31] For sure, their words are not always matched by deeds, but the language and intentions of previously sceptical countries has changed.[32]

And then there's Britain. James Lovelock's story demonstrates the positive role we have played in galvanising international action to protect the climate. As we will see, no country has done more. But while we score well in terms of virtue, we score poorly in terms of economics. Modern digital economies will need energy-hungry data banks, digital networks, and power for electric cars, but the UK has some of Europe's highest energy prices.[33] Until we put in place a plan to address this, we are unlikely to persuade others to follow suit.

James Lovelock lived to the age of 103. In the run-up to his hundredth birthday, I happened to be doing something closely related to his work. I was in Brussels, hosting a private dinner at the British ambassador's residence. It was a rather small dinner – in fact there were only two guests, myself and Enzo Moavero Milanesi, the Italian foreign minister. My objective was to persuade Italy to stand aside so that Britain could host COP26, a crucial climate change conference that marked five years since the Paris Agreement.

Moavero Milanesi is an extremely urbane Italian of the old school, always impeccably dressed and extremely courteous. He has a background in both academia and the European Commission, and became foreign minister for the rather Italian reason that, as a member of neither party in the governing coalition, he was acceptable to both.

COP26 was due to happen in Europe, and Italy was the only other country to have expressed an interest. I believed Britain would do a good job hosting it. But I needed to find a way to head off Italy, which as an EU member would get the support of other European countries if it sought it. Hence the need for a deal. Over the course of the dinner I established that Italy wanted to play a part in COP26 – perhaps hosting one element of the conference – but was happy for the UK to take the lead. A sort of understanding emerged. A few weeks later Theresa May announced that Britain would host COP26 in Glasgow.

From a diplomatic point of view, I was delighted. But just why were we interested in hosting a very expensive conference that cost £250 million?[34] For sure, I believed it would be a helpful showcase for the kind of can-do diplomacy we wanted to be associated with post-Brexit. But it was mainly because no country has done more to combat climate change and I wanted to play to our strengths.

That commitment has come right from the top. Over many decades as both prince and monarch, King Charles has campaigned more visibly and consistently on the risks to the planet than anyone else alive. Back in 1970, he gave a speech in which he warned about the impact of growing pollution from 'gases pumped out by endless cars and aeroplanes'.[35] He has said that people thought he was 'rather dotty' at the time, but since then his thinking has become mainstream.[36] His concerns were echoed by someone else of great influence, namely Margaret Thatcher. She was hardly Prince Charles's political soulmate, but she happened to be the first UK prime minister with a background in science. Perhaps that was why, in 1988, she became the first world leader to give a speech on the risks of climate change.

She first spoke publicly on the issue on a warm September evening nearly a decade into her time as prime minister. It was at the most venerable of British scientific institutions, the Royal Society. Because there was so little interest in the topic, there were no TV cameras present – even for the established world leader that she was by then. She often relied on the glare of TV cameras to illuminate her script, but that night, perhaps fittingly, she had to deliver her message by candlelight. She had been instrumental in implementing the ban on CFCs, but they weren't the only thing warming the planet, she said. It was a range of greenhouse gases, including carbon dioxide and methane, that were 'creating a global heat trap which could lead to climatic instability'.[37] She continued the theme the following year, in an address to the UN. She told delegates that we faced the insidious danger of 'irretrievable damage to the atmosphere, to the oceans, to earth itself'. Climate change 'could alter the way we live in the most fundamental way of all', she said, arguing that the world would only succeed in tackling it through a vast international effort.[38] Cooperation was key. As she said at the opening of the Met Office Hadley Centre for Climate Science and Services, 'The fact is that you cannot divide the atmosphere into segments and say, "All right! We will look after our bit, and you look after yours!"'[39] She argued there needed to be a binding international agreement ahead of the UN Conference on Environment and Development in Rio in 1992.

By the time that conference happened, she had been ejected from office. The UK was represented by John Major, along with a small team of cabinet ministers. He was the first G7 leader to commit to attending and helped secure the UN Framework Convention on Climate Change.[40] Tony Blair continued the effort, putting the UK to work negotiating the Kyoto Protocol,[41] and Gordon Brown passed the Climate Change Act 2008, making the UK the first country to legislate for a legally binding framework to tackle climate change. David Cameron then became prime minister after travelling to the Arctic for a much-satirised photoshoot which saw him pulled across the tundra by huskies on a sled. True to his word, he introduced major initiatives to make renewable energy cheaper, including generous subsidies for solar power and wind turbines. After that, Theresa May passed a law making a net zero economy a legally binding requirement, with an independent committee to monitor progress. Boris Johnson, supported ably by Alok Sharma, then made the UK the first country to incorporate international aviation and shipping into the UK's carbon budgets. There was some watering-down of targets under Sunak, but they were largely reinstated by Starmer.

Other countries have also played a major role in the climate movement. France used the weight of its diplomatic network, one of the most extensive in the world, to secure the Paris Agreement in 2015. Sweden introduced one of the first carbon taxes thirty years ago,[42] and gave the world Greta Thunberg. Denmark has long been a beacon of environmentalism, with abundant offshore wind farms, cutting-edge recycling facilities and a cycling culture which has massively reduced cars in its cities. Over 90% of new cars sold in Norway are electric,[43] and it gets nearly all its energy from hydroelectric sources[44] (while quietly increasing oil and gas exports).

But Britain has consistently been one of the loudest and most credible voices on the issue, not least because of the strength of its science base. Alongside geniuses like Lovelock, the UK hosts a number of globally recognised centres of climate expertise including the Climate Research Unit (CRU) and the Tyndall Centre for Climate Change Research. It also includes the Hadley Centre, whose task is – in Thatcher's words – 'not to predict the weather for a few weeks ahead, but to predict it for a century ahead'. The Hadley Centre and the CRU have jointly established the world's first integrated land and marine global temperature record, which dates back to 1850.[45] Britain also boasts some of the most active climate campaigning organisations – and not just on one side of the argument. Global Justice Now, Just Stop Oil and Extinction Rebellion (XR) were all founded in Britain, as was the climate-sceptic Global Warming Policy Foundation set up by former Chancellor Nigel Lawson.

Because of a sustained political consensus on the issue over more than three decades, Britain has halved its emissions since 1990.[46] That is a bigger reduction than any other major economy. It is a record that is somewhat flattered by the fact that it is a production rather than consumption measure and we now import many of our most carbon-intensive products. But it is nonetheless a major achievement. As a result, Britain is ranked third globally in the global Climate Change Performance Index, ahead of every other large economy and behind only Denmark and the Netherlands.[47] We do rather less well on biodiversity because, as the first country to industrialise, we switched much land over to high-intensity agriculture or industrial use. But we have – at least partially – made up for this with the help of islands we continue to own across the globe where we have designated vast swathes of territorial waters as marine protected areas (MPAs). In fact, Britain has designated for protection more ocean than any country except Australia, including 836,000 km^2 around the Pitcairn Islands and 445,000 km^2 around St Helena.

Reduction in Emissions: G20 Countries, 1990–2023

Country	G20 Rank	Overall Rank	Change
UK	1	12	-49.31%
Germany	2	20	-43.48%
France	3	26	-30.79%
Italy	4	29	-28.47%
Russia	5	30	-28.40%
Japan	6	49	-14.57%
US	7	54	-4.05%
Canada	8	70	19.93%
South Africa	9	75	26.31%
Australia	10	78	37.68%

Source: Pierre Friedlingstein et al., 'Global Carbon Budget 2024', *Earth System Science Data* 17, no. 3 (2024): 965–1039, https://doi.org/10.5194/essd-2024-519 (data file: https://globalcarbonbudgetdata.org/downloads/jGJH0-data/National_Fossil_Carbon_Emissions_2024v1.0.xlsx)[48]

By far the biggest reason for Britain's success in reducing emissions has been a dramatic shift in energy policy. Energy accounts for around three quarters of emissions, so how it is generated matters.[49] In the decade to 2024 the UK succeeded in reducing the proportion of electricity generated from coal from 40% to zero.[50] On windy days, wind turbines now provide up to two thirds of our electricity.[51] Britain's renewables sector is now one of the largest and most competitive in Europe, almost entirely digital and constantly being shaken up by vibrant challenger companies.

But this has not fed through into lower energy prices – and this remains the biggest gap in the UK's approach. Voters generally care about the environment and will support a government that acts pragmatically and proportionately. But they care even more about the economic consequences of high energy bills. In a digital age any country unable to access the energy it needs cheaply will be at a profound disadvantage. America has managed higher growth than any other large economy partly because of access to low-cost (and not necessary green) energy. With natural gas prices one fifth of European levels,[52] it has seen its GDP per head rise three times more over fifteen years. Indeed its energy costs are now so low that it is now repatriating many energy-intensive industries that were previously based abroad – the opposite of what is happening in the UK. No requirement for Middle Eastern or Russian oil or gas also made the US much stronger, in geostrategic terms, after the invasion of Ukraine – just as dependency made Europe weaker.

So what should the UK do? Shale gas, irrespective of environmental considerations, could only supply our needs temporarily.[53] But we should surely use the North Sea oil we still have to its fullest extent. Locally supplied oil and gas has a lower carbon footprint than imports from the Middle East and should be part of any energy transition, as well as an important source of investment and jobs. Doing so is also sensible insurance against a future energy crisis.

North Sea reserves, however, will not last for ever, nor is using them ultimately consistent with a zero-carbon economy. But any longer-term solution will need to be broader than wind and solar, both of which are subject to Britain's highly changeable weather. This 'intermittency' can be addressed with battery storage or standby gas – but both add to costs. Advances in technology may come to the rescue but, for now, by far the safest bet is proper investment in nuclear power.

France has long understood this. Even though nuclear power already supplies two thirds of its electricity, it is currently embarking on its biggest expansion for decades, planning to build up to fourteen new reactors by 2050. Even before the results of such investment bear fruit, French electricity prices are more than 30% lower than in the UK.[54]

But progress in the UK has been patchy. Partly because of inordinate planning delays, the new nuclear power plant I approved for Hinkley Point C may end up being the most expensive anywhere in the world, nearly double what the same plant would cost elsewhere. Planning reforms are urgently needed.

The most promising way to reduce the cost of nuclear energy, though, may be through a new technology that we already have in the UK. The small modular reactors (SMRs) used in nuclear submarines can provide the power needs of a city the size of Oxford or Guildford. They are much easier to find land for than larger reactors, and can be readily manufactured by UK suppliers such as Rolls-Royce. With Grant Shapps, then Energy Secretary, I set up a competition to see whether they are feasible. If they are, we should move fast to get them up and running as part of a longer-term plan to build a more reliable and weatherproof national grid.

In the UK, we have tended to focus more on the altruistic importance of saving the planet than on the economic need for cheap energy. The emphasis needs to change – but the two objectives are not incompatible. Either way will be expensive. That means a trade-off which we should be honest about: higher energy bills for a while to unlock cheaper energy in the future. When I was Chancellor we ended up spending nearly £100 billion to support families through the energy crisis caused by the invasion of Ukraine. How much wiser it would have been to spend that money on nuclear power two decades earlier to insulate ourselves from global energy shocks.

As we do that, we can also play to Britain's long-standing strengths as a practical climate change advocate. Nearly half of our aid budget has been assigned to climate priorities[55] and we can unlock even more support through the senior positions we hold on the boards of international financial institutions such as the IMF and the World Bank. London has become the global hub for green finance, ranking top of the 2024 Global Green Finance Index,[56] something I bolstered with the Edinburgh and Mansion House reforms. Foreign Secretary David Lammy is setting up a Global Clean Power Alliance to make the most of our influence in this area. That alliance should explore refocusing climate targets on carbon consumption rather than CO_2 production, as advocated by Professor Dieter Helm.

We can also help others when it comes to biodiversity. Kew Gardens houses over 50,000 plant species and is one of the largest botanic gardens in the world.[57] Its herbarium has 8.5 million plant and fungal specimens, one of the largest anywhere, and it also has the world's largest plant DNA and tissue banks.[58] The Natural History Museum, under the leadership of Doug Gurr, has developed the leading global methodology for measuring biodiversity, which is being shared readily with other countries. What gets measured gets done – and the UK can help with the measuring.

Professor Nick Stern of the London School of Economics is one of the world's most respected climate experts and author of *The Economics of Climate Change: The Stern Review*, published in 2006,[59] the same year that Al Gore published *An Inconvenient Truth*. Although the latter was more famous, the former may have had a bigger impact on many governments because it set out clearly why addressing the risks to the planet can help rather than hinder economic growth.

Nearly two decades later, the numbers are starting to move in Stern's direction. Massive innovation now means renewable energy is often cheaper than oil or gas. The cost of solar energy capacity has plummeted from nearly £100 per watt fifty years ago to just 15p per watt today.[60] Renewable prices are still falling – just as prices are rising for coal and gas, with the need for ever deeper and more remote extraction. Texas, hardly a beacon of climate activism, is now building more solar farms than anywhere else in the US because the energy they produce is so cheap and reliable.[61]

What worried Prince Charles and Thatcher three decades ago has transformed into a global movement to protect the climate, much of it thanks to British leadership. By halving our own emissions we have shown other countries what is possible. Less well understood is the economic prize: plentiful, cheap, clean energy for consumers and businesses in a digital age. Get this right and, even without oil or gas reserves, we will start to unlock economic competitiveness in a way that only the US has managed to date. Our booming renewables industry is a good start, but will only provide the cheap energy we need if accompanied by the same ambition for nuclear power. Just as defending ourselves properly can be good business, so too can saving the planet.

5
Free Trade Advocate

On a hot summer's day in 1980, Japanese businessman Masataka Okuma arrived in London.[1] The Nissan executive was there to meet government ministers to discuss the prospect of manufacturing cars in the UK. The meeting was in many ways surprising – not least to Okuma himself. Just three years earlier, he had written off investing in Britain due to its appalling industrial relations, numerous strikes and faulty cars made by a part-nationalised British Leyland. The number of cars being made in the country had halved in just eight years.[2] Meanwhile the British government had been not just championing its own company but also restricting imports, including those from Japan.

In other words, Okuma thought, Britain was the worst possible location for a European car plant.[3]

But someone else thought differently. Ever since her days as leader of the opposition, Margaret Thatcher had been pushing to liberate a car industry that she saw as being smothered by state ownership and protectionism. She wanted to regenerate areas of the country that had been blighted by unemployment and was not squeamish about foreign investment playing its part. During her first trip to Japan in 1977, Thatcher visited several Japanese companies, including Nissan's high-tech plant in Zama. She was impressed with what she saw and returned to the UK inspired.

In early 1980, Government officials reapproached Nissan, initially seeking international investment into British Leyland. But Nissan came back with a more radical counter-proposal. Was the UK interested in a brand-new plant? They had long considered investing in Europe but never before in the UK. Could they be persuaded to change their mind? Officials were sent to Japan to visit Nissan, where they met Okuma. The visit to London a month later was agreed.

Okuma began to appreciate that, contrary to his initial instincts, there were in fact advantages in investing in the UK. It had oil reserves, giving it a secure energy supply. It had a reasonably large domestic market. It had a components sector of sorts. But crucially, it was a big enough fish inside the EEC to resist the inevitable opposition to a Japanese car plant that would come from more protectionist members. Okuma left the UK that summer promising that Nissan would submit a more detailed plan in the following months. The UK became the unexpected frontrunner for Nissan's European investment.

Six months after his first visit, Okuma was back in London. Although it was colder, the conditions for investment had warmed. Inside the company, there was still opposition from some quarters citing the 'British disease', as Britain's domestic problems were nicknamed. But there was enough goodwill to move forward to the next stage. Okuma gave a press conference asking for public support. He emphasised that because the proposed plan would involve a lot of new jobs in the north-east, Nissan should be seen as a local firm.

In its sales pitch, Britain presented a direct contrast with France, which at the time was responsible for a number of protectionist stunts designed to damage Japanese manufacturing. In one famous example, the French government, in breach of European trading laws, had ruled that all imported video recorders must be cleared through one of its smallest customs offices, situated in the town of Poitiers. Miles from the port of arrival, with only nine members of staff, the office would take weeks to undertake the necessary customs checks for just one lorryful of Japanese video recorders.[4] Meanwhile, Thatcher continued to hammer home Britain's historic role in supporting free trade – and said Japan should do the same.

The remaining obstacles were knocked down one by one. Reluctance from other car manufacturers was a good thing, thought Thatcher – they needed the competition. Nor would she let

Margaret Thatcher at the new Nissan factory

Chancellor Nigel Lawson's abolition of tax breaks for the purchase of industrial machinery kibosh the plan – Nissan would be given a special (and somewhat secret) exemption. Negotiations went back and forth about whether the plant would be unionised. They stalled temporarily during the Falklands War, but then restarted.

Okuma retired before the process he had initiated was completed. But on 8 July 1986, six years after his initial visit to London, a white T12 Bluebird 2.0 GTX rolled off the production line, marking a new era of British car production. Its registration was JOB 1.

Nissan director Toshiaki Tsuchiya personally inspected JOB 1. That night, he invited some of the local staff round to his home. The cultural differences caused some bemusement. When served a jellied Japanese dish called *konnyaku* the staff asked why on earth anyone would eat something that tasted like rubber. But to everyone's surprise, it was the similarities rather than the differences between the Japanese and British workers that shone through. As Toshiaki recalled, 'Until then I was sure that Japanese employees were the most loyal, but I was surprised to see that actually it was the same or even higher at Nissan Motors UK.'[5]

Meanwhile, the French looked on with deep suspicion. They saw the Sunderland Nissans as a mortal threat to their own car companies. So their government made a concerted effort to have the cars manufactured in Sunderland counted as Japanese exports, so they would be exposed to trade restrictions. But Okuma's hunch paid off: because of Britain's weight in the EEC, Thatcher was able to see off French protectionism. Nissan cars made in Britain were classed as British. Success in Sunderland inspired Honda and Toyota to follow suit, opening their own plants in Swindon and Derbyshire (although the Honda plant has since closed).

By 2010, with around 400,000 vehicles leaving the factory floor each year, the Nissan plant was the most productive in Europe.[6] Since 1986 it has produced over 10 million vehicles, exporting 80% of those to over a hundred different markets around the globe.[7] One in three British-manufactured cars is now produced in Sunderland – indeed, at one point the city was producing more cars than the whole of Italy. Nissan's gamble turned out to be the start of a British manufacturing revolution.[8]

Because EEC membership had helped to draw Nissan to the UK, many feared Brexit would drive it away. Indeed, after the referendum Nissan duly warned that operations in Sunderland would become 'unsustainable' if Britain left the EU without a trade deal. But a deal was agreed, crucially with no tariffs or volume caps in either direction. Japanese car manufacturers today are far more worried about competition from Chinese electric vehicles than Brexit.

When I became Chancellor, I was well aware of the transformation the original Nissan investment had brought to UK manufacturing, so I made it a major priority to secure the next phase of their investment. I met the Nissan chief executive, Makoto Uchida, several times to stress my personal commitment to a new deal. After exhaustive negotiations led by a superb Treasury official, Kristen McLeod, we came to an agreement. The Autumn Statement of 2023 focused on growth and investment, with the flagship measure a new tax incentive called 'full expensing', designed to boost investment in new factories. A year later the numbers showed it did just that.[9] But the very next day I was able to announce that Nissan would produce their next three electric car models in Sunderland. The plans they unveiled included manufacturing the new version of the bestselling Qashqai SUV, a model which will now be exported from Sunderland back to

Japan. All the new electric cars will use batteries produced locally, meaning they are not affected by EU tariffs. Both Uchida and Rishi Sunak came with me to Sunderland to mark a momentous new investment.

The Nissan story is a poster child for the benefits of international trade and investment. But although Britain has been the world's greatest champion of free trade, we have become rather a lone voice of late. Led by the US, other major economies have moved in a more restrictive direction. Even before Donald Trump's new 'Liberation Day' tariffs, the trend towards tariff liberalisation and elimination had stopped in its tracks and the number of protectionist interventions had been soaring.

Author and Rishi Sunak announcing Nissan's electric car investment in 2023

Rise in Harmful Trade Interventions, 2009–24

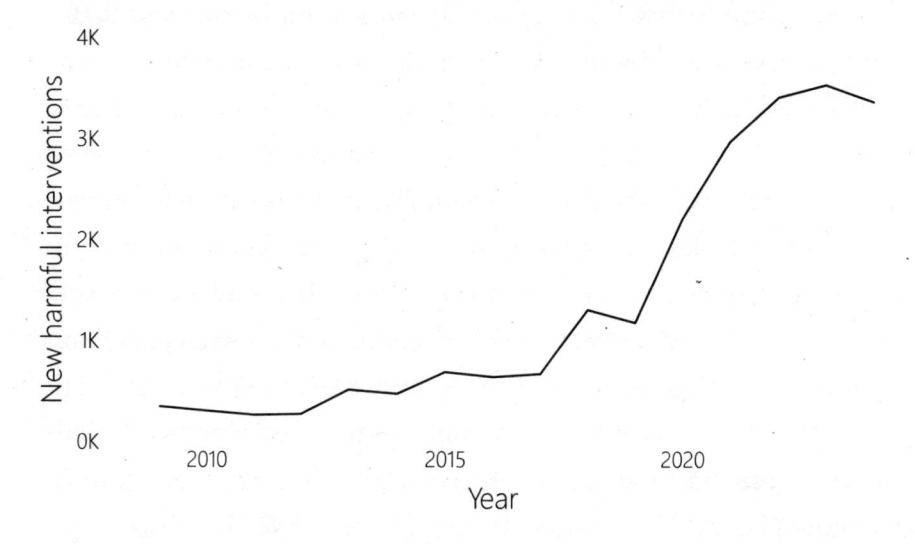

Source: 'Global Dynamics Interventions Data', Global Trade Alert, January 2025, https://www.old.globaltradealert.org/global_dynamics/area_all/year-to_2024/day-to_1231[10]

Many of them were driven by Trump in his first term, who said subsequently that tariffs are 'the most beautiful word in the dictionary'.[11] The president has at least been consistent, railing against Japanese imports as far back as the 1980s.[12] He has certainly never bought into David Ricardo's concept of comparative advantage, the idea that free trade benefits countries even if they have a trade deficit. In public and in private, he remains obsessed with reducing US trade imbalances, particularly with China but also with countries like Germany. Nor is it just mercantilism: the dollar's status as a reserve currency, combined with currency manipulation by many countries exporting to the US, has prevented the dollar devaluation that should theoretically correct a trade deficit. The result has been a United States increasingly indebted to other parts of the world which continue to build up dollar reserves. To no avail: according to the Centre for Economics and Business Research, '[t]he era of unfettered free trade is over. Instead, protectionism is here to stay.'[13]

It would also be wrong to say that hostility to globalisation was driven exclusively by Trump. Hillary Clinton railed against the Trans-Pacific Partnership in the 2016 presidential campaign. Biden kept most of Trump's tariffs and introduced the Inflation Reduction Act to bring clean energy industries onshore. At the same time, Chinese mercantilism on technology, which it describes as part of a 'dual circulation strategy', has kept its markets in strategic sectors firmly closed. The EU, never a fan of free trade outside the single market, has imposed tariffs on solar panels and electric vehicles from China. The pandemic and Ukraine made even free trading nations like the UK sensitive to supply chain risks in critical areas such as energy and medicines.

The nature of such interventions varies. Ninety-five per cent of China's interventions are subsidy-based. Until Trump, the US tended to use local content requirements. The EU regularly resorts to tariffs. Export restrictions including licences, quotas and bans are still not as common as other interventions, but have been growing.[14] Alongside traditional trade barriers, there has also been an increasingly restrictive environment for trade in services and digital products caused by what are called 'non-tariff barriers'. Among the most common are regulations such as GDPR and data localisation requirements.

The overall impact has been stark: in the 1990s and early 2000s, trade grew at nearly double the rate of global GDP. Since the financial crisis, it has only grown at the same pace, meaning that trade has now stopped being the engine of global growth.[15] Even worse, protectionism probably led to deaths during the pandemic: India imposed export restrictions on the world's largest vaccine producer, the Serum Institute, at a stage when less than 2% of Covid vaccines had been administered in Africa.[16]

The last time the world reverted to protectionism was in the 1930s. The Smoot–Hawley Tariff Act of 1930 led to a global trade war that turned recession into depression. Unemployment was over 20% in the UK[17] and around 25% in the US,[18] and in Germany it reached 34%,[19] directly contributing to Hitler's rise.[20] By contrast, after 1945 the world had learnt those lessons, leading to a very different outcome. Massive growth in global trade made a decisive contribution to the biggest ever increase in global prosperity. In one of the most unnoticed and underrated achievements of humanity, the proportion of the world's population living in extreme poverty has dropped from 44% in 1981 to just 9% today.[21] The rich world has benefited massively too: global investment flows and scientific exchange have unlocked remarkable progress in medicine, science and technology.

For the world to turn the clock back would therefore be an extraordinary act of self-harm. The *Economist* calculates that a full decoupling between a US-led western and China-led eastern block would reduce global output by nearly 5%. China would come off worst, with a GDP decrease of nearly 10%.[22] But tariffs of 60% on Chinese goods would also add several points to inflation in the US, increasing the cost of living for many ordinary families who voted for Trump.

But there is huge political support for Trump to do just that. It comes from widespread scepticism about 'globalisation', now a pejorative word blamed for a multitude of ills. It has become a particular bogeyman in economically deprived communities – I often found it thrown back at me in the UK election campaign as a reason not to vote for the Conservatives. The reality is that it has massively increased spending power, with cheaper clothes, TVs, computers and other consumer goods.

But even though lower prices have benefited poorer families, the overall benefits of a globalised world have been uneven. Well-connected cities such as London, Singapore and San Francisco have flourished, albeit with big wealth disparities. Other parts of advanced nations have been left behind and sometimes struggled to grow at all. Even among developing countries, the benefits have varied: China has increased its exports one hundred and eighty times over since 1980, with India and Bangladesh managing around a third of that.[23] But sub-Saharan African countries have barely increased their exports at all.[24] For them, the promise of globalisation is as hollow as it is in the UK's 'red wall' areas or in the US's Rust Belt states.

The answer, though, is not to give up on global trade but to make sure its benefits are spread more widely. Analysis by the WTO shows how powerful this can be if you get it right: over two decades, the doubling of exports from low- and middle-income countries – from 16% to 32% of global trade – led to the number of people living in extreme poverty falling by three quarters.[25] There has been no equivalent fall in Rust Belt states, the north of England or many other left-behind regions in advanced economies. Their scepticism about the supposedly unalloyed benefits of free trade should not be a surprise.

Geopolitics has also forced a reassessment of previous assumptions about global trade. Russia's invasion of Ukraine highlighted the risks of energy dependency on a hostile power. China's increasing determination to challenge the democratic order makes it wise to avoid technological dependency. The pandemic made everyone understand the importance of secure supply lines in an emergency. These are reasonable concerns and some new barriers to trade are therefore inevitable. But as we strengthen economic security, it would be a mistake to unlearn the broader lessons discovered by David Ricardo and Adam Smith. Quite simply, we cannot afford to lose the economic growth they unlock.

The stakes are particularly high for a medium-sized trading nation like the UK that has always flourished on the back of openness to international markets. But sitting outside a large trading block, do we have the clout to stop a drift towards protectionism that could be disastrous for our economy? It turns out that, once again, with some nimble diplomatic footwork, we can have a big influence on the way the issue unfolds – if we choose to do so.

Britain has long been a champion of free trade. The story of Nissan in Sunderland is part of a broader transformation of the UK economy driven in significant part by foreign investment, now widely understood to boost GDP, increase productivity and create jobs. The UK has prospered as a result: in 2023 the value of foreign direct investment (FDI) stock in the UK was $3 trillion, second only to the US.[26] UK companies associated with foreign investment directly or indirectly account for nearly a third of all jobs.[27] Even after Brexit, Britain continues to attract broadly the same proportion of big FDI projects in Europe as before.[28] It also protects its economy with fewer trade barriers than nearly any other major economy.

The UK's free trade instincts did not start with Thatcher. Like most countries, we started off as mercantilists keen to protect our farmers and manufacturers from competition. But in the eighteenth century, Adam Smith's ideas about free trade and laissez-faire economics started to gain traction. David Ricardo, just three years old when Smith published *The Wealth of Nations*, built on those intellectual foundations with his theory of comparative advantage. Their intellectual logic combined with political pressure to lower food prices, with the result that by the middle of the nineteenth century, most protectionist measures had been scrapped – the first time any country took such a decision unilaterally. The hated Corn Laws, used by landowners to keep grain prices artificially high, were abolished. Cheap raw materials fired up the workshop of the world and poorer families benefited from lower food prices. The British empire played its part. For all its faults, as Niall Ferguson writes in *Empire*, no organisation in history did more to promote the free movement of goods, capital and labour.[29] By the end of the nineteenth century, trade had tripled.

There were setbacks, notably in the 1930s, as we have seen. But when the world's nations regrouped after the Second World War, they wisely chose not to turn inwards. Free trade was seen as a solution to the wreckage of war and a way to prevent conflict in the future. In 1948, negotiations began for the General Agreement on Tariffs and Trade (GATT). The world embarked on a free trade journey unlike any other in human history.

GATT was buttressed over many years by the protection of global shipping lanes offered by the US Navy, the world's biggest. It eventually led to the creation of the WTO in 1994. At the heart of the WTO is the concept that trade can only be liberalised if there is a transparent rules-based system in which countries are obliged to treat each other with reciprocity, something that gave it a peculiarly British flavour. Its particular genius is the concept of 'most favoured nation status', which means that if a WTO member reduces tariffs on imports from one member, it must do so for all. Although the rule excludes free trade agreements, it reduced the discrimination and favouritism that previously characterised trade agreements.

FREE TRADE ADVOCATE

Thatcher continued to rage against protectionism wherever she found it, particularly the notorious Common Agricultural Policy. She also championed what will remain Britain's biggest legacy to the EU, namely the creation of the single market, largely set up on the back of a White Paper drafted by her former Secretary of State for Trade, Lord Cockfield. It replaced tariffs on goods (at the time 32% on salt, 37% on china, 14% on cars, among others) with just one tariff: zero. Air travel was made easier, professional qualifications were recognised across member states and product rules were harmonised.

The UK economy's service sectors, such as the legal system, have benefited richly from the country's openness. Because it is perceived as fair and dependable, English law remains the preferred legal basis for governing trade disputes even when neither contracting party

Arbitration Caseloads by Location, 2023

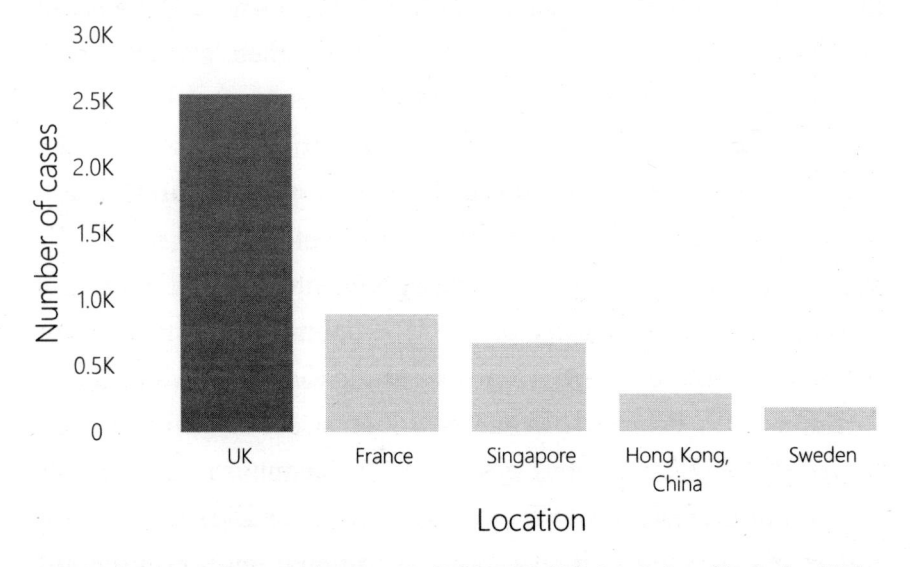

Source: 'International Data Insights Report 2nd Edition 2024', The Law Society of England and Wales, 10 September 2024, https://www.lawsociety.org.uk/topics/research/international-data-insights-2024 [30]

133

has a connection with the UK. As well as in general trade, it is used particularly in finance, insurance and maritime dispute resolution, whether through arbitration or in the courts. An important factor behind this is judicial independence and the UK's non-political process for appointing judges, highly respected for their ability to adjudicate complex cases. This has led to the UK's legal sector becoming one of the largest in the world, with London consistently taking the global top spot in commercial judgments, arbitration caseloads and arbitrator appointments.[31]

Brexit has inevitably interrupted UK trade flows into the EU, at least for the moment. At time of writing, the value of imports in real terms has decreased by 1% and exports by 11%. While that appeared to confirm the suspicions of some that it would cause lasting economic damage, non-EU exports decreased by a similar amount.[32] In fact, the post-Brexit trade deal agreed between the EU and UK mandates zero tariffs and zero quantitative restrictions on bilateral trade, which means that the additional friction that now exists often boils down to bureaucracy, such as customs forms or border checks. That has a big impact on just-in-time supply chains for manufacturers. But it should ease over time with better use of technology – and potentially a thawing of relations under the new government. If and when that happens, the 'trade intensity' of the UK economy, which many economists link to productivity, should return to close to previous levels.

But a much bigger challenge now looms as a result of Trump's tariffs. If the UK ultimately negotiates an exemption, its economy will still be damaged by lower growth in other countries. But if it is not exempted, there will be a serious additional impact on the just over 2% of GDP accounted for by goods exported to the US.[33] That creates a difficult call for the government. If Britain does not retaliate, it looks weak. If it does, higher prices for business and consumers will make the damage worse.

There is of course a perfectly reasonable logic to retaliation, even for people who believe in free trade: without it, there is little pressure on the country introducing tariffs to reverse course. That is why China and the EU are likely to respond with measures designed to inflict equivalent damage on the US economy. But it would be the wrong course of action for the UK: goods exports to the UK from the US only account for 0.3% of American GDP,[34] hardly a big enough stick to make Trump think twice. It may be the wrong course of action for China and the EU as well: goods exports from the US to each of them account for just 0.5% and 1.3% of American GDP respectively.[35]

After Brexit, Britain has the autonomy to make its own choices. That autonomy could include a trade deal with the US, something about which the Trump administration has generally been enthusiastic. The compromises necessary to secure any deal, particularly with respect to our agricultural sector, will be far from easy. But there is surely more chance of doing so if the US administration does not see us as dancing to the EU's tune on retaliatory tariffs.

It is also worth asking whether Trump has a point. He argues that tariffs boost inward investment by forcing global companies to reshore manufacturing and he is already able to point to billions of dollars of additional investment in the US to prove his point. In the UK, too, European quotas on Japanese exports were one of the original reasons for Nissan's investment. Free-trade purists believe that any barriers reduce competition, innovation and productivity growth but the theory often works imperfectly in the real world where there can be a tension between increasing trade and boosting investment.

Ultimately what matters for competitiveness is openness to the brightest and best ideas from around the globe. Both trade and investment play a role in this. Sometimes it will be a finely balanced judgement as to which should be prioritised. But if the result of Trump's tariffs is that the US becomes more closed to innovation from around the world, it will lose out. If the UK stays open to new ideas, it will remain prosperous.

Our most successful sectors – financial services, technology, life sciences, the creative industries and education – have always benefited from that openness. We have become the world's second largest exporter of services[36] by being the world's most open services economy (among the big economies) – and therefore the most internationally competitive. The same logic applies to manufacturing: if we put up fewer barriers to goods imports, we may suffer initially from additional exports being diverted from the US. We might look enviously at the new factories being built in the US. But ultimately, if we hold our nerve, British manufacturers will derive competitive advantage from lower import prices and more innovation than in countries that put up trade barriers. That in turn will spur more investment. It's an approach that has made smaller countries like Singapore extraordinarily successful. Singapore-on-Thames could work for us as well when it comes to trade policy – even without removing our social safety net.

Some argue that, post-Brexit, the UK can no longer claim to be a champion of global free trade. In fact, the opposite is true. As an autonomous player in a more protectionist world, we have both a strategic interest in trade liberalisation and the agency to do something about it. That should not only be a key priority for our relationship with major trade blocks like the US and the EU. It also makes the long-standing links we have with countries like Japan, Canada, Australia, South Korea, Taiwan and Switzerland more important.

Like us, such medium-sized economies are instinctively in favour of free trade and against protectionism. Like us, they do not have the option of self-sufficiency when it comes to sourcing key supplies. But what is striking is that, combined with us, that relatively small list of countries accounts for 13% of total global trade. That is remarkably similar to the 11–12% represented respectively by the US, EU and China.[37] If that grouping can find a way to speak as one voice, it has the potential to be a much bigger voice in global trade negotiations. In that context, Britain's decision to sign up to the Comprehensive and Progressive Agreement for Trans-Pacific Partnership trade agreement (CPTPP) was significant because it has anchored the UK in an alliance which includes many of the very same countries.

The UK should therefore actively build alliances to argue not just against protectionism but in favour of further liberalisation, particularly on the non-tariff barriers that now affect 10% of trade between the largest economies. US withdrawal from the WTO could paradoxically make things easier.

As a country with a large technology sector, the UK is also well positioned to champion another big opportunity for trade liberalisation, namely in the digital sphere. Boosting e-commerce increases trade not just in digital services but also in the physical goods that depend on electronic payment systems. We should champion agreements in areas such as data sharing, vital for the development of AI, as we did successfully in the recent UK–Japan Digital Partnership[38] and the AI safety summit in 2023.[39] The logical place to start is an agreement with the US, which they have suggested they are open to.

If the world's largest and third largest tech ecosystems can agree a set of rules, they are likely to be followed by others in time.

Finally, the UK should also work with other countries to adopt a pragmatic approach to economic security. Concerns about energy dependency on Russia or technological dependency on China are real and justified. As both a military power and a free trading nation, Britain should help chart a workable approach to trade with China that fully protects our and our allies' security interests. But full decoupling is in neither side's interests – and makes an unwinnable conflict more likely. Most importantly of all, we should fight hard to sustain free and open trade between democracies. The more trade deals we sign with friends and allies the better.

In the end, our calculation should come down to first principles. Britain has prospered and will continue to prosper through being the world's most open large economy. That openness, whether it comes from lower barriers to imports or a warmer climate for foreign investment, has delivered more competition, more productivity and more innovation than could ever have been achieved through subsidies or state ownership. For sure, we need to be much better at making sure all parts of the country benefit from the prosperity it unlocks. But even if the rest of the world turns its back on free trade, we should not.

So, just as we saw in the chapters on security and democracy, our diplomatic and economic interests are aligned: using our influence to prevent a return to protectionism supports an economy that has always flourished with more international trade and investment. Free trade, which has delivered for us – and others – the biggest ever increase in human wealth, is rather friendless at the moment. If it chose to, the country of Adam Smith could help once again win the argument he made two hundred and fifty years ago.

6

Pandemic Prevention

On 9 March 2020, Martin Landray was travelling on the number 18 bus from Marylebone to Euston.[1] The UK's first Covid lockdown was just weeks away. Landray is an expert on clinical trials and next to him on the double-decker was another eminent epidemiologist, Sir Jeremy Farrar. Farrar had worked on public health in Vietnam for many years, sat on the government's SAGE advisory committee, and was director of the Wellcome Trust, the health research foundation, which was where they were both headed.

They talked about a new respiratory disease, SARS-CoV-2, which had originated in China and had now reached the UK. At that stage, life was still pretty normal in Britain, as demonstrated by the packed bus they were sitting in. But the new coronavirus was raging in the north of Italy and crippling its health system. The two scientists agreed it would spread throughout the UK within a fortnight, and that they needed to start searching for treatments – fast.

Landray had already sounded the alarm a couple of weeks earlier. Emailing Farrar about an unrelated matter, he had added at the bottom some words about the new virus. Everyone was thinking

Sir Martin Landray

about social distancing and travel restrictions, he said, but at some point people were going to start thinking about treatments. If we weren't careful, a large range of drugs would get thrown at patients, but no one would have any idea which ones worked and which ones didn't. Was anyone thinking about randomisation?

Randomisation is an approach to clinical trials whose origins lie in the eighteenth century, when Scottish naval doctor James Lind was attempting to find a cure for scurvy. He tested potential cures for sailors by comparing them to what we would now call a 'control group', a second group of sailors not receiving the cure. Using that novel approach he discovered, to general surprise, that the best cure was lemons.

British scientists and inventors continued to develop this approach over many years – indeed, centuries – and in 1946 the UK became the first country to use what we now call a randomised controlled trial. In that case, the trial concerned the effectiveness of a drug called streptomycin in treating pulmonary tuberculosis.[2] The methods they used laid the foundations for a massive change in the way research was practised across the world.[3]

Two and a half centuries after Lind's experiment, Landray followed up his conversation on the double-decker by getting in touch with Professor Peter Horby, another expert in new and emerging diseases. Horby had just returned from Wuhan in China, where he had tried to set up a drugs trial to treat the new SARS-like disease. He had failed, ironically because the speed of China's lockdown meant he couldn't find the number of patients he needed.

Ordinarily, such trials would take around a year to get off the ground. But the two medics knew that in a global emergency things had to be different. To get a trial up and running quickly they needed to make it easy for doctors and nurses to co-opt patients – which they did by making the trial part of a patient's regular clinical care rather than a separate study.

Within nine days of writing the protocol – which set out the aims and parameters of the trial – they had recruited their first patient. Within a month the government and the National Institute for Health and Care Research agreed that other clinical research networks should switch their efforts to supporting the study. It was then rolled out to more than 175 hospitals throughout the UK. Every single NHS hospital ended up taking part, including an extraordinary 10% of all patients hospitalised with Covid.[4] The trial made full use of a strong network of research nurses and high-quality NHS patient data.

By this point the pandemic was tearing through populations across the world, so the pressure to deliver was huge. Britain had, in its early stages, abandoned South Korean-style test and trace and dithered over a lockdown. As a result, our infection rates were among the highest, and there was rising public concern. The worst affected patients were being put on ventilators, with a survival chance of just 50%.[5] There were no treatments and no vaccines – indeed, at that stage no one even knew if a working vaccine would be found.

The trial investigators kept cool heads and picked their drugs carefully. One of them was the malaria drug hydroxychloroquine, which America had already tested on hundreds of thousands of patients and which France and Brazil had started using. Trump extolled its virtues, and many called for it to be used in the NHS. But Landray, Horby and everyone else in the study were not going to be bounced: hydroxychloroquine would be tested exactly like the other drugs in the trial, now officially named the Randomised Evaluation of COVID-19 Therapy (RECOVERY) Trial. If it worked it would be mandated. If it didn't it would be banned.

Hydroxychloroquine turned out to be useless.[6] America's Federal Drugs Agency immediately changed its licensing rules to prohibit its use.[7]

But at the same time, positive results were emerging from an unexpected source, an anti-inflammatory drug called dexamethasone. It had two big advantages: it was cheap and it was already stocked in the cupboards of all pharmacies. Amazingly, it worked – the first time any drug had been shown to save lives. Better still, it worked best on the sickest patients. The discovery of dexamethasone was a chink of light at a moment when the pandemic had already taken nearly 40,000 lives in the UK. But despite the urgency, the two professors deliberately held back from saying anything publicly. For another week they probed and double-checked the data.

In that period, the grim daily death toll was solemnly announced from an adapted state room in 10 Downing Street. On 16 June, in the very same room, chief scientific advisor Sir Patrick Vallance unveiled the findings to TV cameras.[8] As Landray puts it, the steroid's results were announced at lunchtime, it was in use by teatime and saving lives by the weekend. The newly knighted Sir Peter and Sir Martin are estimated to have saved a million lives across the globe.[9]

But that wasn't the end of the RECOVERY trial. In February 2021, Landray and Horby announced that an arthritis drug, Tocilizumab, had also proved effective, not just by helping patients on ventilators but also by reducing the odds of them needing one in the first place.[10] Subsequently, in the US another drug called Regeneron was also found to be effective.[11] Two of the big three treatments found to work for Covid had their origins on that red double-decker London bus. The world took note. As *The New York Times* put it: 'The United States has produced little pathbreaking clinical research on treatments to reduce cases, hospitalisations and deaths,' while 'progress on therapeutics research has been a very different story in Britain'.[12]

Perhaps better known is Britain's contribution to vaccine discovery, which was spearheaded by another Oxford-based scientist, Professor Sarah Gilbert.[13] Just a week after Landray and Farrar's double-decker conversation her group revealed that, with the help of Oxford's Jenner Institute, they had identified a Covid vaccine candidate and were preparing for its first clinical trial.

Dame Sarah Gilbert

Their research into this potential vaccine had begun just ten weeks earlier, when Chinese scientist Zhang Yongzhen bravely ignored intense pressure from his own government and made the virus's genetic structure public.[14] Gilbert had previously worked on the vaccine for MERS using funding provided after the Ebola outbreak of 2015–16 through the UK Vaccines Network, at the time chaired by a little-known civil servant called Chris Whitty. That work formed the blueprint for her team's Covid vaccine candidate and gave them an enormous head start: they knew its design was safe and that it triggered an immune response. They also knew it could be manufactured in large quantities and could be stored at 'fridge temperatures' (2–8°C).

As Covid spread further, Gilbert sought the help of Professor Andrew Pollard, director of the Oxford Vaccine Group, who had experience running large-scale vaccine trials. Those trials began on 23 April. A week later, it was announced that the university had agreed a deal to develop and distribute the vaccine with the Anglo-Swedish pharmaceutical company AstraZeneca.[15] Over a thousand immunisations (both vaccines and placebos) were given to healthy adult volunteers between the ages of eighteen and fifty-five. The results, published that July, showed that it induced a strong immune response, especially after two doses.

The study then expanded beyond the UK, even reaching as far as Brazil. On 23 November the results were revealed: no hospitalisations or severe disease had occurred in the vaccinated groups. On 30 December, as the miserable pandemic year drew to a close, the vaccine was approved for use. On 4 January 2021, the first doses were administered to the general public.

UK regulators, usually criticised as being too slow and bureaucratic, showed themselves to be the nimblest in the world. Led by Dr June Raine, the MHRA – the country's official medicines regulator – took the groundbreaking step of doing multiple workstreams in parallel rather than sequentially. That meant that Britain became the first country to approve a vaccine tested in clinical trials. They started by licensing the Pfizer-BioNTech mRNA vaccine developed in Germany, and the Oxford AstraZeneca vaccine followed shortly after.

The Oxford AstraZeneca vaccine was based on an older technology than Pfizer-BioNTech's mRNA vaccine, but it had one crucial advantage: as a so-called viral vector vaccine, it didn't require the ultra-cold storage needed by mRNA vaccines. That meant it was more practical to distribute in countries with only basic health infrastructure. It was also cheaper because of a little-known but commendable act of altruism: both the University of Oxford and AstraZeneca agreed to distribute it to poorer countries at cost. As a result, after six months it was already authorised for use in 178 countries, compared to 106 for the Pfizer-BioNTech vaccine.[16] At that time, including its generic copies, half of the doses allocated via the WHO's COVAX initiative were Oxford–AstraZeneca.[17] In its first year around 3 billion doses are estimated to have saved 6.3 million lives.[18]

During the pandemic, vaccines and treatments discovered in the UK likely saved more lives globally than those from any other country. The UK press focused remorselessly on failings in other aspects of the country's response, but British scientific capabilities were central to the global effort. Nor was it just new vaccines and treatments: genome sequencing at the Wellcome Sanger Institute in Cambridge enabled us to identify new variants quicker here than anywhere else. At one point, nearly half of global Covid genome sequencing was happening in the UK. Britain also put its money where its mouth was, allocating more funds to initiatives such as COVAX than any other country apart from the US, Germany and Japan.[19] No other country made a bigger contribution to the global fight against Covid.

Yet just a few years on, progress in preparing for the next pandemic has stalled.

The WHO says that over seven million people died because of Covid.[20] But those numbers would have been much higher if it hadn't been for some unexpected luck. Part of the reason that vaccines became available so quickly was that, as mentioned earlier, work on a viral vector vaccine in the same disease category was already underway in Oxford. At the same time, relatively new mRNA technology being developed for cancer treatment turned out to work better for Covid vaccines than many thought possible. We may not be so lucky next time. There are still many infectious disease classes for which we don't have vaccines, including the Marburg virus, Rift Valley fever and Lassa fever.[21] Finding vaccines can be phenomenally difficult – after forty years of trying, we have still failed to discover one for HIV. Despite the over-use of antibiotics, we still have many more weapons in our armoury for bacterial infections than viral ones. That means there is still no effective treatment for Mpox, MERS, or even measles. Lateral flow tests, which told people within minutes if they were infected, were a key part of our pandemic response. But progress in diagnostic capabilities for other disease categories has been much more limited.

Yet the threat of another pandemic has not gone away. The UK Covid-19 Inquiry has highlighted that whereas influenza and coronaviruses are of particular concern when preparing for epidemics and pandemics, there is always the threat of 'Disease X', a term defined by the WHO as 'a serious international epidemic [...] caused by a pathogen currently unknown to cause human disease'.[22] Particularly worrying are respiratory pathogens with high adaptability and transmissibility that can spread without visible symptoms. Increasing urbanisation and globalisation mean that when one emerges, it will spread fast.

At the same time other threats to health are starting to loom larger. Bacterial infections are becoming very effective at resisting the antibiotics we throw at them. We are starting to lose the race to develop the new second- and third-line antibiotics needed for when this happens, with more than a million people dying every year because they cannot access an antibiotic that works. A recent study in the *Lancet* found that this could double to two million every year by 2050. In that same year, another eight million deaths could occur from associated causes while infected with drug-resistant bacteria.[23] On current trends, by the middle of the century antimicrobial resistance could become as big a killer as cancer.[24]

Yet the focus of most governments has moved on. Leaders are concentrating on economic growth, immigration and Ukraine. The US Secretary for Health and Human Services, Robert F. Kennedy Jr, is a known vaccine sceptic who has described Covid vaccines as the 'deadliest vaccine ever made', a claim starkly contradicted by scientific evidence.[25] President Trump is withdrawing from the WHO, so when it comes to preventing the devastating impact of another pandemic, leadership is unlikely to come from the US. Is there a role for cash-strapped Britain, blessed with a superb science base, but whose politicians have so many other problems to grapple with? We have many strengths when it comes to helping the world prevent another pandemic, but are UK capabilities still in the top rank? They are – and, if we want it to be, good health can also be good business.

Britain has a long track record when it comes to tackling deadly diseases. Ebola is a virus many times more deadly than Covid. It causes severe blood-clotting, which often leads to fatal internal bleeding. Horribly painful, it spreads via direct contact with bodily fluids such as blood, saliva, urine and semen. In 2015, there was a deadly outbreak in West Africa – it did not become a global pandemic but could easily have done so.

As Health Secretary, I was deeply involved in our national response. We set up airport screening systems to check people coming back from the affected countries. We modelled what would happen if someone with Ebola showed up at an NHS hospital, and made sure every hospital had proper isolation rooms with supplies of PPE. We increased the number of specially equipped intensive care beds available.

But we also played a major role in tackling the disease at source. Because the WHO had been unable to mobilise the response needed in West Africa, it was decided that three developed countries would take individual responsibility for helping stamp it out. Britain took responsibility for Sierra Leone, France for Guinea and the US for Liberia. We sent out more than 1,500 military personnel, 150 NHS volunteers, 100 Public Health England staff, as well as supplying vehicles and PPE.[26] The Royal Navy also sent one of its larger support vessels, the RFA *Argus* and its three helicopters and 100 hospital beds.[27]

In July 2014, the government of Sierra Leone declared the Ebola outbreak a public health crisis. By the time Operation Gritrock began there were an estimated twenty deaths a day. Despite a heroic attempt to stem the spread of the virus, cases were increasing. One of the biggest risks was British healthcare and aid workers bringing the virus back to the UK. They showed extraordinary courage, working in red zones where there was a 70% mortality rate for those infected. One, a nurse called Pauline Cafferkey, did catch the virus. Thankfully, she survived after life-saving treatment at the Royal Free in London.[28]

Although the number of daily deaths seems small compared to the Covid pandemic, Ebola was in some ways more worrying because the chance of surviving the disease was so much lower. There were considerable risks for the UK when it rolled its sleeves up and got stuck in: if any more personnel had become infected and transmitted the virus back home, the decision would have been heavily criticised. Nonetheless, after a huge effort spanning nearly a year, Ebola was all but eradicated in Sierra Leone. The French and Americans were equally successful in Guinea and Liberia. Clear allocation of responsibility and operational autonomy led to a highly successful operational outcome.

So, how do the UK's capabilities stack up today?

When it comes to our science base, Britain often boasts about having nurtured more Nobel Prize winners than anywhere except the US. Less well known is that nearly a third of them have been awarded to scientists born outside Britain but affiliated with a UK institution or resident in the UK,[29] demonstrating just how successful we have been in attracting the brightest minds to our shores. The traffic goes the other way too: the 2024 Nobel Memorial Prize in Economic Sciences was shared by three academics working in US universities, of whom two were born in Britain and the third was educated here.[30] In recent years the international spread of Nobel recipients has become much broader – but in science in particular, the UK still wins a disproportionately high number of awards. British-based scientists also write many of the most respected scientific articles, with the UK ranking second on Scimago's 'H index' – a measure of scientific productivity and impact.[31]

That happens largely because, as discussed in chapter two, the UK continues to have many top-ranked universities. When it comes to scientific research, world-leading institutions such as Oxford, Cambridge, UCL and Imperial form part of a network which includes the Wellcome Trust, one of the largest medical charities in the world, Cancer Research UK, the world's largest independent funder of cancer research,[32] and the British Heart Foundation, again

Citations and Impact by Country

Country	Overall Rank	Citable documents	Citations per document	H index
US	1	609 674	0.92	3 051
UK	2	201 255	1.14	1 928
Germany	3	179 861	1.00	1 690
Canada	4	113 461	1.07	1 562
France	5	110 009	0.99	1 514
Australia	6	105 340	1.31	1 377
Netherlands	7	64 918	1.22	1 373
China	8	1 018 423	1.05	1 333
Italy	9	137 096	1.10	1 333
Japan	10	124 330	0.76	1 301

Source: 'Country Rank', Scimago, 2024, https://www.scimagojr.com/countryrank.php
Note: Metrics based on Scopus data as of March 2024. Document and citation figures are from 2023.

one of the largest funders of cardiovascular research.[33] Increasingly, that network now includes US-style spin-outs from university research departments.

This means that the UK is playing a major role in many of the scientific discoveries that are shaping a new medical revolution. When the first working draft of a human genome sequence was unveiled in 2000, one third of the base pairs were sequenced at the Wellcome Sanger Institute in Cambridge.[34] As Health Secretary, I set up Genomics England and launched the '100,000 genome project',[35] the world's first large-scale national effort to sequence whole genomes for cancer and rare disease research as part of a national health system. Many people have had rare diseases diagnosed as a result, and personalised therapies for certain cancer patients have become possible. Cameron became the first world leader to have an entire sequenced genome proudly sitting on a USB stick on his desk.

Prior to that, the UK was responsible for a number of crucial genomic firsts, including the discovery of the double-helix structure of DNA by James Watson, Francis Crick, Maurice Wilkins and Rosalind Franklin in 1953.[36] Another Brit, double Nobel Prize-winner Frederick Sanger, developed the first widely used method for DNA sequencing in 1977.[37] Cloning[38] and IVF[39] were also pioneered in the UK; mRNA was discovered by teams of scientists working across the UK and the US; and Oxford Nanopore Technologies is using its groundbreaking capabilities to sequence ultra-long strands of DNA and RNA to develop the world's first real-time pandemic surveillance system.[40]

Institutions such as the London School of Hygiene and Tropical Medicine (LSHTM) and the Liverpool School of Tropical Medicine have also been responsible for training many of the world's leading health experts. In the last contest to become director-general of the WHO, every finalist had done some of their training in the UK. That included the winner, Dr Tedros Adhanom Ghebreyesus, who got two degrees in the UK: an MSc in the immunology of infectious diseases from the LSHTM and a PhD from Nottingham.[41]

But it is the NHS, for all its well-publicised failings at home, that offers the biggest prize for scientists worrying about our ability to fight lethal disease. When it comes to medical innovation its centralised structures, often associated with lumbering bureaucracy, also give access to large amounts of high-quality patient data more quickly than other systems. The RECOVERY trial showed how effectively those structures allow clinical trials to be scaled up very quickly. Landray says the UK is among the top five countries globally for the quality of its scientific research – but the very best for the way that same research links seamlessly into both pharmaceutical companies and a major healthcare system.

Doing so needs the consent and support of patients. As a not-for-profit system, the NHS maintains a high degree of trust with patients, meaning there is more willingness to take part in trials. It also means less 'vaccine hesitancy' during pandemics or other health scares.

This builds on a long tradition. Britain has played a major role for centuries when it comes to life-saving discoveries for humanity. British doctor Edward Jenner noticed that milkmaids infected with cowpox were immune to smallpox, a discovery which formed the basis of the first vaccine for the disease in 1796.[42] Dr John Snow famously discovered the link between dirty water and cholera in the 1854 London cholera outbreak.[43] In 1928, Alexander Fleming discovered penicillin,[44] often considered the single medical innovation that has saved more lives than any other. Since then, the groundbreaking discoveries have continued: British epidemiologists Sir Richard Doll and Austin Bradford Hill identified the link between smoking and lung cancer;[45] Sir Harold Ridley invented the intraocular lenses now used to replace natural lenses in cataract operations;[46] Ian Donald pioneered the use of ultrasound in obstetrics;[47] John Charnley did the first total hip replacement;[48] and the UK's Louise Brown became the world's first ever 'test tube baby'.[49] The NHS also completed the first ever successful combined heart, liver and lung transplant,[50] the world's first minimally invasive surgery and the world's first gene therapy trials for children born without an immune system,[51] and made the world's first bionic hand.[52]

Britain has also made sure the benefits of such discoveries are spread far and wide. The number of children in sub-Saharan Africa dying before they are five is down from 25% in the 1960s[53] to a little over 5% today[54] – a remarkable advance which, according to Chris Whitty, owes much to UK efforts to improve access to clean water, sanitation and vaccinations. British-led research into malaria, pneumonia and meningitis has also saved many lives. The UK also uses technical and financial assistance to help local governments strengthen health systems in countries like the DRC, Ghana and Nepal.[55] In the last decade, the UK-funded Health Partnership Scheme supported the training of more than 90,000 health workers in thirty countries.[56] UK contributions have fallen since the pandemic, but only the US has regularly given more to global health projects.[57]

Such a long tradition of health innovation has also been good business. Off the back of it, the UK has become Europe's largest hub for life sciences. It gets the most venture capital funding[58] and has two of the world's top twenty pharmaceutical companies.[59] Success stories include Oxford Nanopore Technologies, which was spun out from the University of Oxford in 2005 and developed the world's first nanopore DNA and RNA sequencing platform;[60] through their portable DNA sequencer, they have tracked variants of Ebola, Zika and Covid.[61] Other rising stars include companies like bit.bio, which reprogrammes human cells for use in drug discovery, and Perspectum, which offers highly innovative digital diagnostics.[62]

Much of the strength in life sciences is centred in Cambridge, home to a cluster of around six hundred life science companies.[63] They are closely linked and cross-fertilise with the university, ranked only below Harvard in the world for life science research.[64] British giant AstraZeneca has its headquarters there, the German company

BioNTech, responsible for the Pfizer-BioNTech vaccine, chose Cambridge as the global headquarters for its revolutionary mRNA research into a cancer cure, and other heavyweights with offices in the city include Thermo Fisher Scientific, Sanofi, Amgen and Illumina. Plans for an Oxford–Cambridge railway, the 'OxCam arc', will unlock more housing and make the city even more attractive for investors.

I have witnessed the UK's influence on global health issues first hand. As Health Secretary, my focus was on reducing preventable deaths caused by medical error (which I have written about in my first book, *Zero*). I made some progress, but as it is a global issue I persuaded the WHO to set up an annual World Patient Safety Day, which takes place on 17 September and each year focuses on a different aspect of avoidable death reduction. Other countries have made big contributions to global health resilience, particularly the US and Germany. But Britain remains one of a select group of countries whose contribution to improving global health has been defining.

What needs to happen now, if we want to avoid another global health catastrophe? Because of our strength in life sciences, we are in the fortunate position of being able to benefit economically from whatever the world decides to do.

The obvious starting point is to make urgent progress on vaccines, treatments and diagnostics. We saw how British research into MERS helped speed up a vaccine for Covid because they are from the same viral family, so we need to make sure research is underway for vaccines in every major disease category – a task UK universities and pharmaceutical companies are extremely well suited to deliver.

Secondly, we need to develop a new class of antibiotics. Bacterial infections are gradually becoming immune to the current class of drugs. Without new ones, we risk medical catastrophe, because the clock would be turned back to before Fleming's discovery of penicillin in 1928. Dame Sally Davies, who worked with me when she was chief medical officer, has led international efforts to address this issue and persuaded world leaders to commit to a target to reduce deaths linked to antimicrobial resistance.[65] But British research and universities can play a big role. As part of that, Lord Ara Darzi has launched the global Fleming Initiative, to be based at the Fleming Centre being built at St Mary's Hospital in London.

Finally, and perhaps more challengingly, we need to improve global cooperation. Globalisation is the reason why the Covid virus spread so fast. Only global cooperation will stop a repeat. This has obviously become more difficult following President Trump's decision to withdraw the US from the WHO. But neither the US nor any other country can stop a virus getting over its borders, so there needs to be a body able to muster the international collaboration necessary to prevent one from originating, particularly in poorer countries where the risks are higher. That can only be the WHO. Reforming rather than scrapping it is the answer.

That means addressing structural failures that prevent the WHO from accessing countries to investigate an outbreak, as happened with Covid in China. But it also means raising standards of biosecurity in laboratories from which pathogens could escape. The highest level of biosafety is 4, known as BSL-4, but it is not always used where it is needed – the SARS virus, for example, escaped from BSL-3 laboratories in Singapore, Taiwan and China.[66] The world may ultimately need a pandemic treaty to implement this. That is unlikely to happen with President Trump, but as a major WHO funder the UK can play a crucial role in mandating the organisation to raise safety standards in its member countries.

If that sounds like a dull but worthy bureaucratic objective, it is worth remembering that just a few short years ago the pandemic cost around seven million people their lives. The economic cost, estimated at $10–15 trillion,[67] has meant higher debt, higher taxes and more strained public finances for all us – something I had to confront in my baptism of fire when I became Chancellor. And the more we and others take the necessary steps, the greater the benefits to Britain's booming life science economy. It is now the biggest in Europe, with more than 300,000 of the world's most sought-after scientists working here.[68] The UK's science base has made it a global leader in key fields such as genomics, vaccine development and biotechnology. The more the world invests, the more Britain benefits. So just as with other big global challenges discussed in this book – security, climate, migration and democracy – doing the right thing for the world can be profitable too.

7

Human Rights Voice

My eyes welled up.

I was sitting at home, mobile clutched to my ear, talking for the first time to Nazanin Zaghari-Ratcliffe. She had been allowed out of Evin Prison in Tehran for just one weekend on furlough. Having been wrongfully imprisoned for over two years, she was currently staying with her parents under house arrest. Her hope – later dashed – was that temporary freedom might end up being permanent.

It was a balmy August afternoon and this conversation – I had recently become the new Foreign Secretary – had been organised by her husband, Richard. We had never met or spoken before, but over that half-hour call she was surprisingly open with me. In particular, she was concerned about whether a prolonged absence would affect her relationship with her husband. I told no one about the call, because I wasn't sure how it might affect her chance of getting a permanent release.

I had arrived at the Foreign Office a month earlier. I had no knowledge of the Middle East – or, if I am honest, interest in it. My principal objective was to concentrate on the relationship with the

US and threats from Russia and China. I remember telling Alistair Burt, my wise minister of state, that I didn't want to spend any time on it. 'You decide what to do and I will back you,' I said rather optimistically. But like every Foreign Secretary, I discovered that was impossible. However much I wanted to concentrate on other priorities, the Middle East sucked me in. It ended up taking around half my time.

I knew a little of Nazanin's case, because Richard's uncle and brother were constituents of mine and had previously come to meet me. I had told them the key question was whether the Foreign Office were really trying to get her home, or just going through the motions. Little did I know that a year later the answer to that question would be a decision on my desk.

Richard's experience in dealing with my predecessor had not been a happy one. In 2017, Boris Johnson had mistakenly told the Foreign Affairs Committee that Nazanin had been in Iran to train journalists, something her family feared would be used by the Iranian authorities to extend her sentence.[1] The Foreign Office saw the whole issue as a messy headache. Worse, it was getting in the way of important geostrategic issues, such as Iran's compliance with a treaty which had been painstakingly negotiated to stop it building nuclear weapons.

So when Richard requested a meeting with me, the Foreign Office was extremely suspicious. Officials strongly advised me not to meet someone who had ignored their recommendation not to go public about Nazanin's detention. They worried that as a result he had turned his wife into a 'prize' for whichever government or minister secured her release. They saw him as a troublemaker and even warned me he might secretly record our conversation.

I rejected the advice.

My experience as Health Secretary taught me that sometimes the British establishment can shut out people who have been wronged by the state. I remembered Scott and Sue Morrish, who lost their three-year-old son Sam to sepsis and were refused a meeting with their local hospital to discuss it. They described how the shutters of the establishment came crashing down. Trying to get answers to their questions was like talking to a brick wall. My special adviser Christina Robinson wondered if Richard was being blocked in the same way. There was also another reason I wanted to meet him: if Britain wants to champion the rule of law, I believe we should practise what we preach. Getting Nazanin home would demonstrate our commitment to habeas corpus. Unlike in an autocracy, in a democracy like the UK every single citizen matters.

So, amidst much nervousness, I met Richard, first in a group and then one to one.

The man I met was quite different to what I had been led to expect. Modest, softly spoken and eminently reasonable, he was keen to engage constructively. He was also surprisingly realistic about the limits of Britain's influence. Nonetheless, he wanted reassurance that we really were doing everything we could to get Nazanin home. Underneath his gentle demeanour was an iron determination.

There was something else unusual about Richard: he was not just passionate about getting his wife home – he also wanted to use her case to improve things for other families going through the same nightmare. In particular, he wanted to smash the practice of hostage-taking as a weapon of diplomatic leverage. Because he bravely went public about Nazanin's detention – unlike other families similarly affected – he exposed to the world the extent to which

Iran was using the practice. In the end, other families followed his lead and demolished the conspiracy of silence on the issue. Iran now rightly pays a much greater price for its inhuman approach to diplomacy.

There was, however, a particular complexity in Nazanin's case. Iran made it clear that a condition for her freedom, alongside that of two other British-Iranian nationals, Anoosheh Ashoori and Morad Tahbaz, was the repayment of a historic debt owed by the UK. The money was owed for some Chieftain tanks that had been ordered by the previous Iranian regime under the Shah, paid for in advance, but never delivered in full after the revolution. It was cash for hostages and an appallingly cynical thing to do – but was it a ransom?

The answer to that question mattered, because Britain has a long-standing (and wise) policy not to pay ransoms. We know that, if we do, it increases the likelihood that other British citizens will be kidnapped. In this case, I concluded that however despicable it was for Iran to use Nazanin, Anoosheh and Morad as pawns, settling the issue could not be considered 'paying a ransom'. The money, around £400 million, was owed to Iran. What's more, it should have been paid a long time ago.

I therefore started to make the argument inside government that the debt should be paid. The Treasury was broadly neutral, perhaps because Chancellor Philip Hammond had been Foreign Secretary when Nazanin was detained. Gavin Williamson, then Defence Secretary, was extremely hostile – concerned that the money could be used to finance terrorism through Hezbollah or other Iranian proxy forces in Yemen, Syria or Lebanon. But when he was replaced by Penny Mordaunt, it became clear that the MOD would not block a deal, even if they remained unenthusiastic.

Meanwhile, I met the Iranian foreign minister in New York to try to make some progress on the diplomatic side. Javad Zarif is an urbane, smart operator. He speaks excellent English and was educated in the US. Our one-to-one discussion lasted half an hour. Not once did he try to suggest that Nazanin was guilty of the charges against her. He wanted to engage, probably to maintain Britain's support for the Iran nuclear deal which Donald Trump had just pulled out of. We discovered he ultimately had little influence inside the Iranian regime. As foreign minister, he was charged with engaging with the outside world – and no more. Judicial decisions were controlled by the hardline Revolutionary Guard, the IRGC, who reported not to the president but to Iran's Supreme Leader.

So I travelled to Tehran in a further effort to move things forward. Because British Airways do not fly there, we had to go on Iran Air, and had the curious experience of being surrounded by Iranian agents in the neighbouring business class seats. My security-conscious Foreign Office officials warned me that they were not regular businessmen so we were careful not to look at confidential papers or hold sensitive conversations. When I arrived, I found that Tehran was an unexpectedly beautiful and bustling city. There were no Western brands available in the markets, which made it feel like an exotic, undiscovered gem, somewhere with the potential to be a great world city – as indeed it once was.

I knew I would not be allowed to meet Nazanin. Instead, I asked the smooth Mr Zarif to pass her a gift. It was a copy of Nelson Mandela's autobiography, *Long Walk to Freedom*, which I had inscribed with a personal message to give her some encouragement. Needless to say, she never received it. We wondered if a meeting with Ali Shamkhani, the secretary of the Supreme National Security

Council, would be more productive, because he was thought to have greater influence. He certainly projected power and did indeed promise to give Nazanin access to her own doctor, something we knew she desperately wanted. But that too never happened. For Iran, the whole issue was only about one simple transaction – you pay the debt and we'll release the hostages. What made it harder was that it was a transaction with a country they deeply mistrusted. History weighed heavily with them, not least the UK's support for the previous regime under the Shah. We were very much 'little Satan' alongside the US's 'big Satan'.

Yes, we owed the money, and yes, I was trying to get it repaid. But I still believed that to link a diplomatic dispute over money to the fate of innocent citizens was unconscionable. In the twenty-first century the freeing of a blameless hostage should never be part of a financial transaction between countries. I said as much in a media interview at the UN, and my comments were unexpectedly met with much jubilation from Nazanin's family and supporters. It turned out to be the first time a British Foreign Secretary had acknowledged that she was innocent. In saying so, I had inadvertently torn up a weaselly rule that 'we do not comment on the judicial processes of other countries'.

While I tried to get the wheels of Whitehall grinding to get the debt paid off, I also made it clear to Iran that the status quo was not an option: there needed to be progress towards releasing the hostages and there would be consequences if there was not. It was not always easy to find 'consequences' that kept the pressure up. But I needed to do something, because nothing changed after my return from Tehran; they made not even the smallest of goodwill gestures, such as providing the medical access we had requested for Nazanin or an improvement to her cell conditions. So I notched up the pressure by changing our travel advice: from then on all British-Iranian nationals were advised not to travel to Iran. I knew that would annoy Iran, because many dual nationals were engaged in trade that brought in much-needed foreign currency.

Again, nothing happened.

My next step was to agree to Richard's request to give Nazanin formal diplomatic protection. This legally elevated her detention to a 'state-to-state dispute' – the first time in over a century such status had been granted to a private citizen. Again, I had to overrule official advice to do it. The change was of symbolic rather than practical significance, because Iran did not recognise Nazanin as British. As a result, the Foreign Office was concerned it would raise expectations that we could not satisfy.

I was hesitant too, but for a different reason. What if Iran chose to retaliate by arbitrarily lengthening Nazanin's jail sentence? After careful reflection, I decided the only people who should make that call were Nazanin's family. So I spelt out the risks to Richard. But he was resolved. As he told me later, he wanted to know that Nazanin's suffering would always be the government's suffering too. I heard the announcement on the radio on a visit to Scotland. I told my private secretary that I hadn't slept the night before, because I was so worried about what might happen. She told me she hadn't either.

Ultimately, there was no additional sanction from Iran. But neither did my efforts bear fruit before I stepped down as Foreign Secretary. I had, however, turned her case into a top priority for the Foreign Office. The sustained media coverage orchestrated by Richard meant it stayed there.

I also made standing up for wrongly imprisoned Brits a key priority. As part of that, I asked the Foreign Office to draw up a list of other innocent victims. Initially, I was told that was not possible, on the basis that the UK could not 'second-guess' court decisions made in other countries. But after a lot of badgering, I got what I wanted. We carefully reviewed whether we were doing all we could. Not every case was as clear-cut as Nazanin's, but at least the principle was established: if we believed a British citizen had been unjustly treated, we would use diplomatic capital to get them home.

From the back benches, I continued to press her case, including in a direct exchange with Boris Johnson at a parliamentary committee. In the end, to her credit, it was Liz Truss who managed to get the deal done when she was Foreign Secretary. Nazanin and

Author finally giving the Mandela autobiography to Nazanin Zaghari-Ratcliffe

Anoosheh finally came home on a dark morning in March 2022. Morad returned the following year. I met Nazanin over a happy barbecue at my house in Surrey. I gave her – finally – a copy of Mandela's book. Her long walk to freedom was over.

It should not have taken such an effort to get Nazanin home. The fact that it did exposed the gaping divide between our values and those of countries like Iran. But when a renegade country is building a nuclear bomb, attacking Israel and supporting terrorism across the Middle East, it can sometimes be hard to get the machinery of government to focus on the rights of a single person. Nazanin was British, so we had an obligation to do so. But what about the human rights of people who are badly mistreated by their own governments? Should a country like Britain be willing to risk relationships in defence of our values? There can be a diplomatic price for doing so. But even in the most challenging situations there is usually something that can be done.

The global outlook for individual rights and freedoms is currently rather depressing. Executions are rising, often used by autocratic regimes to crush dissent. Use of the death penalty has doubled since 2020 – even before accounting for executions in China, Vietnam and North Korea, who don't publish their data.[2] At the same time, many countries are increasing their restrictions on media freedom, putting publishers under greater pressure than they have been for many years. The number of journalists behind bars – a good proxy – has more than tripled since the turn of the century.[3]

At the same time, religious persecution is becoming more common. Minority Christian communities are among the most persecuted – with an estimated 380 million suffering high levels of harassment for their beliefs[4] – but Jews, Yazidis, Muslims and Hindus are also in the frame. The result is that while 20% of the population of the Middle East used to be Christian, the number has now fallen to just 5%.[5] In 2018 I asked Philip Mounstephen, then Bishop of Truro, to assess the situation for me and recommend some actions the Foreign Office could take,[6] and he did a seminal piece of work which is still echoing around the corridors of power today.

The UK is often accused of colonial attitudes, and castigated for historical shortcomings. We haven't always made the right choices, but we do have a long track record of championing individual rights at home and abroad. That originates from a peculiarly British suspicion of the dangers of an over-mighty state. John Stuart Mill talked about the 'tyranny of the majority'; Isaiah Berlin characterised individual rights as 'negative liberties': the idea that you should be able to think, say or do what you like provided it does not impinge on the liberty of others to do likewise. At crucial moments in history, a law has been changed in Britain with far-reaching impact elsewhere, most famously when it came to the abolition of the slave trade following campaigning by William Wilberforce.

Wilberforce was an MP for forty-five years. He never held government office. Yet he changed history more than nearly any other MP has done or probably ever will. He campaigned patiently and courageously over eighteen years to abolish a trade which Britain had been instrumental in setting up. Working with the Society for the Abolition of the Slave Trade, he got hundreds of petitions submitted to Parliament, including one from Manchester in 1788 signed by nearly a fifth of the city's population. He was also a devout Christian, so alongside powerful speeches in Parliament he mobilised churches across the country to put pressure on MPs through their own constituencies. Given the majority of MPs owned shares in companies that profited from the slave trade, it was a remarkable achievement to persuade them to vote against their own financial self-interest. In 1807 he did just that, aided by the first holder of the office of Foreign Secretary, Charles James Fox. Even better, Britain used the Royal Navy to enforce the new law across the globe.

The abolition of the slave trade needs to be put in due perspective: prior to that, British ships transported more than three million slaves across the Atlantic.[7] But it was nonetheless one of many milestones when British history was defined by the advance of individual rights. The signing of Magna Carta and the Suffragettes are well known, but there are many others – such as the establishment, largely thanks to British lawyers, of the original Geneva Conventions for war combatants and prisoners in the nineteenth century.

Public pressure has often played a critical role, just as it did for Wilberforce. It has often been buttressed by civil society organisations, of which the UK boasts some of the best known. One of them was set up by a barrister called Peter Benenson, who, in early 1961, was disgusted by the fact that two Portuguese students had been arrested and sentenced to seven years in prison simply for raising their glasses in a toast to freedom.[8] It was an act of defiance against the autocratic regime then in control of the country. Benenson was a former Bletchley Park codebreaker and the type who didn't take no for an answer.[9] He considered going to the Portuguese embassy to protest, but realised that would be futile. So he asked himself instead how autocratic regimes would react to a more concerted worldwide protest.

Thus was conceived the novel idea of a one-year international letter-writing and media campaign to free political prisoners. He launched it in the *Observer* on 28 May 1961, with an article entitled 'The Forgotten Prisoners', which described powerfully the plight of prisoners of conscience who did not advocate violence.[10] He argued that all such prisoners should get an amnesty – hence the name of his organisation: Amnesty International. He established an office in London to collect information on such cases and publicise them through journals and newsletters. It is not known what happened to the Portuguese students, but the one-year Appeal for Amnesty campaign has now been going for sixty years. Thousands of political prisoners have been released as a result.

In the process, Amnesty International has become a huge organisation with hundreds of employees and around ten million members in 150 countries. Its influence has occasionally been tarnished by misjudgements, but it remains one of the most influential global voices for human rights. It sits alongside numerous other UK-based campaigning organisations such as Open Doors, Article 19, the Aegis Trust, Thomson Reuters Foundation, Redress, Anti-Slavery International, Equal Rights Trust, Liberty, Justice and Reprieve.

Their work has been made possible because of a modern, legal conception of human rights which Britain also helped craft. It arguably originated in the Atlantic Charter signed by Roosevelt and Churchill in 1941, of which the sixth principle affirmed individual rights for 'all men in all lands'.[11] That may sound anodyne, but it was the first time an international agreement between two countries referred not just to state interests but to the rights of individual citizens.

After that, Britain set up or helped set up the ECHR (discussed in the migration chapter), followed by the International Covenant on Civil and Political Rights in 1966 and the International Criminal

Court in 1998.[12] British lawyers appear before the International Court of Justice (ICJ), the UN's ultimate court for inter-state disputes, more frequently than those from nearly anywhere else.[13]

More recently, the UK was one of the first large countries to legalise disability rights and make same-sex marriage possible. David Cameron still considers the latter, which happened in 2013, one of his proudest achievements. For better or worse, London probably has more practising human rights lawyers than anywhere in the world, perhaps alongside New York. One of them went on to become the current occupant of No. 10.

We are by no means the only country with a long-standing interest in human rights. Germany, as well as being the only nation to pay reparations for genocide, has set up special units for investigating war crimes.[14] Its legal system allows prosecution regardless of when or in which country a war crime was committed, which means that it prosecutes not only people who worked as administrators in concentration camps, but also ISIS members responsible for more recent crimes. Sweden also has a long-standing tradition of championing human rights. Its law also allows for cases to be tried outside the country in which they were committed – which is why the Iranian official Hamid Nouri was arrested in Germany for a notorious prison massacre in his own country.[15] Denmark is renowned for campaigning against the use of torture with its global Convention Against Torture Initiative.[16] France has put a huge diplomatic effort into promoting the universal abolition of the death penalty.[17] And the US too has played a hugely important role, most famously with Eleanor Roosevelt's responsibility overseeing the drafting of the Universal Declaration of Human Rights in 1948.[18]

In this book, I look at the many links between economic and political strength – whether it is on security, democracy, the climate or migration. Frequently, what is good for Britain's global influence also supports its economy. When it comes to championing human rights, the trade-off is starker. Other countries rarely welcome being told how to run their affairs, especially by former colonial powers. It may not cost us much economically to have an argument with Iran or North Korea – but the story is very different with China, the UAE or Turkey. The complexity of those trade-offs became painfully clear to me when I became the first Western foreign minister to visit Saudi Arabia after the brutal strangling of *Washington Post* journalist Jamal Khashoggi.

In 2017 the crown prince of Saudi Arabia, Mohammed bin Salman, known as MBS, became the kingdom's de facto ruler after deposing his cousin.[19] He was just thirty-one at the time. Since then, he has remained a paradox to Western eyes. His economic and social reforms, including allowing women to drive and travel abroad alone, have given the world hope that he might modernise Saudi Arabia. But he has continued with brutal punishments for lawbreakers, zealous use of the death penalty and the ruthless hunting down of political opponents – as Khashoggi found to his cost.

At the same time, Saudi Arabia continues to be a vital strategic partner for the UK. We rely on Saudi intelligence to prevent terror attacks, including one tip-off that allowed us to intercept a bomb smuggled in a printer to East Midlands Airport. We have significant commercial interests in the country, including the lucrative multi-billion pound Al-Yamamah arms contract for the supply of Typhoon jets which supports many jobs in factories in Blackburn.

The Saudis have tried to distance themselves from Salafism,[20] which, among other things, gave the world Osama bin Laden, and remain key allies against Iran. If human rights were top of my mind after the Khashoggi murder, they could not be my only consideration. We need to look to our interests as well as our values – and sometimes choose between them.

How should I use the little influence I had? Diplomacy is often about balancing competing objectives, and this was the ultimate test. For the sake of British jobs and security I couldn't jeopardise the partnership. But for the sake of British values, I couldn't gloss over a murder.

I needed to make the cool-headed calculations with which every diplomat is familiar. Where was the balance of advantage in this relationship? Who needed who more? Did Britain carry any sway? Saudi Arabia was in a difficult position and needed all the friends it could get. But it had the unstinting support of Trump, who saw the Saudis as central to his anti-Iranian alliance. They were also being assiduously courted by China.

The meeting didn't start till around midnight, something that was apparently quite normal. In the royal palace, I sat between MBS and our ambassador, Simon Collis. A Foreign Office Arabist of the old school, Simon was not just fluent in Arabic but had lived most of his working life in the Middle East. His wife is Syrian and he had converted to Islam. Instead of sitting quietly, he joined in the discussion and reinforced the points I made with great vigour. He was one of the most impressive diplomats I ever worked with.

As was reported, I was direct with my concerns about what happened to Khashoggi. I made it clear that if a strategic partnership was to continue the UK would need to know it would not and could not happen again.[21] But I did not overplay my hand. Instead, I decided to use the limited leverage the UK had to try and bring the conflict that Saudi Arabia was pursuing in Yemen to an end. I also signalled our support for media freedom by launching – with Canadian foreign minister Chrystia Freeland – a global campaign to protect and defend the rights of journalists and the importance of a free press.

Some will disagree with those calls. Many continue to oppose arms sales to Saudi Arabia as a matter of principle. But in the context of an important security ally in the middle of big social reforms, it was a reasonable position to take. The diplomatic leverage we had also made an impact. A month later, I travelled to Stockholm for the first ceasefire in Yemen for three years, and became the first Western foreign minister to meet a Houthi representative. As so often with protracted conflicts, things have gone backwards since then. But at least that ceasefire turned into an eventual decision by both Saudi Arabia and the UAE to disengage from the war. It also showed that the UK could raise sensitive human rights issues in a delicate diplomatic context.

How you wield power depends on a careful assessment of how much leverage you have with the person you are seeking to persuade. Sometimes public pressure works best, as in 2018, when I demanded the release of British citizen Matthew Hedges from jail in the UAE. On other occasions private discussions are the only way possible if access is to be maintained – as with China. Sometimes it is best to act unilaterally, whether formally or through a personal approach. At other times it works best to drum up support with allies to pass a motion at the UN. Sometimes you assess yourself as having substantial influence, and sometimes you have to be honest that you don't.

Occasionally, the only way is through diplomats behind the scenes. In 2019 I appointed the UK's first ever human rights ambassador, a capable civil servant called Rita French, to do just that. Over the past five years, largely unknown at home, she has used her position to say things that ministers have not been able to – and got things done. She helped to persuade Sierra Leone to abolish the death penalty and has championed women human rights activists detained in Saudi Arabia. She has regularly amplified the voices of Afghan and Iranian women suffering brutal repression. And at the UN Human Rights Council, she has demanded accountability for atrocities in Syria, Ukraine, Sudan, Myanmar and Xinjiang.

But we should be honest: if we want to be a powerful player in the world, we will often need to act in accordance with our interests – including economic interests. In a new cold war, we will need allies, and they will not all be cosy European democracies. Nonetheless, whatever the realpolitik, and however limited the options, there is always a way to raise a difficult issue if you look for it. A country like Britain should never abandon its principles even if the way we apply them will vary from case to case.

At his trial in 1964, when he potentially faced the death penalty, Nelson Mandela famously said that the ideal of a democratic and free society was one he hoped to live for, but if necessary was prepared to die for. Few of us will ever face that stark choice. But we do face an easier one: whether to speak out, or not. In her meetings with Gorbachev, Thatcher always asked after the health of imprisoned dissident Andrei Sakharov. It apparently infuriated the Soviet leader. But given what happened subsequently, who knows – it may just have had some impact. The moment you stop trying, the battle is lost.

8

The Next Silicon Valley

Nothing can prepare a Chancellor for the drama of a budget.

Treasury officials rather blandly call them 'fiscal events'. It's bureaucrat-speak for those rare moments in the political calendar when Chancellors emerge from the shadows to cut taxes – or put them up. During the rest of the year it is other ministers who have the thankless task of defending the government in the media. Sometimes I would listen to the *Today* programme in my flat in No. 11 and feel rather guilty as some poor minister was defending the government for not putting enough money into his or her area. Often the same person had lobbied me previously for money and I had turned them down.

But the vanishing act only lasts so long. When a fiscal event comes round, whether a budget or an Autumn Statement, Chancellors more than make up for long periods of silence. At such moments we vainly hope to emerge into the spotlight triumphantly, dispensing largesse like Santa Claus right at the centre of the Westminster universe. It never quite works out that way. Instead you just feel terrified that your carefully crafted plans might unravel.

At a budget, a Chancellor's relationship with voters becomes very personal. Every commuter, office worker and taxi driver knows their monthly pay depends on what you decide. Holidays, house purchases and home improvements are put on hold while people wait to see what it means for their family finances. Even the most vanilla politician becomes a rather important figure in people's lives. People I had never met would send me prayers in the post. Others would shout 'Good luck!' (or something less repeatable) as they passed in the street. They may not have liked me but they knew me. And long after you leave the job they remember you – for better or worse.

On the day itself, you carefully rehearse for a moment of ritual theatre. Chancellors have held up a red box outside the door of No. 11 Downing Street for more than a century. The world's media are out in force, penned behind Downing Street barriers. The box you hold up is not the actual red box you use for ministerial papers. Nor, sadly, is it a historical one. In fact, it is a replica, produced after the original started falling apart. A civil servant called Michelle gave me instructions with military precision. No one messed with Michelle.

On one occasion, in the heat of the moment, I forgot Michelle's instructions. After parading my red box in front of the cameras I was supposed to get into a car to be driven to Parliament. Instead, I turned round to the door of No. 11 to go back inside. After a pregnant pause the door opened and an official gingerly told me my mistake. So I walked in briskly, turned right down the corridor and came straight back out of the No. 10 door as if nothing was wrong. No one noticed.

Fiscal events are also one of the few occasions when the parliamentary authorities reserve seats in the visitors' gallery for family members. One of my autumn statements was on my wife's birthday, so I was able to wish her a public happy birthday from the Dispatch

Box. On another, my eight-year-old daughter fell sound asleep right next to all the journalists – to their delight. More poignantly, my brother came to see me deliver my first budget when he was fighting cancer. He had no hair, because of chemotherapy. He didn't survive to see the next budget, but his oldest son came in his place, which meant the world to me.

For the world outside, Budget Day is when the theatre happens. But inside No. 11 the drama happens in the weeks that precede it. That's when all the crucial decisions are made. Every Chancellor approaches those decisions differently. George Osborne was fascinated by the power interplay between the Treasury and other government departments. Gordon Brown composed his budget speeches before he knew what decisions he would take, using speechwriting to organise his thoughts. My personal hero was Nigel Lawson, who understood better than any Chancellor how the tax system shapes society's social contract. His landmark 1988 budget made the country immensely more hard-working and entrepreneurial (although it also triggered a recession).

For me, the purpose was straightforward. In every budget, a Chancellor becomes, briefly, the most powerful person in the country. The key is to use that power to overcome short-term pressures, in order to wrestle through longer-term reforms that stand the test of time.

As I tackled a nightmare £72-billion black hole in my Autumn Statement of 2022, the short-term necessity was to plug the gap. The longer-term goal was to create stability and set the scene for growth. I knew I needed to give people hope. My own background as an entrepreneur had convinced me that technology was a major opportunity for the UK. So, after some hesitation, I included a passage in the speech saying the UK should aim to become the world's next Silicon Valley. It was a bold and unexpected ambition. But was it credible? I rather expected to be ridiculed.

Rather to my surprise, I wasn't. The UK's technology sector is one of our great and largely unnoticed success stories. And one of the reasons is the remarkable story of someone many people have never heard of.

Demis Hassabis had always been curious about the secrets of the human mind.[1] He was born in London to a Singaporean mother and a Greek Cypriot father. Before he started school he was reading fluently and had learnt to play chess. He was the type of child who constantly bombarded his parents with questions. By the time he was thirteen, Demis had not only become a chess master but, for his age, the second best player in the world. Chess, he said later, was PE for the mind.

But Demis had already decided that chess would not be his career. Why use all that brainpower on chess moves instead of real problems? When it came to the biggest scientific problems, brainpower was the key – particularly if it could be unlocked artificially via computers. Thus started his fascination with AI.

His journey from child chess prodigy to AI researcher began at the age of eight, when he used prize money from a tournament to buy his first computer, a ZX Spectrum. He then taught himself to code. His first foray into AI came at the age of eleven, when he programmed his Commodore Amiga to play video games against himself. He began to see the potential of computers as a kind of magical extension to the brain.

Demis completed his A levels at the age of sixteen and won a place at Cambridge. But the university wouldn't allow him to start his degree before he was eighteen, so he pursued his curiosity about computing intelligence in the gaming industry. He won a competition for a job at game developer Bullfrog Productions[2] and later became the lead programmer on the 1990s classic *Theme Park*. It had AI as a core component.

After graduating from Cambridge with a double first, Demis returned to the gaming industry, this time at Lionhead Studios, and then founded his own company, Elixir Studios. Demis's games always had some form of AI involved, and he became very adept at creating AI that could make human-like decisions. He then completed a doctorate in cognitive neuroscience at UCL.

By that stage, Elixir had closed its doors. But in 2010 Demis got together with Shane Legg and Mustafa Suleyman to launch something much more ambitious: it was an AI laboratory called DeepMind, which allowed him to combine his interest in neuroscience with his love of gaming.

They needed funding – and knew exactly where they wanted it to come from. Peter Thiel had founded the payments company PayPal, and was an early backer of social network Facebook. But apart from a punt on Spotify, he had rarely invested outside America. 'He felt the power of Silicon Valley was sort of mythical, that you couldn't create a successful big technology company anywhere else,' Demis reflected later.[3] But a conversation between the two men about chess convinced the investor to take a chance on the ambitious Brit. Thiel even allowed the company to stay in London.

It thrived.

DeepMind's early research focused on teaching AI to play simple video games like *Pong* through reinforcement learning. Through

Sir Demis Hassabis

repetitive play, the computer gradually improved its score and came to master each game. They then applied the same approach to more complex games.

Then, in January 2014, came a landmark moment: Google purchased DeepMind for a reported £400 million.[4] It was one of the biggest tech acquisitions in UK history. Part of the deal was that DeepMind's offices were to remain in London, a commitment that Google continues to honour to this day. Demis argues that the UK has many world-class universities which are a magnet for talent, giving DeepMind more access to smart recruits than if it were competing with its peers in Silicon Valley. The London–Oxford–Cambridge 'golden triangle' also fosters out-of-the-box thinking, because of the unique way so many different sectors and disciplines collide. In DeepMind's case that intersection is between the tech sector and world-class neuroscience, particularly at UCL.

The following year something happened which the whole world took note of: DeepMind's lab released AlphaGo, a program that could play the ancient Chinese strategy game Go. After being shown how humans played the game, AlphaGo played it against itself thousands of times to hone its skills. It was then pitted against one of the world's best Go players, Lee Sedol, who had won the world title eighteen times. Two hundred million people watched worldwide as Lee was beaten 4–1 by the computer.

The bar was raised again when DeepMind released AlphaGo Zero. This new program no longer needed to be trained using amateur gamers. Instead, it taught itself from scratch by playing over and over against itself – refining its skills at a pace that humans simply cannot match. The new approach meant it quickly overtook the capabilities of previous versions. This led to the creation of AlphaZero, which can play Go, chess and shogi. AlphaZero took just four hours to teach itself to play chess better than any human challenger. It then resoundingly beat the world's best computer chess programme, Stockfish.

Being in the UK was also good for Demis's interest in life sciences. He started to get curious about the potential of applying similar levels of raw computing power to solve long-standing problems, and in 2016 teamed up with a leading London teaching hospital, the Royal Free, to develop a mobile app called Streams, which used historic patient data to determine the risk of acute kidney injury. They had a setback when the Information Commissioner's Office ruled the Royal Free had breached data protection law, but results published in 2019 showed the app had not only improved quality of care but also reduced cost.[5]

A few years later, that led DeepMind to unlock a much bigger biomedical advance – so significant, in fact, that it led to Demis receiving a Nobel Prize.

Many diseases, including dementia and Parkinson's, are caused by changes in the way proteins alter their structures in a process known as 'folding'. If we can predict how proteins become biologically active, such diseases can potentially be prevented or cured. Scientists have been trying to solve the 'protein folding problem' for half a century. No one imagined that Demis, with his background in computer games, would use a new algorithm developed by DeepMind to attempt just that. But DeepMind's AlphaFold tool started predicting protein structures more accurately than had ever been done before, and it also shed light on the structure of SARS-CoV-2 during the pandemic. By July 2022, AlphaFold had predicted structures for nearly all catalogued proteins known to science. Instead of cashing in on this extraordinarily valuable database, DeepMind made it open access to everyone, meaning that scientists from all over the world can access it.

AlphaFold was described as 'the first time a serious scientific problem had been solved by AI'.[6] It won Demis the Nobel Prize in Chemistry in 2024, together with Dr John Jumper, who worked with him on AlphaFold, and US-based Professor David Baker, who worked independently on computational protein design.[7] Demis has also been knighted, in recognition of his contribution to British science. He has come a long way from gaming.

If the world has reason to be grateful to DeepMind, the company also makes clear its gratitude to the UK. It has maintained its commitment to staying in London. It has fostered Stanford-style partnerships with many UK universities with public–private connections that had previously been rare. As a result, British university spin-offs in technology and life sciences are now starting to look much more like those in the US.

Britain's combination of top universities, access to capital and talented entrepreneurs like Demis has given it Europe's biggest innovation ecosystem. It has become a vital part of our economy. But how realistic is it for the UK to become the world's next Silicon Valley?

Britain has long been a pioneer of computing innovation. In the 1840s, Ada Lovelace, daughter of the poet Byron, published the first algorithm for Charles Babbage's 'theoretical computing machine'. This is why some people call her the world's first computer programmer – but the real breakthrough came over a century later, during the Second World War.

The existential threat posed by the Nazis broke down long-standing silos between politicians, academia and business. Alan Turing, working in total secrecy with his colleagues at Bletchley Park, created the world's first programmable electronic computer: it was called Colossus and its job was to crack the Enigma codes used by the Nazis to encrypt messages. Colossus's decoding of those messages may have shortened the war by two years.

Turing was shamefully prosecuted for homosexuality, leading to his tragic suicide at the age of forty-one. We will never know what else he might have achieved. But after the war, other programmers took his work to the next stage. In 1948, the Manchester 'Baby' became the world's first stored-program computer. Then, in 1951, came the world's first 'business computer', developed for the needs of a company called J. Lyons and Co. It was called the Lyons Electronic Office, or LEO.[8] The year 1955 saw the first fully transistorised computer in Europe, the Harwell CADET.⁹ Atlas, one of the world's first supercomputers, was built in the UK in 1962.¹⁰

Many of those instrumental in such milestones were less well known than Turing. One was Dina St Johnston, who worked at computer manufacturer Elliott-Automation, where she learnt to program. She realised that there was no technical support available for computer users, so – working from a dining room table in a converted pub – she founded Vaughan Programming Services. It was the UK's first software house. Eventually, the company wrote programs for British Rail, the BBC, Unilever, Texaco and Kellogg's, among others.¹¹ Had she been alive half a century later she would have become much wealthier and more famous.

Another modest British innovator did become famous. Tim Berners-Lee was working for CERN in Geneva in 1989, when he made a suggestion for a way for colleagues to share information about their work. He called it 'Mesh'. There was little interest in it, but a year later he started writing code for what he then renamed the 'World Wide Web'.¹² Although his research was conducted mainly in Switzerland, the US defence establishment put in place hardware that made his vision possible. He never made anything like as much money as the many billionaires his creation unleashed. He was, however, feted with a star appearance at Danny Boyle's acclaimed London 2012 Summer Olympics opening ceremony, for which I was responsible as Culture Secretary. The 'father of the internet' has become well known for passionately campaigning for governments to ensure the internet remains a public good. He has also practised what he preaches, by refusing to seek royalties from his world-changing idea.

Sir Tim Berners-Lee at the London 2012 Opening Ceremony

Nor has British innovation stopped there. The invention of e-commerce is often attributed to the British entrepreneur Michael Aldrich, whose system of connecting a shopper's television with a transaction-processing computer via their telephone is considered a forerunner of online shopping. The advent of the World Wide Web turned a nation of shopkeepers into the world's biggest online shoppers: today, Brits spend more money shopping online than consumers in any other major economy apart from the US.[13] For a long time, we were even spending more than Americans.

Normally, our national story is about brilliant inventions which other countries go on to make money from. But in the case of technology, something different is happening. The UK tech sector is a huge and rather underrated success story. In 2021 Britain became the only European country to have one hundred 'unicorns' – tech companies worth more than $1 billion.[14] In 2022, its ecosystem exceeded the $1 trillion mark, only the third in the world to do so after the US and China.[15] In 2023, Elon Musk told me that London and San Francisco have become the world's two leading hubs for AI, although China is giving both a run for their money. British tech start-ups hoover up more venture capital than France and Germany combined,[16] and when it comes to AI, only the US and China have more start-ups.

British universities have played a key role in the revolution. As mentioned earlier, three of the world's top ten universities are in the UK, more than anywhere else except the US.

Newly Funded AI Start-Ups by Country, 2013–2023

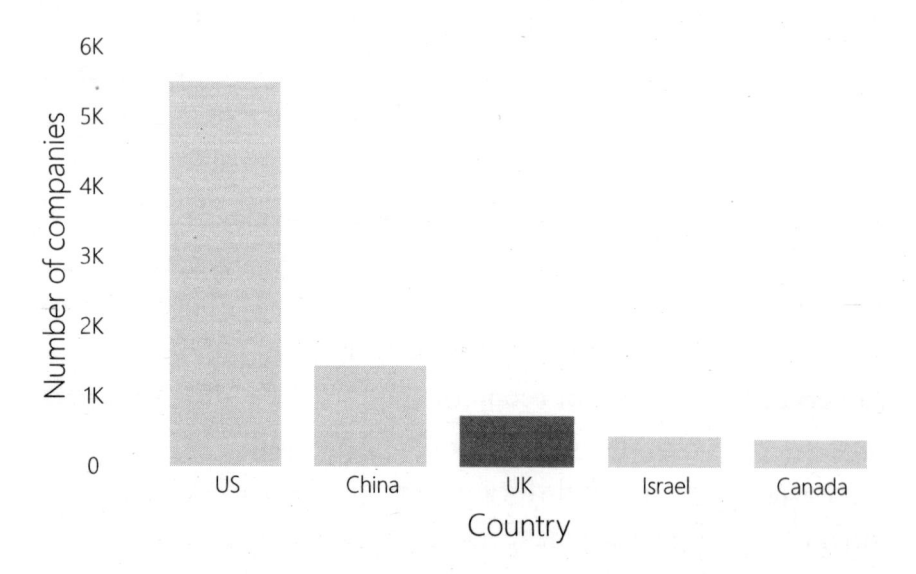

Source: Quid via Nestor Maslej et al., 'The AI Index 2024 Annual Report', AI Index Steering Committee, Institute for Human-Centered AI, Stanford University, April 2024, https://hai.stanford.edu/ai-index/2024-ai-index-report, p. 252[17]

Top 10 Universities, 2025

Institution	Overall Rank	Country
University of Oxford	1	UK
Massachusetts Institute of Technology	2	US
Harvard University	3	US
Princeton University	4	US
University of Cambridge	5	UK
Stanford University	6	US
California Institute of Technology	7	US
University of California, Berkeley	8	US
Imperial College London	9	UK
Yale University	10	US

Source: 'World University Rankings 2025', *Times Higher Education*, 4 October 2024, https://www.timeshighereducation.com/world-university-rankings/latest/world-ranking

Global Innovation Index 2024

Country	Overall Rank	Score
Switzerland	1	67.5
Sweden	2	64.5
US	3	62.4
Singapore	4	61.2
UK	5	61.0
South Korea	6	60.9
Finland	7	59.4
Netherlands	8	58.8
Germany	9	58.1
Denmark	10	57.1

Source: World Intellectual Property Organization et al., *Global Innovation Index 2024: Innovation in the Face of Uncertainty* (World Intellectual Property Organization, 2024), https://doi.org/10.34667/TIND.50062, p. 18

They continue to file many more patents than similar-sized countries. They produce more graduates in AI-relevant courses than anywhere else in Europe.[18] Spin-outs are becoming more common even outside the Oxford–Cambridge–London 'golden triangle', particularly following a seminal piece of work by Oxford's vice chancellor, Irene Tracey. As a result, the UK is ranked the fifth most innovative economy in the world.[19]

Something else could also power up our Silicon Valley ambitions: we are going to have to spend a lot more on defence. That was the catalyst that got the original Silicon Valley off the ground.

The successful launch of the Soviet Union's Sputnik 1 satellite in 1957 triggered panic in the US. To help compete in the arms and space race with the Soviet Union, the engineering faculty of Stanford University was asked for assistance. Its dean of engineering was a visionary patriot called Fred Terman. He saw the request as a big opportunity not just to serve his country but also to reconstruct his department's curriculum for the longer-term benefit of his students. So he set up Stanford Industrial Park. He leased chunks of university land to high-tech start-ups. He also persuaded William Shockley, inventor of the transistor, to leave Bell Labs and base his new company in Palo Alto. To make sure the new ventures could attract Wall Street capital, he generously shared intellectual property rights.[20]

The combination of private capital and lucrative government contracts was explosive. New companies took off and Silicon Valley was born. Stanford developed unique capabilities including pioneering the world's smallest computational and communications devices – which kept on getting smaller. Defence giant Lockheed Martin set up its missile and space division nearby. NASA opened a big research centre and funded companies like Fairchild Semiconductor with generous contracts. The Pentagon research agency DARPA also played a key role, remaining to this day one of the world's largest funders of computer science research.

That support for the tech sector has continued. Under the guidance of former Google CEO Eric Schmidt, a new organisation called the Defense Innovation Unit (DIU) is speeding up the adoption of AI and other cutting-edge technology by US troops on the frontline. It now invests nearly a billion dollars annually in innovations of potential use to the Department of Defense.[21] Because of the prospect of big defence contracts, that funding then attracts massive additional private equity and venture capital. Such investments make sure there are plenty of disruptors snapping at the heels of the 'magnificent seven' – Apple, Microsoft, Nvidia, Amazon, Meta, Tesla and Alphabet – and keep Silicon Valley on top of its game.

A much smaller country has pulled off a similar trick. Under Prime Minister Benjamin Netanyahu, Israel has used military research to turn itself into one of the world's leading technology hotspots. Netanyahu told me a few years ago that when he came to office, Israel's technology was essentially like North Korea's – all military. He had to increase defence spending to 5% of GDP, but saw that as an opportunity to nurture a civilian tech sector. At the same time, he fostered close partnerships between defence contractors and the Israeli army to allow rapid and flexible adoption of new innovations without endless wrangling over contracts. As a result, technology has given Israel battlefield advantage and grown its economy. It is now the dominant regional power – a textbook example of the link between economic dynamism and political clout. But it was Netanyahu's next comment that really got me thinking: Britain, he said, could do the same.

I got to know the British tech sector, not as a politician but as an entrepreneur, when I co-founded a publishing company called Hotcourses with my best friend Mike. As ambitious twenty-somethings, we started producing chunky directories of courses and colleges which weighed a ton. We didn't make a profit for five years but had a lot of fun. It was the early 1990s, and we became fascinated by the new search engines being launched by Yahoo, AltaVista and Google. We wondered if our directories would work better online, like the new search engines. So we decided to take the plunge into a totally new world. The first step was to raise some money, but we were turned down by every venture capitalist in London. Rather ridiculously in retrospect, they only wanted to invest in blue-sky rather than existing businesses. We were much too dull.

In the end we raised a small amount from some angel investors. It was just about enough. We set about building from scratch what became the world's biggest database of courses, colleges and universities. As the world went online, we began to eclipse our larger competitors, who remained stuck publishing magazines. We on the other hand stopped printing altogether. When we finally sold the company, it employed seventy people in London and two hundred in India. It continues to thrive.

By coincidence, my first job in the cabinet, Culture Secretary, made me responsible for the technology sector. At the time, broadband speeds were painfully slow, particularly in the countryside where it was often non-existent. I decided to prioritise the roll-out of faster broadband. I had previously visited Singapore and South Korea and been wowed by the infrastructure they were putting in place. So a month after coming to office – without any approval from the Treasury – I announced that by the end of the parliament the new government would build the best broadband network in Europe.[22]

I might have expected a punishment beating for making such a major funding commitment. But George Osborne was preoccupied with his first budget and, to his credit, always understood the strategic importance of the tech sector. My partner in crime was Rohan Silva, a smart visionary who was then working as an adviser in No. 10 (and is now himself an entrepreneur). Soon, our tech ambitions became a central part of the government's economic strategy. It largely delivered: Ofcom's European Broadband Scorecard 2015 showed that the UK did indeed have some of the cheapest and fastest broadband in Europe.[23] We still have more work to do on fibre but on that too are catching up fast.[24]

Good broadband alone, however, won't turn us into California, Israel or Taiwan. So Rohan and I travelled to Silicon Valley for inspiration. A leading venture capitalist in Sand Hill Road compared the can-do culture on the West Coast to East Coast conservatism: 'Over there they think people over twenty-five are smart but here we think people under twenty-five are.' We both noticed the UK didn't even get a mention.

Another investor said they would open an office in London if there were more early-stage companies in the UK. So our next step was to push through, with George Osborne's support, changes to the tax and visa regimes. The Enterprise Investment Scheme (EIS) was made more attractive and the Seed Enterprise Investment Scheme (SEIS) was set up to incentivise wealthy investors to back the highest-risk smallest start-ups. We also focused on building up a tech cluster in East London. This began in an area initially known as Silicon Roundabout, based in old industrial buildings in Shoreditch. After the Olympics, it became 'Tech City'. It would have been more natural for the political establishment to back a new cluster outside London – but we knew that London's appeal was central to the success of our vision. In time, though, the benefits spread and 'Tech City' became 'Tech Nation'. We secured commitments from companies such as Google, Facebook, Intel and McKinsey to invest in the UK. We also took Mark Zuckerberg to meet David Cameron. It was the first and only time I saw Zuckerberg wear a tie.

After the 'Big Bang' in 1986, the City transformed itself into one of the world's two dominant hubs for financial services. If we do the same for technology, we could banish our long-standing productivity issues, transform our national finances and greatly enhance our global prestige. The foundations have been put in place but it is the work of more than one parliament. Luckily, the vision has strong cross-party support, including from Rachel Reeves. The government's recent AI review, written by Matt Clifford, will see public sector GPU computing capacity expand twentyfold by 2030, introduce an easier visa path for AI talent and establish AI growth zones with full access to the copious power they need.[25] Of course, it needs to be delivered, but the ambition is superb.

If we really want to be the world's next Silicon Valley, however, there is a big weakness we need to tackle head on: the UK's failure to produce technology companies of a globally significant size.

*

THE NEXT SILICON VALLEY

For many years Britain has failed to turn innovative start-ups into giants. Cambridge boasts one of the world's top semiconductor design companies, Arm – but it is listed in New York. DeepMind is owned by Google. Mike Lynch, described before his tragic death as Britain's Bill Gates, sold his company Autonomy to Hewlett Packard (in what became a highly controversial transaction). In the different subsectors that comprise the technology industry, the UK has disappointingly low numbers of top 100 companies.

Number of Publicly Traded UK Companies in Top 100 by Sector

Category	Number of UK Companies
AI*	1
Biotech	5
E-commerce	6
Electronics	1
Internet	3
IT services	3
Medical devices	2
Pharmaceuticals	5
Renewable energy	3
Semiconductors	1
Software	1
Telecommunication	5

Source: 'Companies Ranked by Market Cap', CompaniesMarketCap.com, https://companiesmarketcap.com
Note: * As of writing, there were only 57 publicly traded companies worldwide that were included in the AI subcategory on CompaniesMarketCap.com.

The reason has often been a lack of capital. At the start-up stage, that issue has been partially addressed through the EIS and SEIS schemes. But the fastest-growing companies can still struggle to get funding to scale up to the next level. Wall Street has traditionally been a much easier place than the City to raise funding for high-growth companies with low or no profits – as is often the case with technology start-ups.

That hesitancy is in part due to the sleepy conservatism of UK pension funds. They only invest around 4% of their assets[26] in the London stock market, despite sitting on the world's second largest pension pool.[27] An even tinier proportion of their assets goes into the fastest-growing UK technology companies that are still private. Pension funds in countries like the US, Canada or Australia have no such hesitation, which is why they get better returns for their members. The result is that promising British start-ups are more likely to get funding from Canadian pension funds than British ones.

Working with the then Lord Mayor of London, Sir Nicholas Lyons, in 2023 I unveiled a major programme to change this. They were called the Mansion House reforms[28] and included measures requiring or incentivising smaller pension funds to pool their capital in order to develop more professional investment strategies. We also changed the regulations to make sure they focused on overall returns and not just costs. The result will be that the UK finally unlocks huge chunks of the £2.5 trillion of assets held by UK pension funds.[29] That will mean not just better returns for pension fund holders but a new generation of trillion-dollar British tech giants.

Such reforms cannot come a moment too soon. Many others have their eye on the technology prize. France has great strengths in AI, recently hosting a big AI summit and attracting even more investment than the UK. Germany, South Korea and Japan have formidable strengths in robotics. Israel is a global leader in cyber security. And all are dwarfed by the US, which has eight of the world's top ten tech companies.[30] If we need any reminder of the size of the prize, it is worth considering that Amazon's capitalisation alone is about two-thirds of the size of the entire UK economy.

China is also on the march. It is harder to measure Chinese progress, because its tech ecosystem is increasingly isolated behind a walled garden or 'silicon curtain'. But DeepSeek, a Chinese startup set up only in 2023, has now turned heads with its R1 large language model, which is highly effective and less hungry for processing power than US alternatives. It is being spurred on by fierce domestic competition from Alibaba's Qwen. A good proxy for the quality of a country's innovation is the number of patents it files: when it comes to AI, fully three quarters of all patents globally are now filed by China, particularly from Beijing and Tsinghua Universities. Tsinghua is President Xi's alma mater, and publishes more AI research than any other university in the world.[31] His ambition for China to be the global leader in AI by 2030 is taking shape.

But amidst such fierce competition, the UK has two things many of its competitors can only dream of: highly respected universities and a large financial services sector. It has more AI graduates than anywhere else in Europe. That means the talent pipeline from both UK students and international students studying in the UK is extremely strong. And when it comes to financing new start-ups, Britain has the world's second largest financial services sector, meaning there is a lot of capital to tap into. With pension fund reform there will be even more.

The UK also has another key strength: its phenomenal science base means it has a broader tech ecosystem than many countries. That now extends from AI to quantum, from defence to life sciences and from clean energy to the creative industries. Such sectors often cross-fertilise each other, as we saw when Demis Hassabis combined gaming and neuroscience. Another example is the way strengths in financial services and technology have given the UK one of the world's biggest fintech sectors.

Growing that ecosystem will give the UK a pivotal role in one of the biggest challenges facing humanity – how to ensure AI remains a force for good and does not mark the start of a dystopian future in which malign actors use vast computing power for evil purposes.

Mustafa Suleyman, one of Demis's co-founders at DeepMind, wrote recently about a professor at a well-known university describing how a single person with enough intellectual curiosity could now develop the capacity to kill a billion people. He writes about this and other dangers arising from the growth of AI in his recent book, *The Coming Wave*, where he discusses the 'containment problem': the risk with any scientific development that you can never control its speed or direction of travel.[32]

Such issues were a big enough concern to persuade Rishi Sunak to host the world's first governmental summit on AI safety in 2023. It was attended by twenty-eight nations including the US, China and the EU. The discussions highlighted not just the challenges we face but the role the UK can play in preventing AI armageddon, not least with our experience as a military power. But there is much work to do: a report commissioned at the summit concluded that there are severe limitations to our understanding of why general purpose

AI models produce the results they do – and only limited ways to reduce the risks.[33]

That will mean guardrails around the safe use of AI. The key is to make sure new regulations do not end up stifling innovation in the process – as is the case with current EU rules. Regulatory autonomy outside the EU gives the UK the ability to change and adapt the rules nimbly in a way that strikes a more pragmatic balance between innovation and safety – and secures the future of a strategic growth sector.

If I was ever asked, as Chancellor, how the UK would thrive in the decades ahead, I would always talk about the UK's opportunity to be the world's next Silicon Valley. Getting there is by no means a foregone conclusion – it will require focus from successive governments and nimbleness as we compete with others. But given that California's GDP is already bigger than the UK's, the potential for technology to be a major source of wealth is obvious. However, there is a chicken-and-egg question to resolve first: some of the things that will make it possible – investment in universities, life science research and defence – require funding. Where do you find those resources before you have got to the destination?

My next book will focus more broadly on how to overcome our economic challenges. But as we consider Britain's global role in this book, the short-term source of funding can only really come from two places: welfare reform and public sector efficiency. Both are politically challenging – but both offer enormous potential for savings.

The public sector accounts for around 20% of our output. It is the only part of the economy directly under the control of the government. Yet its productivity is growing by a measly long-term average of 0.9% a year, around half the growth rate in the private sector.[34] Public sector productivity is still 7% below pre-pandemic levels and nearly 20% lower in the NHS.[35] According to Treasury analysis supplied to me when I was Chancellor, if that productivity increased by 1% more a year than the current 0.9% – so around 2% in total – something magical would happen: our debt would stop rising as a proportion of GDP.[36] We would be able to increase funding in key areas like the NHS and defence without forever increasing taxes. If we increased it by even more we could even start to consider reducing taxes.

Anyone who has run a business would say that 2% productivity growth a year is more than achievable. Anyone who has run a government knows that in the public sector it is very hard. Unions are extremely effective at putting pressure on governments, not least because any strikes dominate the media. Although I won my battle with the BMA in 2016, the NHS had to endure nearly a year of strikes in the process. One of the first acts – and a greatly mistaken one – of the current government was to spend £9.4 billion on public sector pay demands without asking for a single productivity improvement in return.[37]

Getting 2% productivity growth in the public sector is perfectly possible. I secured agreement from the NHS, our biggest public service, to deliver it for the next five years in return for a big budget investment to overhaul their creaking computer system. It should be entirely possible to do so for other public services, as indeed I had planned to do.

We can also learn a lot from other countries. Estonia has the most digitised state in the world. Elon Musk is trying to reinvent the way the US federal government works. Economic infrastructure such as roads, railways and nuclear power stations is better elsewhere because of lengthy planning delays in the UK, which, to its credit, the government has started to tackle. When it comes to private sector productivity, countries like Germany and South Korea are far ahead of the UK in terms of their investment in robots and automation. Once again, all roads lead to technology – and an often inefficient British state should be one of the biggest beneficiaries.

The second area where short-term funding could be released is welfare. Currently, nearly three million adults of working age are on sickness or disability benefits.[38] Within five years the cost of that will increase to nearly £80 billion a year.[39] It is bad for the economy – and often terrible for the individuals involved, who end up in a benefits silo that can make mental health conditions even worse. Just returning the number of claimants to pre-pandemic levels, in other words where they were in 2019, reduces that bill by £40 billion a year. That is not easy to deliver at a stroke, but a reasonable ambition for a parliament. It would also reduce the pressure to raise migration.

Public sector productivity improvements and welfare reform are challenging policy areas. But in the short term, they are the only show in town. Without them we face the prospect of ever higher taxes and ever diminishing growth. With them, we unlock long-term growth generated by increased defence spending and proper investment in our universities. Both are vital foundations for giving Britain a stronger voice in the world.

A successful economy matters not just because it makes a finance minister's chequebook go further. It also has a powerful, intangible effect in bolstering a nation's credibility, influence and soft power.

When I became Chancellor in the middle of an economic crisis, I received sympathy from fellow finance ministers. I also knew our woes were not helpful to Britain's reputation, to say the least. By the end of my time, when we had tackled inflation, had avoided a deep recession and were growing faster than many others, sympathy turned into respect.

But weathering a storm is not enough. A strong presence in technology – in a technology century – would bolster the UK's soft power and provide the funding for its hard power. Britain has a long way to go before it matches Californian innovation and risk-taking. But it is far from impossible. It means making sure universities solve their current financial issues. It means keeping the UK attractive for entrepreneurs and international investors. It means continuing to invest in areas such as computing capacity, defence innovation, clean energy and broadband. It means making sure innovation hubs like Oxford, Cambridge and Manchester are supported with the housing and transport connections they need. And it means providing more support to areas with good universities where land and housing is cheaper.

Like any entrepreneur, we can succeed if we are hungry enough. And we have every reason to try: if Britain's tech sector was as big as California's, our GDP per head would be around 10% larger, overtaking that of Germany and making us one of Europe's wealthiest countries. We would create thousands of exciting job opportunities for young graduates as well as generating around £60 billion more in tax revenues every year.[40] We would have anchored our economy in the parts of the global economy that are growing fastest.

We would also become a much more powerful voice. Whether it is contributing to global security with the most technologically sophisticated armed forces, defending democracy by stopping election interference, preventing climate change with advanced clean energy solutions or stopping innovations in AI from falling into the wrong hands, we would be bigger and bolder on the global stage.

The result, for UK citizens, would be a series of virtuous circles: a bigger defence budget helping to turn the UK into the world's next Silicon Valley; vaccine research preventing a global pandemic and creating life sciences jobs; clean energy fulfilling our climate obligations as well as providing lower energy prices. Investing wisely in areas that bolster our global influence adds to our economic strength – and builds the stronger economy that is ultimately the source of political clout.

9
A Global Vocation

'This time you had better bloody accept the job,' the Chief Whip snapped down the phone. It wasn't how I'd envisaged being asked to become Foreign Secretary. But there was a reason for his directness: six months earlier, during a fraught reshuffle, I had refused to budge as Health Secretary. This time the vacancy was more senior. It was caused by Boris Johnson's dramatic resignation over Brexit. A loyal Chief Whip wanted to make sure that I was not going to embarrass Theresa May a second time.

He needn't have worried.

For me, the Foreign and Commonwealth Office is one of the greatest offices of state. Through an extensive network of embassies and consulates, it protects our interests and projects our values – all with British 'keep calm and carry on' professionalism. Coming as I do from a proud naval family, I needed no persuading. Of course I'd bloody accept the job.

After face-to-face formalities with the prime minister, I walked through the arch that connects a comparatively modest Downing Street to the gleaming grandeur of the Foreign Office. I was led up what is called the Grand Staircase by the most senior civil servant in the department, the permanent under-secretary, Sir Simon McDonald. I paused in front of a bust of the Labour Foreign Secretary Ernest Bevin. Bevin was probably the greatest post-war Foreign Secretary. He played a pivotal role in setting up NATO and faced down Stalin to ensure West Germany remained free. No pressure then.

Sir Simon is the epitome of a diplomat: urbane, experienced and smart. He gently slipped into the conversation that I was the sixty-fourth holder of the post of Foreign Secretary. In other words, while the position was special, I was not. The Foreign Secretary's office is by far the grandest in Whitehall, much more imposing than the prime minister's. Settling down to work in a vast oak-panelled room with gilded bookshelves and antique furniture you feel a bit like you are in the middle of the British Museum. Its calm splendour was a striking contrast to the permanent sense of crisis at the Department of Health which had been my life for six years.

Of course, that splendour has a purpose: it has long been used to impress on visiting foreigners that they are in the presence of a great power. That felt somewhat optimistic, as we teetered helplessly at the time with a weak economy and hung parliament.

During that year, I had to glad-hand more than my fill of world leaders and foreign dignitaries. On my first full day I met Angela Merkel, in London for a conference of Balkan leaders. When I introduced myself as Britain's new Foreign Secretary she said wryly, 'Congratulations… if that's the right word.' To my surprise, more often than not on my travels I found that other countries had a whole lot more respect for the UK than we have for ourselves. So in the months that followed I found myself wrestling with the question that confronts every Foreign Secretary: is the grandeur of the office – both physical and metaphorical – a delusion?

In order to answer that question, I started writing this book. Halfway through writing it, in an unexpected twist of fate, I became Chancellor of the Exchequer. When I got round to finishing the book after stepping down from office, I found that being responsible for the economy made me change my central argument in two ways: first of all, if we want to punch above our weight in the world, we need to explain how we are going to pay for it. Secondly, the book needed to recognise more explicitly the iron link between economic strength and political influence. A strong voice needs a strong economy, because without it you really are left like the Wizard of Oz hiding behind a curtain. Nonetheless, even now, with multiple economic challenges, we should not underestimate the clout we have. Whether on security, democracy, migration, trade, climate change, human rights, health or technology, we have a lot to contribute to global solutions, as the earlier chapters demonstrate.

Indeed, sometimes British influence emerges in the unlikeliest of situations.

It had been 281 days since journalist Wa Lone had tasted freedom. In the notorious Insein Prison in Yangon, he sat disconsolately in his cell. Beatings, torture and disease were rife. His and his colleague Kyaw Soe Oo's crime had consisted of reporting the news without fear or favour. It was, he thought, perfectly safe to do so, because after fifty years of censorship the government of Myanmar, formerly Burma, had said it would allow a free press. Wa had leapt at the opportunity to do what journalists love to do most, namely hold their government to account.

He may have hoped that working for the internationally respected Reuters news agency would give him some protection. He was wrong. When he and his colleague wrote about a massacre of the Rohingya people by the feared Burmese army, known as the Tatmadaw, they crossed a line.

The Rohingya are a Muslim minority in a predominantly Buddhist country. They live in the west of Myanmar in Rakhine State. For forty years they have been denied citizenship rights[1] and treated as 'not really Burmese'. In effect, they have been in a stateless limbo. Decades of persecution by the Myanmar authorities culminated in a wave of violence by a group of Rohingya militants in September 2017. Eight police officers and one immigration officer were killed. Myanmar's authorities seized the chance to instigate a broader crackdown.

In the village of Inn Din, hundreds of men, women and children were driven from their homes and fled to a nearby beach for shelter. From there they were forced back to the village, interrogated and held overnight in a school. The next morning, they were moved to nearby scrubland, where they were executed. The lucky ones were shot. Two were reportedly hacked to death.

Thanks to courageous reporting by Wa and Kyaw, the world found out.[2] The two journalists did their job painstakingly. They gathered first-hand accounts from survivors. They got hold of photographs showing men bound, kneeling and with their captors standing behind them brandishing rifles. Other pictures showed bloodied corpses piled on top of each other in a mass grave.

The reporting directly implicated the Tatmadaw. The army did not turn the other cheek.

A GLOBAL VOCATION

Three months after the massacre, both journalists were invited to a Yangon restaurant to interview a policeman who claimed to be a whistleblower. The policeman passed them some documents. As they left, they were arrested and charged with breaching the Official Secrets Act – for possessing the very documents they had just been handed. The meeting had been a set-up. Wa and Kyaw were then interrogated remorselessly, including with sleep deprivation.[3]

But then something unexpected happened.

The police captain in charge of the entrapment operation decided to do something brave – and at great personal risk. Instead of sticking to the official line, he surprised everyone by testifying at the trial that there had been a plot to frame the journalists. It was a brief ray of sunshine and there was suddenly hope the case would be dropped

Wa Lone leaving court

209

as a result.[4] Alas, the captain soon found himself in hot water for his honest testimony, and was sentenced to one year in prison for violating the Police Disciplinary Act.[5] Wa and Kyaw were each sentenced to seven years in prison.[6]

Such events are not uncommon. Currently, there are nearly six hundred journalists in prison worldwide, many with similar stories.[7] But it was particularly unfortunate that this should happen in a country taking its first halting steps towards democracy. Only a year earlier its former military rulers had agreed – finally – to allow free elections. Instead of the army, voters overwhelmingly chose Aung San Suu Kyi, a brave democracy campaigner who had been imprisoned by the junta for a total of fifteen years.[8] Because her late husband was British, the constitution did not allow her to be head of state. But as leader of the victorious political party she was able to exercise de facto control by sitting behind a nominated prime minister. Nonetheless, her power was severely constrained because the army and police remained outside the control of the new government. She ruled in an uneasy alliance with the head of the Tatmadaw, General Min Aung Hlaing.

It was an imperfect arrangement to say the least. But it was an improvement on the military dictatorship that preceded it. The world hung its hopes on the Oxford-educated Nobel Prize winner. Her years of house arrest and stints in Insein Prison made her Myanmar's Nelson Mandela. Yet, uncomfortably, she found herself presiding over a genocide in one part of the country and the persecution of journalists in another.

Just two weeks after their sentencing but nine months after their arrest, as Wa and Kyaw languished in their cells, the new British Foreign Secretary arrived in Myanmar. I had come to meet Aung San Suu Kyi.

A GLOBAL VOCATION

I had high hopes and was looking forward to meeting a world figure. Far from being critical of her failure to condemn the genocide in Rakhine, I understood the delicacy of her position and planned to cut her some slack. Even though I was concerned about what had happened, I thought an imperfect democracy was better than no democracy at all.

To meet her I travelled to Naypyidaw, Myanmar's brand-new purpose-built capital. It had only been in use since 2005, when the idiosyncratic military dictatorship decided to move from Yangon (formerly Rangoon).[9] They wanted to make a decisive break with colonial times, so thousands of civil servants were instructed to relocate nearly two hundred miles away to a supposedly gleaming new seat of government. But compared to the buzz of Yangon it was a ghost town. Characterless modern buildings replaced fading colonial splendour. In place of the magnificent Shwedagon Pagoda there sat a rather underwhelming replica. Foreign VIPs like me travelled in a motorcade with outriders, who were utterly pointless because the roads were empty.

I arrived at the government building and was ushered up to the first floor. As is common for diplomatic meetings, two armchairs were placed in the middle of a horseshoe of chairs so the two 'principals' could sit next to each other. Their respective delegations then sit in a line down each side. As sometimes happens, it was agreed I would spend time alone with Aung San Suu Kyi at the start of the meeting to allow 'chemistry' to be established. There was no particular time limit to this first encounter, but obviously the longer it went on the better the two principals were considered to be getting along.

To break the ice, I told her that my 79-year-old mother was born in colonial Burma. Her father worked for the British pharmaceuticals

Author with Aung San Suu Kyi

company ICI, and was posted there before the war. Aung San Suu Kyi seemed to warm to this personal link and asked me whether my mother was in good health. After pleasantries, we moved to business. As a world-famous democracy campaigner, she would understand the importance of human rights, or so I thought. But just as when she later testified in front of the ICJ, she robustly defended the military against accusations of genocide. She also believed the Myanmar courts were more than capable of dealing with any injustice.

I was disappointed – as was the world after her ICJ appearance. And not for the first time on that trip.

The day before I had been escorted by the Tatmadaw on a visit to Rakhine State. As we flew over the region in a Russian-built helicopter there was no sign of any of the burnt-out villages written about by Wa and Kyaw. Perhaps they had been overgrown by lush vegetation. More likely the helicopter route had been chosen to avoid them.

I had also visited huts set up to process Rohingya refugees returning from Cox's Bazar in Bangladesh, where so many had fled in fear. But despite the effort put into building and staffing them, there was not a refugee in sight. That was as the government intended, because they didn't really want any of the 'foreigners' they had booted out to come back. Nor did the refugees want to return, despite the squalor they were living in: why risk travelling across the border from Bangladesh if the genocide might be repeated? Miserable, disease-ridden border camps in Cox's Bazar were a safer bet.

After visiting the Potemkin processing centre, I went on to meet some Rohingya in one of the 'villages'. As I stood next to the soldiers accompanying me, the villagers told me that they had been treated 'excellently' and there had been 'no genocide'. The fear in their eyes told me the opposite was in fact the case.

I told all this to Aung San Suu Kyi. It was to no avail.

But I didn't give up. If I wasn't making progress on the Rohingya genocide, maybe I could do something about Wa and Kyaw, the two imprisoned journalists. They were represented, at Reuters's expense, by Amal Clooney, a formidable human rights barrister. She advised me that the best way to get them out was by requesting a presidential pardon during Myanmar's traditional New Year festival, known as Thingyan.

So I made the request. Again, a brick wall. Why was I challenging due process in the Burmese courts? I calmly told Aung San Suu Kyi that there had been no due process, that the two journalists had been framed and that the court was a sham. But the lady was not for turning.

Our ambassador to Myanmar sat next to me. Dan Chugg was one of our most capable diplomats. He was quite well known for being in a documentary about Boris Johnson's time as Foreign Secretary, in which he surprised everyone by getting his guitar out and playing it. As a consummate professional, he handed me a carefully crafted single sheet of paper listing all the flaws in the legal process. He knew we were far more likely to succeed in challenging process than in challenging principle. He also guessed that anything longer than a page would not be read by Aung San Suu Kyi. I secured a commitment from her that she would read the one-pager herself.

'Give my best wishes to your mother,' she said softly as I walked out of the door.

I did just that – and my mother was thrilled. But we did not forget our mission. Over the months that followed, with Amal's help, I organised for others to lobby her privately. That included Lord Ara Darzi, a former UK health minister who had built a hospital in Yangon. We even thought about flying out Ed Llewellyn, former chief of staff to Cameron, who was friends with her and who was our ambassador to France at the time. But it was not necessary. Eight months later, around the time of the Thingyan festival, we hit the jackpot: the two journalists were released after 511 days in prison.[10]

So the trip to Myanmar was not fruitless. On the other hand, strictly speaking, the fate of two imprisoned Burmese journalists wasn't anything to do with the UK. They weren't British or reporting about Britain. No jobs back at home were at stake. It had no bearing on Brexit and frankly made no difference to our global standing. No one else really cared. In some ways, it was actually against our interests to raise such issues. A request from a former colonial power on a human rights issue could easily sour relations (as indeed it did – we were denied official contact for several months after my visit). Without such 'lectures', a country led by an Anglophile democracy campaigner who had lived in Oxford for many years might be a natural ally – but get the tone wrong, and she could cosy up to her big neighbour, China, which never asks awkward questions on human rights.

When I thought about the trip further, I realised a curious thing. Despite the randomness of the visit, despite the lack of national interest, despite the absence of any trade opportunities, no one was in the least surprised that I should want to go there. Britain is neither an imperial power nor a superpower, but it wasn't seen as remotely out of the ordinary for its Foreign Secretary to be holding another country to account for a genocide. On the contrary, this was the kind of thing Britain just *did*.

And among the 193 UN members, not many others do. Few would ever stick out their neck so visibly on a matter of principle in which there was no national advantage. Not that they mind when we do it. When Baltic states are worried about Russian aggression, when Asian countries are worried about China's incursions in the South China Sea, when Israel is attacked by swarms of drones from Iran, after turning to the US it is often Britain they come to next.

We have become so used to being a global champion for democratic values that we don't even question it ourselves. The most left-wing MPs will stand up and ask the Foreign Secretary what Britain is going to do about something happening on the other side of the world – as if we still had an empire. Often, they are the same people who, in another context, criticise our past and belittle our global influence. But if they really believed we were powerless, they wouldn't be asking the question.

All advanced democracies have lost confidence in recent years. But in dangerous times, underestimating our capabilities is as big a mistake as overestimating them. When you combine the hard power of our military, the reach of our diplomatic network, the influence of our universities, the strength of our technology base and the soft power of our media and culture, few countries match Britain's ability to shape global events.

Of course, wherever we can, we should seek the leadership of the US, as the world's most powerful democracy. No country has done more to make the world more free and more prosperous. None has more capability to protect the progress made. But whatever we think about President Trump's views on particular issues, it is not realistic or reasonable to expect American leadership on every issue. Sometimes we will need to put together different alliances of like-minded countries, whether in Europe or with friends in similar countries, such as Australia, Canada or Japan.

It is not always easy to quantify the extent of Britain's influence. But numerous think tanks, universities and expert organisations try to do just that. And the UK is nearly always in the top ten.

Like other countries, we have been through a difficult period in which we've had to cope with 'black swan' events such as a global financial crisis, a pandemic and an energy shock. But our economy remains one of the most open and innovative of any large country. We have more leading universities than anywhere else apart from the US – helping to earn us fifth place globally for innovation. We have particular strengths in the industries that will grow the fastest this century, including the world's third largest technology ecosystem. That is one of the reasons why in 2024, according to an annual survey of chief executives, the UK overtook China and Germany to be the second most attractive destination for investment globally after the US.[11]

Nor is the widespread assumption about the inevitability of British relative economic decline born out by the facts. The Centre for Economics and Business Research (CEBR) is one of the few organisations to do long-term growth projections. They say that today the UK is the sixth largest economy in the world and by 2039 – when their forecast period ends – it will still be the sixth largest. Our GDP per head is twenty-second globally but perhaps a fairer comparison is where we stand among the twenty largest economies, where we are fifth after the US, Australia, Germany and Canada. The CEBR say that by 2039 the UK will continue to have the fifth highest GDP per head in the G20.[12]

Our governments – including ones in which I served – have made many mistakes. But our democracy is no more flawed than others, and more healthy than many. The UK media is the fourth freest in the G20 and the country is in the top ten globally for internet freedom. Perceptions of corruption are the fifth lowest. Compared to our peers, the UK remains one of the freest and least corrupt countries on the planet.

When it comes to security and the rule of law, as discussed earlier, the UK armed forces need considerable investment. But they still remain the second most powerful in NATO and in the top ten globally. The global influence they give us is buttressed by a still considerable aid budget and the enormous soft power coming from the strength of our universities and the reach of our culture. We also take our responsibilities as a global citizen seriously: we have reduced emissions by more than any other large country, and are one of the most generous when it comes to giving to charity.

Top 10 Economies by Size: 2024 and 2039

Rank	2024	GDP (current USD trillion)	Rank	2039	GDP (current USD trillion)
1	US	29.15	1	US	53.46
2	China	18.33	2	China	44.77
3	Germany	4.69	3	India	12.81
4	Japan	4.02	4	Germany	7.49
5	India	3.88	5	Japan	6.33
6	UK	3.59	6	UK	6.25
7	France	3.16	7	France	4.99
8	Italy	2.37	8	Brazil	4.06
9	Canada	2.20	9	Canada	3.74
10	Brazil	2.16	10	Indonesia	3.71

Source: 'World Economic League Table 2025', CEBR, December 2024, https://cebr.com/world-economic-league-table/

Freedom

Country	G20 Rank	Overall Rank	Score
Canada	1	5	97
Japan	2	11	96
Germany	3	18	95
Australia	3	18	95
UK	5	29	92
France	6	41	89
Italy	6	41	89
Argentina	8	52	85
US	9	54	84
South Africa	10	66	81
South Korea	10	66	81
Brazil	12	80	72
India	13	97	63
Mexico	14	104	59
Indonesia	15	108	56
Turkey	16	139	33
Russia	17	173	12
Saudi Arabia	18	180	9
China	18	180	9

Source: 'Freedom in the World 2013–2025 Raw Data', Freedom House, 2025, https://freedomhouse.org/report/freedom-world

Generosity

Country	G20 Rank	Overall Rank	Donated Money (% of Adults)
Indonesia	1	1	90%
UK	2	6	67%
US	3	13	61%
Canada	4	15	60%
Australia	5	16	59%
Germany	6	29	52%
Saudi Arabia	7	38	43%
Russian Federation	8	42	42%
France	9	45	41%
South Korea	10	49	40%

Source: 'World Giving Index 2024', Charities Aid Foundation, 2024, https://www.cafonline.org/docs/default-source/inside-giving/wgi/wgi_2024_report.pdf

The data quoted in this book is by no means exhaustive. It also changes from year to year, so it would be a mistake to attach too much weight to any individual assessment. It should also be said that because this book is about Britain's global role, it doesn't look at how the UK does on social indicators that do not cross borders: in some, such as health outcomes, we do worse than other advanced economies; in others, such as educational standards, we do better (in England if not Scotland or Wales).

Some studies do attempt to look at the overall levels of well-being in different countries. The official UN Human Development Index looks at health, education and living standards. The World Happiness Report asks people in different countries how happy they consider themselves to be, a subjective measure that generally correlates closely with other well-being indicators. The UK doesn't do too badly in either. While it is often ahead of other large economies, it usually lags behind some of the smaller and more prosperous European countries such as Switzerland, the Netherlands and the Nordics. Finland has come top of the World Happiness index for the last eight years.[13]

So should we just aim to be Finland? Or indeed any other country with a higher GDP per capita, better public services and a superior overall ranking for well-being? Many in Britain would like to do just that. On the left, there is suspicion that overseas military projection is a hankering for an imperial past. On the right, there is growing isolationism. Both are declinist about Britain's prospects. Former Conservative cabinet minister William Waldegrave, for example, believes that we should abandon our permanent seat at the UN Security Council and accept our fate as a modest, middle-ranking country.

Often, such an approach is couched as 'realism'. Rather than withdrawing from global cooperation, why not make a difference in small but important areas where we can?

That is a false choice. Britain already makes a difference in numerous worthy areas and has a long track record of doing so. As Foreign Secretary, William Hague launched a global campaign to stop sexual violence being used as a weapon of war, a highly successful initiative which continues to this day. Boris Johnson organised a big campaign to stamp out the illegal wildlife trade, attracting seventy countries to its launch in London. Theresa May made enormous progress championing the stamping out of modern slavery. I myself launched campaigns to promote freedom of religion and belief and media freedom, both of which continue.

Human Development Index

Country	Overall Rank	Score
Switzerland	1	0.967
Norway	2	0.966
Iceland	3	0.959
Hong Kong, China (SAR)	4	0.956
Denmark	5	0.952
Sweden	5	0.952
Germany	7	0.950
Ireland	7	0.950
Singapore	9	0.949
Australia	10	0.946
Netherlands	10	0.946
Belgium	12	0.942
Finland	12	0.942
Liechtenstein	12	0.942
UK	15	0.940
New Zealand	16	0.939
UAE	17	0.937
Canada	18	0.935
South Korea	19	0.929
Luxembourg	20	0.927

Source: United Nations Development Programme, 'Human Development Report 2023/2024: Breaking the Gridlock – Reimagining Cooperation in a Polarized World' (United Nations, 2024)

A GLOBAL VOCATION

World Happiness

Country	G20 Rank	Overall Rank	Ladder Score
Mexico	1	10	6.979
Australia	2	11	6.974
Canada	3	18	6.803
Germany	4	22	6.753
UK	5	23	6.728
US	6	24	6.724
Saudi Arabia	7	32	6.600
France	8	33	6.593
Brazil	9	36	6.494
Italy	10	40	6.415
Argentina	11	42	6.397
Japan	12	55	6.147
South Korea	13	58	6.038
Russia	14	66	5.945
China	15	68	5.921
Indonesia	16	83	5.617
Turkey	17	94	5.262
South Africa	18	95	5.213
India	19	118	4.389

Source: John F. Helliwell et al. (eds), 'World Happiness Report 2025', Wellbeing Research Centre, 2025, https://worldhappiness.report/ed/2025/

But valuable though they are, such initiatives cannot in themselves address the scale of the dangers now facing the world. If the UK did decide to emulate Finland or Switzerland, who would lead the charge on European security? Or the global struggle between autocracy and democracy? Or climate change? Or reforms to reduce uncontrolled migration? It might seem beguiling to stand back and applaud as others get their hands dirty on our behalf – but in reality, there is no 'free rider' option. On the contrary, if we pull up the drawbridge others will follow suit – not least isolationists in the US.

So, interesting though it is to consider where the UK sits in rankings of global power, this is not in the end an argument about British exceptionalism. It is about whether countries that have influence are actually prepared to use it. For all its flaws, liberal democracy remains the best system ever invented for human happiness, prosperity and freedom. The more we fulfil our responsibilities the more others will follow suit, and pressing global issues will get tackled. The twentieth century showed what happens when you leave things too late. Are we prepared to learn the lessons?

No desire to live up to international responsibilities can duck the gritty question of how to fund them. The UK faces the same demographic pressures and rising expectations as many other countries. But as this book also shows, we are different: with its extraordinary science and technology base, Britain is in the lucky position of being able to make the exercise of global responsibilities a source of prosperity. Investing in technology to support a modern military will give our economy a crucial edge in the age of AI. Backing the science necessary to stop a future pandemic will unlock profitable new vaccines, treatments and medicines for the UK's burgeoning

The author's first meeting with Dr Henry Kissinger. He later became a great friend.

life sciences sector. Tackling climate change in a smart way will cut energy costs, making British business more productive and competitive. With energy and application, it is perfectly possible for us to become the world's next Silicon Valley and generate enormous wealth in the technology century.

Of course, there are many pitfalls along the way. The biggest of all, as Henry Kissinger said frequently, is self-doubt. So in a dangerous world, it is surely time to swap lazy declinism with a proper understanding of the extent and source of our global influence. If Britain wants to be a force for good, we have much to bring to the table.

LETTER TO
SIR KEIR STARMER

Dear Keir,

Around a year on from your massive general election victory, you probably feel like you are only just coming up for air. You haven't had an easy start, but if it's any consolation, I can't remember a time when any of the governments I served in were actually popular. Bricks never stop flying your way, but that is just the job.

It is an understandable political strategy to spend a lot of airtime rubbishing your opponents, but people want to hear leaders offering solutions. You showed that with your decision to reverse Labour's policy on defence and commit to 2.5% by 2027. In the end the only thing that matters is substance: the extent to which you actually change the country for the better. With a huge majority and a full parliamentary term you have the potential to be as bold as the Attlee or Thatcher governments. Attlee is remembered for founding the NHS and NATO. Thatcher for unleashing the economy and defeating the Soviet Union. They both combined big domestic reforms with a clear sense of Britain's global vocation.

I am a lifelong Conservative and always will be. So I want my country to succeed – even under a Labour government. It is probably unrealistic to expect you to cut taxes (although, if you want the economy to grow, please don't keep putting them up), but you can at least make sure that the money the government spends contributes to the long-term transformation of the economy. Defence spending can turn us into a technology superpower. Medicine spending can make us a life science giant. Education spending can give us the best-qualified graduates.

Be careful when the civil service tell you about the need for trade-offs. You will no doubt be told to choose between domestic priorities like the NHS and international priorities like defence. Most governments please no one by doing a bit of both. Of course you have to balance the books, but if you are willing to take radical decisions on welfare reform and public sector productivity, you could boost our much-needed defences, fund infrastructure that turns the UK into the world's next Silicon Valley alongside building countless hospitals and schools. That would transform Britain's place in the world. It would fund high-quality public services for generations to come. And it would be remembered long after you are gone.

That is because the real trade-off is not between one department and another but between the short and the long term. Laying the foundations for long-term growth, prosperity and influence may not affect the OBR forecasts but will affect our children's future. With your enormous majority and the time you have left, you are one of the few prime ministers who could actually make that happen. Politicians rarely regret being too radical but usually wish they had done more with their power when they had it.

I know that, like me, you want Britain to be a force for good. With a smart approach to policy-making, pursuing global responsibilities can make us more – not less – prosperous. Right now, a really dangerous world needs Britain to find its voice. Given the extraordinary potential we have as a country, I hope you help it do just that.

JEREMY HUNT

POSTSCRIPT

I would like to thank the many people who helped me put this book together. I first started writing it in the summer of 2021 and numerous people have guided my initially rather half-baked instincts into the arguments in this book. From the start I have been lucky to have the brilliant sinologist Anthony Jarvis as my researcher, who has been incredibly thorough and diligent, digging out stories and facts that bring the core messages to life. He was supported in the early days by the very able Jessica Cunniffe. Thank you also to my editor Jack Ramm, who challenged me, as ever, in the right ways, and to the brilliant Gesche Ipsen, who managed to find typos even after we had read the manuscript a thousand times. The whole team at Swift – Mark, Ruth and Diana – were their usual delight to work with. My agent Jonny Geller has also been a constant source of wise advice – somehow I feel Jonny and I are on the same part of life's journey together, and I have really appreciated that.

I am also grateful to numerous experts who helped me understand some of the issues which I only skated over in office. On defence, David Richards and Nick Carter were both superb (and I hope my father forgives the army bias in who I consulted), alongside Karin von Hippel. On democracy, diplomacy and China I was given excellent insights by former colleagues Simon McDonald and Kim Darroch as well as Charlie Parton, Tim Davie from the BBC and Max Lu from the University of Surrey. On trade, Dan Hannan, Greg Hands and Cheryl Schonhardt-Bailey helped me understand what a free trading nation should want to do next. On climate change, Nick Stern, Alok Sharma, Doug Gurr, Dominic Lawson, Michael Dawson and Mike Hulme gave me many practical and helpful suggestions. On migration, Alex Chalk and Geoffrey Cox lent me their superb legal brains (free of charge). Andrew Mitchell and Paul Collier helped me understand the role of international development. When it comes to pandemic prevention, Martin Landray, Chris Whitty and Sally Davies were excellent critical friends. On human rights, Richard Ratcliffe and Nazanin Zaghari-Ratcliffe as well as Simon Collis and Rita French gave me many constructive suggestions, as did Demis Hassabis and Ro Silva on technology and Paul Johnson on the economic arguments. Anthony Seldon and David Blair kindly gave me much time and great insights as well. Jeffrey Archer also gave me valuable encouragement. All the opinions and no doubt many mistakes are mine and not theirs.

I also want to thank the fantastic civil servants – too many to name – who I worked with in four government departments over fourteen years. Civil servants are often accused of trying to frustrate the wishes of their political masters, but I never found that. Any large organisation will have stronger and weaker performers, but my experience was that as long as politicians are clear about what they want, civil servants do their best to deliver. Quite properly, I rarely if ever knew which party they voted for. That is not to say we do not need big reform in the civil service – we do. But the short-termist, media-obsessed way the system works is a problem politicians need to tackle head on – rather than shunt the blame onto 'the system' and the people trapped in it. Working alongside them were the best

POSTSCRIPT

special advisers I could have ever hoped for: I cannot mention them all by name but Adam Smith and Christina Robinson in particular gave me help I will never be able to repay.

Finally, I need to thank my incredible wife Lucia. She has been my rock. I know it hasn't been easy bringing up a family among the maelstrom of British politics, but she is the love of my life, without whom nothing would have been possible. And to my kids, I love you to bits so please don't go into politics…

NOTES

Introduction

1   In the 2025–26 financial year, a change of 1p to the basic tax rate is £6.5 billion. Source: 'Direct Effects of Illustrative Tax Changes Bulletin (January 2025)', GOV.UK, 28 January 2025, https://www.gov.uk/government/statistics/direct-effects-of-illustrative-tax-changes/direct-effects-of-illustrative-tax-changes-bulletin-january-2025.
2   Mehreen Khan, 'Bank Could Cut Interest Rates Three Times This Year, Says IMF', *The Times*, 21 May 2024, https://www.thetimes.com/business-money/economics/article/imf-warns-hunt-against-cutting-national-insurance-again-7dvhpqc5x.
3   Elizabeth Clery, John Curtice and Curtis Jessop (eds), 'British Social Attitudes: The 41st Report', National Centre for Social Research, 2024, https://natcen.ac.uk/publications/british-social-attitudes-41-national-identity.
4   Tim Wallace and Ben Wright (eds), '"A Very Nice Life for a Lot Less Money": Why Young People Are Fleeing High-Tax Britain', *Daily Telegraph*, 20 October 2024, https://www.telegraph.co.uk/business/2024/10/20/britain-gloomy-poor-highly-taxed-young-people-packing-bags/.
5   William James, 'Trump Says Brexit to Be "a Great Thing", Wants Quick Trade Deal with UK', Reuters, 16 January 2017, https://www.reuters.com/article/world/trump-says-brexit-to-be-a-great-thing-wants-quick-trade-deal-with-uk-idUSKBN14Z0XT/.

1. Security Anchor

1. Human Rights Watch, 'Sierra Leone: Getting Away with Murder, Mutilation, and Rape', 1999, https://www.refworld.org/reference/countryrep/hrw/1999/en/39219.
2. Alfred B Zack-Williams, 'Child Soldiers in the Civil War in Sierra Leone', *Review of African Political Economy* 28, no. 87 (1 March 2001), http://www.jstor.org/stable/4006694.
3. Kieran Mitton, 'Elite Bargains and Political Deals Project: Sierra Leone Case Study', UK Government's Stabilisation Unit, 2018, https://assets.publishing.service.gov.uk/media/5c191317e5274a465849a1ae/Sierra_Leone_case_study.pdf.
4. This account of British intervention in Sierra Leone is mostly based on the following sources: David Richards, *Taking Command* (London: Headline, 2014); Steve Heaney and Damien Lewis, *Operation Mayhem* (London: Orion, 2014); 'Operation Barras', National Army Museum, https://www.nam.ac.uk/explore/operation-barras; and Will Fowler, *Certain Death in Sierra Leone: The SAS and Operation Barras, 2000* (Oxford: Osprey, 2010).
5. BFBS Creative, 'The Pathfinders: Jungle Battle in Sierra Leone – Tea & Medals', 23 June 2022, https://www.youtube.com/watch?v=YMZ5F-Ya9mQ.
6. 'UK Armed Forces Deaths: Operational Deaths Post World War II: 3 September 1945 to 29 February 2024', Ministry of Defence, 4 April 2024, https://assets.publishing.service.gov.uk/media/6605529d91a320001182b1b2/UK_armed_forces_operational_deaths_post_World_War_2_2024.pdf.
7. 'Defence Expenditure of NATO Countries (2014–2024)', NATO, 2024, https://www.nato.int/nato_static_fl2014/assets/pdf/2024/6/pdf/240617-def-exp-2024-en.pdf.
8. Dina Smeltz, 'American Support for Active US Global Role Not What It Used to Be', Chicago Council on Global Affairs, 22 August 2024, https://globalaffairs.org/research/public-opinion-survey/american-support-active-us-global-role-not-what-it-used-be.
9. Joshua Jamerson, 'GOP Sparring Over U.S. Role in Ukraine War Colors Ohio Senate Race', *Wall Street Journal*, 16 April 2022, https://www.wsj.

com/articles/republican-debate-over-war-in-ukraine-plays-out-in-ohio-senate-race-11650118454.
10 In 2024, Fitch forecast the UK's budget deficit to be 4.4%, whereas for France it was expected to be 6.1%. See more information here: 'Fitch Revises France's Outlook to Negative; Affirms at "AA-"', Fitch Ratings, 11 October 2024, https://www.fitchratings.com/research/sovereigns/fitch-revises-france-outlook-to-negative-affirms-at-aa-11-10-2024; 'Fitch Affirms United Kingdom at "AA-"; Outlook Stable', *idem*, 20 September 2024, https://www.fitchratings.com/research/sovereigns/fitch-affirms-united-kingdom-at-aa-outlook-stable-20-09-2024.
11 Sabine Kinkartz, 'What Is Germany's Debt Brake?', DW, 11 July 2024, https://www.dw.com/en/what-is-germanys-debt-brake/a-67587332.
12 Vladimir Putin, 'On the Historical Unity of Russians and Ukrainians', 15 July 2021, http://en.kremlin.ru/events/president/news/66181.
13 Donald J. Trump (@realDonaldTrump), Twitter, 21 March 2018, https://x.com/realDonaldTrump/status/976532956557737984. The full tweet reads: 'I called President Putin of Russia to congratulate him on his election victory (in past, Obama called him also). The Fake News Media is crazed because they wanted me to excoriate him. They are wrong! Getting along with Russia (and Others) is a good thing, not a bad thing.......'
14 Max Jeffery, 'Ben Wallace: Britain Is "Highly Unlikely" to Send Troops to Ukraine', *Spectator*, 18 December 2021, https://www.spectator.co.uk/article/ben-wallace-britain-is-highly-unlikely-to-send-troops-to-ukraine/; 'Ukraine', *Hansard*, 25 January 2022, https://hansard.parliament.uk/commons/2022-01-25/debates/1AB76A45-585A-402CAD27-2C6B8897B8D0/Ukraine; Reuters, 'Biden Says Putting U.S. Troops in Ukraine "Not on the Table"', YouTube, 8 December 2021, https://www.youtube.com/watch?v=607ZFFUCGTQ.
15 Charles Lichfield, 'Windfall: How Russia Managed Oil and Gas Income after Invading Ukraine, and How It Will Have to Make Do with Less', Atlantic Council, 30 November 2022, https://www.atlanticcouncil.org/in-depth-research-reports/issue-brief/windfall-how-russia-managed-oil-and-gas-income-after-invading-ukraine-and-how-it-will-have-to-make-do-with-less/.
16 'GDP (constant LCU) – Russian Federation', World Bank, 2025, https://data.worldbank.org/indicator/NY.GDP.MKTP.KN?locations=RU.

17 Sergey Vakulenko, 'Russia Has the Resources for a Long War in Ukraine', Carnegie Russia Eurasia Center, 16 May 2024, https://carnegieendowment.org/research/2024/03/v-usloviyah-voennogo-bremeni-glavnye-voprosy-o-nastoyashem-i-budushem-rossijskoj-ekonomiki.

18 Office of the Director of National Intelligence, 'Assessment of the Effects of Sanctions in Response to the Russian Federation's Invasion of Ukraine', September 2023, https://www.odni.gov/files/documents/FOIA/DF-2023-00313-Assessment-of-the-Effects-of-Sanctions-in-Response-to-the-Russian-Federations-Invasion-of-Ukraine.pdf.

19 Siri Aas Rustad, 'Conflict Trends: A Global Overview, 1946–2023' (PRIO Paper, 2024), https://www.prio.org/publications/14006.

20 Shawn Davies et al., 'Organized Violence 1989–2023, and the Prevalence of Organized Crime Groups', *Journal of Peace Research* 61, no. 4 (1 July 2024): 673–93, https://doi.org/10.1177/00223433241262912.

21 'Defence Expenditure', NATO.

22 Peter E. Robertson, 'Military PPP Data', Military PPP, 3 March 2025, https://militaryppp.com/blog/.

23 Compiled by James Rogers, 'Audit of Geopolitical Capability', The Henry Jackson Society, January 2019, https://henryjacksonsociety.org/wp-content/uploads/2019/01/HJS-2019-Audit-of-Geopolitical-Capability-Report-web.pdf.

24 '69743 – List of Countries AF Training Provided to [Dataset]', UK Parliament, 6 July 2020, https://questions-statements.parliament.uk/writtenquestions/detail/2020-07-06/69743.

25 'Was the UK the First Country to Send Main Battle Tanks to Ukraine?', Full Fact, 19 December 2023, https://fullfact.org/live/2023/dec/sunak-liaison-tanks-ukraine/.

26 Peter Dickinson, 'Britain Becomes First Country to Supply Ukraine with Long-Range Missiles', Atlantic Council, 11 May 2023, https://www.atlanticcouncil.org/blogs/ukrainealert/britain-becomes-first-country-to-supply-ukraine-with-long-range-missiles/; Claire Mills, 'Security Guarantees to Ukraine', House of Commons Library, 22 July 2024, https://researchbriefings.files.parliament.uk/documents/CBP-9837/CBP-9837.pdf.

27 David Maddox, 'British Army Set to Shrink to Smallest Size since before Napoleonic Wars', *Independent*, 15 October 2024, https://www.independent.co.uk/news/uk/politics/british-army-smallest-john-healey-b2629481.html.

NOTES TO PAGES 42–44

28 'Defence Key Figures 2024', Ministère des Armées, July 2024, https://www.defense.gouv.fr/sites/default/files/ministere-armees/Chiffres%20cl%C3%A9s%20de%20la%20D%C3%A9fense%20-%202024%20UK.pdf.

29 'Rapporto Esercito 2023', Ministero della Difesa, 2024, https://www.esercito.difesa.it/Rapporto-Esercito/Documents/2023/ok_RE23_A4_ITA.pdf.

30 'Personalzahlen der Bundeswehr', Bundeswehr, 30 November 2024, https://www.bundeswehr.de/de/ueber-die-bundeswehr/zahlen-daten-fakten/personalzahlen-bundeswehr.

31 David Axe, 'Britain Spent So Much on Two Giant Aircraft Carriers, It Can't Afford Planes or Escorts', Forbes, 28 June 2020, https://www.forbes.com/sites/davidaxe/2020/06/28/britain-spent-so-much-on-two-giant-aircraft-carriers-it-cant-afford-planes-or-escorts/.

32 '"We're Going to Need a Bigger Navy"', House of Commons Defence Committee, 14 December 2021, https://committees.parliament.uk/publications/8205/documents/85026/default/.

33 'UK Armed Forces Equipment and Formations 2024', Ministry of Defence, 27 February 2025, https://www.gov.uk/government/statistics/uk-armed-forces-equipment-and-formations-2024.

34 In 1982, the Royal Navy's active surface fleet had 4 light cruisers, 12 destroyers and 43 frigates. Source: John Evelyn Moore, ed., *Jane's Fighting Ships 1982–83* (London, UK: Jane's Publishing Company Ltd, 1982).

35 'UK Armed Forces Equipment and Formations 2024', Ministry of Defence; 'Military Formations, Vessels and Aircraft: 2013', Ministry of Defence, 19 February 2015, https://www.gov.uk/government/statistics/military-formations-vessels-and-aircraft-2013.

36 'Chief of the Defence Staff, General Sir Nick Carter Launches the Integrated Operating Concept', GOV.UK, 30 September 2020, https://www.gov.uk/government/speeches/chief-of-the-defence-staff-general-sir-nick-carter-launches-the-integrated-operating-concept.

37 Harrison Kass, 'Nuclear Aircraft Carriers in the U.S Navy: Most Expensive Warships Ever', Center for the National Interest, 26 October 2024, https://nationalinterest.org/blog/buzz/nuclear-aircraft-carriers-us-navymost-expensive-warships-ever-207813; Eric Tegler, 'With a Sight, Sound and Radar Picture, Saildrone Could Build an AI Database of Everything

in the Ocean', Forbes, 16 August 2021, https://www.forbes.com/sites/erictegler/2021/08/16/with-a-sight-sound-and-radar-picture-saildrone-could-build-an-ai-database-of-everything-in-the-ocean/.
38. Simon Staffell, 'The Integrated Review: A Technological Revolution at the Heart of UK Defence and National Security', RUSI, 12 March 2021, https://rusi.org/explore-our-research/publications/commentary/integrated-review-technological-revolution-heart-uk-defence-and-national-security.
39. Claire Mills and Esme Kirk-Wade, 'The Cost of the UK's Strategic Nuclear Deterrent', House of Commons Library, 22 August 2024, https://researchbriefings.files.parliament.uk/documents/CBP-8166/CBP-8166.pdf.
40. 'Defence Expenditure', NATO.
41. 'PM Announces "Turning Point" in European Security as UK Set to Increase Defence Spending to 2.5% by 2030', GOV.UK, 24 April 2024, https://www.gov.uk/government/news/pm-announces-turning-point-in-european-security-as-uk-set-to-increase-defence-spending-to-25-by-2030.
42. Tom Watling, 'Inside Russia's Dozens of Attempts to Kill Ukrainian President Volodymyr Zelensky', *Independent*, 7 May 2024, https://www.independent.co.uk/news/world/europe/zelensky-assassination-ukraine-putin-russia-b2541002.html.
43. According to NATO, the UK spent an estimated 2.33% (£64.58 billion) of GDP on defence in 2024. Increasing this to 3.4% would require nearly £30 billion. Source: 'Defence Expenditure', NATO.
44. In the 2025–26 financial year, a change of 1p to the basic tax rate is £6.5 billion. Source: 'Direct Effects of Illustrative Tax Changes Bulletin (January 2025)'.
45. NATO, 'Wales Summit Declaration Issued by NATO Heads of State and Government (2014)', NATO, 5 September 2014, https://www.nato.int/cps/en/natohq/official_texts_112964.htm.
46. 'Defence Expenditure', NATO.
47. In 2024, NATO Allies in Europe spent a total of $380 billion on defence. Source: 'Secretary General Welcomes Unprecedented Rise in NATO Defence Spending', NATO, n.d., https://www.nato.int/cps/en/natohq/news_222664.htm.

2. Democracy Champion

1. Lindsay Maizland and Clara Fong, 'Hong Kong's Freedoms: What China Promised and How It's Cracking Down', Council on Foreign Relations, 19 March 2024, https://www.cfr.org/backgrounder/hong-kong-freedoms-democracy-protests-china-crackdown.
2. Chinese Human Rights Defenders, 'CHRD Communiqué Alleging Torture of Chinese Lawyer Wang Quanzhang', 26 August 2020, https://www.nchrd.org/2020/10/chrd-communique-alleging-torture-of-chinese-lawyer-wang-quanzhang-august-26-2020/.
3. 'Wang Quanzhang – Chinese Human Rights Defenders', Chinese Human Rights Defenders, 22 January 2016, https://www.nchrd.org/2016/01/wang-quanzhang/.
4. Christian Shepherd, 'Wife of Detained Chinese Lawyer Begins 100-km March to Press for Answers', Reuters, 4 April 2018, https://www.reuters.com/article/world/wife-of-detained-chinese-lawyer-begins-100-km-march-to-press-for-answers-idUSKCN1HB0J6/.
5. 'Wang Quanzhang: China Human Rights Lawyer Trial Begins', BBC News, 26 December 2018, https://www.bbc.com/news/world-asia-china-46684398.
6. South China Morning Post, 'Chinese Human Rights Lawyer Wang Quanzhang Reunites with Family', YouTube, 27 April 2020, https://www.youtube.com/watch?v=FzuWjlYhXcs.
7. Huizhong Wu, 'Chinese Human Rights Lawyer Chased out of 13 Homes in 2 Months as Pressure Rises on Legal Advocates', AP News, 23 June 2023, https://apnews.com/article/china-human-rights-lawyers-beijing-wang-quanzhang-1e327eb9cf0959d6e643d6101618e8c6.
8. Iain Duncan Smith, 'Starmer's Britain Won't Be China's Peer, It'll Be Xi's Puppet', *Daily Telegraph*, 19 November 2024, https://www.telegraph.co.uk/news/2024/11/19/starmers-britain-wont-be-chinas-peer-itll-be-xis-puppet/.
9. 'Remarks by President Biden at the United States Naval Academy's Class of 2022 Graduation and Commissioning Ceremony', White House [archive], 27 May 2022, https://web.archive.org/web/20220527173919/https://www.whitehouse.gov/briefing-room/statements-releases/2022/05/27/

remarks-by-president-biden-at-the-united-states-naval-academys-class-of-2022-graduation-and-commissioning-ceremony/.

10. 'World Economic Outlook Database, October 2024 Edition', IMF, October 2024, https://www.imf.org/en/Publications/WEO/weo-database/2024/October; 'GDP, PPP (current international $)', World Bank, 2025, https://data.worldbank.org/indicator/NY.GDP.MKTP.PP.CD.

11. Kenneth Rogoff and Yuanchen Yang, 'China's Real Estate Challenge', IMF, December 2024, https://www.imf.org/en/Publications/fandd/issues/2024/12/chinas-real-estate-challenge-kenneth-rogoff.

12. James Mayger, et al., 'Foreign Direct Investment Into China Slumps to Worst in 30 Years', Bloomberg, 18 February 2024, https://www.bloomberg.com/news/articles/2024-02-18/foreign-direct-investment-into-china-slumps-to-worst-in-30-years.

13. Sam Peach, 'Why Did Alibaba's Jack Ma Disappear for Three Months?', BBC News, 20 March 2021, https://www.bbc.com/news/technology-56448688.

14. C. Textor, 'China: Working-Age Population 1980–2050', Statista, 12 July 2024, https://www.statista.com/statistics/1219212/china-number-of-working-age-persons/.

15. Feng Wang, Baochang Gu and Yong Cai, 'The End of China's One-Child Policy', Brookings, 30 March 2016, https://www.brookings.edu/articles/the-end-of-chinas-one-child-policy/.

16. João da Silva, 'China Economy Slowdown Deepens, Official Figures Show', BBC News, 18 October 2024, https://www.bbc.com/news/articles/crr54x00857o.

17. 'World Economic League Table 2025', CEBR, December 2024, https://cebr.com/world-economic-league-table/.

18. Sebastian Horn, Carmen M. Reinhart and Christoph Trebesch, 'China's Overseas Lending', *Journal of International Economics* 133 (1 November 2021): 103539, https://doi.org/10.1016/j.jinteco.2021.103539.

19. 'International Comparisons of Defence Expenditure and Military Personnel', *The Military Balance* 125, no. 1 (11 February 2025): 520–25, https://doi.org/10.1080/04597222.2025.2445483.

20. Jane Flanagan and Dan Atherton, 'Corrupt Politicians Turning Africa against Democracy', *The Times*, 24 July 2024, https://www.thetimes.com/

world/africa/article/corrupt-politicians-turning-africa-against-democracy-zndj6cfpk.

21 Christian W. Haerpfer et al., 'World Values Survey: Round Seven – Country-Pooled Datafile Version 6.0.' (Madrid, Spain & Vienna: JD Systems Institute & WVSA Secretariat, 2022), doi:10.14281/18241.24.

22 Robert Wike et al., 'Representative Democracy Remains a Popular Ideal, but People Around the World Are Critical of How It's Working', Pew Research Center, February 2024, https://www.pewresearch.org/global/wp-content/uploads/sites/2/2024/02/gap_2024.02.28_democracy-closed-end_report.pdf.

23 John Curtice, Ian Montagu and Chujan Sivathasan, 'Damaged Politics? The Impact of the 2019–24 Parliament on Political Trust and Confidence', National Centre for Social Research, June 2024, https://natcen.ac.uk/sites/default/files/2024-06/BSA%2041%20Damaged%20Politics.pdf.

24 David Klepper, 'Russian Disinformation Is about Immigration. The Real Aim Is to Undercut Ukraine Aid', AP News, 1 March 2024, https://apnews.com/article/russia-election-trump-immigration-disinformation-tiktok-youtube-ce518c6cd101048f896025179ef19997.

25 Shayan Sardarizadeh, Merlyn Thomas and Lucy Gilder, 'Baseless Claim about Kamala Harris Crash Spread by Mysterious Site', BBC News, 4 September 2024, https://www.bbc.com/news/articles/cy4ye15le8xo.

26 'Director General Ken McCallum Gives Latest Threat Update', MI5, 8 October 2024, https://www.mi5.gov.uk/director-general-ken-mccallum-gives-latest-threat-update.

27 'BBC Boss Warns of Russian and Chinese Propaganda after World Service Cuts', BBC News, 14 October 2024, https://www.bbc.com/news/articles/cj9jgmexmx4o.

28 William Hague, 'The Next Big Battlefield Will Be in Our Minds', *The Times*, 14 October 2024, https://www.thetimes.com/comment/columnists/article/the-next-big-battlefield-will-be-in-our-minds-wkspf5g6t.

29 Yana Gorokhovskaia and Cathryn Grothe, 'Freedom in the World 2025', Freedom House, February 2025, https://freedomhouse.org/sites/default/files/2025-03/FITW_World2025digitalN.pdf.

30 Daniel Hannan, 'How to Avoid World War Three', CapX, 2 December 2024, https://capx.co/how-to-avoid-world-war-three.

31 For data file, see https://freedomhouse.org/sites/default/files/2025-02/All_data_FIW_2013-2024.xlsx.
32 The UK ranks fifth in total number of embassies / high commissions. If you count other diplomatic missions, such as number of consulates and permanent missions, the UK ranks seventh. Source: Lowy Institute, 'Global Diplomacy Index', 2024, https://globaldiplomacyindex.lowyinstitute.org/country_ranking.
33 'GDP (Current US$)', World Bank, 2025, https://data.worldbank.org/indicator/NY.GDP.MKTP.CD.
34 Kevin Rudd, *The Avoidable War* (New York: Hachette, 2022).
35 'Corruption Perceptions Index 2024' (Transparency International, 2025), https://images.transparencycdn.org/images/Report-CPI-2024-English.pdf.
36 Allie Funk, Kian Vesteinsson and Grant Baker, 'Freedom on the Net 2024', Freedom House, 2024, https://freedomhouse.org/report/freedom-net.
37 'World Press Freedom Index 2024', RSF, 2024, https://rsf.org/en/index.
38 'The Importance of Scotland to the UK: David Cameron's Speech', GOV.UK, 7 February 2014, https://www.gov.uk/government/speeches/the-importance-of-scotland-to-the-uk-david-camerons-speech.
39 Bill Clinton, *My Life* (New York: Vintage Books, 2005).
40 'Rhodes Scholar Database', Rhodes Trust, https://www.rhodeshouse.ox.ac.uk/scholar-community/rhodes-scholar-database/.
41 Nick Hillman, 'HEPI Soft-Power Index 2024: The US Pulls Further Away, While the UK Stands Still and France Slips Back', HEPI, 9 October 2024, https://www.hepi.ac.uk/2024/10/10/the-us-pulls-further-away-in-the-latest-soft-power-index-while-the-uk-stands-still-and-france-slips-back/.
42 'Summia Tora', Rhodes Trust, https://www.rhodeshouse.ox.ac.uk/scholar-community/rhodes-scholar-bios/rhodes-scholars-class-of-2020/summia-tora/.
43 UNESCO Institute for Statistics, 'Total inbound internationally mobile students, both sexes (number)', https://databrowser.uis.unesco.org/view#indicatorPaths=UIS-EducationOPRI:0:26637, accessed March 2025.
44 Luke Perrott, 'Higher Education Student Statistics: UK, 2022/23 – Where Students Come from and Go to Study', HESA, 8 August 2024, https://

www.hesa.ac.uk/news/08-08-2024/sb269-higher-education-student-statistics/location

45 'The Speech by Bill Clinton, Former US President, to the Labour Party Conference in Blackpool (Part One)', *Guardian*, 3 October 2002, https://www.theguardian.com/politics/2002/oct/03/labourconference.labour1.

46 Eleanor Lawrie, 'Free Speech Row Prof Kathleen Stock: Protests Like Anxiety Dream', BBC News, 3 November 2021, https://www.bbc.co.uk/news/education-59148324.

47 Finlay Malcolm, Bobby Duffy and Constance Woollen, 'Freedom of Speech in UK Higher Education', September 2023, https://www.kcl.ac.uk/policy-institute/assets/freedom-of-speech-in-uk-higher-education.pdf.

48 The total includes leaders from the same country; as such the number of countries with US and UK educated leaders is actually 58 and 52 respectively.

49 'World University Rankings 2025', *Times Higher Education*, 4 October 2024, https://www.timeshighereducation.com/world-university-rankings/latest/world-ranking.

50 David M. Eberhard, Gary F. Simons and Charles D. Fennig (eds), 'Ethnologue: Languages of the World, Twenty-Seventh Edition', SIL International, 2024, https://www.ethnologue.com/insights/most-spoken-language/.

51 Nic Newman et al., 'Reuters Institute Digital News Report 2024', Reuters Institute for the Study of Journalism, 2024, https://doi.org/10.60625/RISJ-VY6N-4V57.

52 'BBC's Global Audience Holds Firm despite Increased Competition', BBC, 18 July 2024, https://www.bbc.com/mediacentre/2024/bbc-global-audience-measure.

53 Caroline Davies, 'Aung San Suu Kyi Praises BBC World Service', *Guardian*, 20 June 2012, https://www.theguardian.com/world/2012/jun/19/aung-san-suu-kyi-world-service.

54 'The Weakest Link', BBC, https://www.bbc.com/historyofthebbc/anniversaries/august/weakest-link.

55 Isobel Lewis, 'How *Taskmaster* Became a Stratospheric, and Very Silly, Success Story', *Independent*, 30 May 2024, https://www.independent.co.uk/arts-entertainment/tv/features/taskmaster-finale-alex-horne-greg-davies-b2553082.html.

NOTES TO PAGES 78–81

56 Peter Conte, 'How *Love Island* Became a Global Phenomenon', Nine.com.au, 2020, //9now.nine.com.au/love-island-australia/love-island-uk-australia-usa-worldwide-show/ace4c990-701e-4ece-91af-c3b50594f4b9.
57 'About *MasterChef*', MasterChef UK, https://masterchef.com/pages/about-us.
58 Patrick Leu, 'Top-Selling Artists Worldwide as of August 2022, Based on Certified Sales', Statista, 29 May 2024, https://www.statista.com/statistics/271174/top-selling-artists-in-the-united-states/.
59 'The Phantom of the Opera', n.d., https://www.thephantomoftheopera.com/.
60 'The Numbers That Show This Has Been a Season like No Other', Premier League, 19 May 2024, https://www.premierleague.com/news/4016793.
61 'Vision for Publishing: The Role of Publishing in the UK's Success', Publishers Association, March 2024, https://www.publishers.org.uk/wp-content/uploads/2024/03/Vision_for_Publishing_pages.pdf.
62 'Factbox – Recent British Royal Weddings', Reuters, 3 May 2018, https://www.reuters.com/article/world/us/factbox-recent-british-royal-weddings-idUSKBN1I40GR/.
63 'Did Several Billion People Watch the Queen's Funeral?', Full Fact, 20 September 2022, https://fullfact.org/news/Queen-funeral-viewing-figures/.
64 'Creative Industries', UK Government: Great Britain & Northern Ireland, https://www.great.gov.uk/international/investment/sectors/creative-industries/.
65 'Ted Sarandos Keynote: Royal Television Society London Convention 2024', Netflix, 17 September 2024, https://about.netflix.com/news/ted-sarandos-keynote-royal-television-society-london-convention-2024.
66 'Written Evidence Submitted by Department for Culture, Media and Sport', House of Commons Culture, Media and Sport Select Committee, 14 November 2023, https://committees.parliament.uk/writtenevidence/125356/pdf/.
67 'Global Soft Power Index 2025' (Brand Finance, 2025), https://brandirectory.com/softpower.
68 Yasmin Rufo and Ian Youngs, 'Theatre, Film and Music Support in Budget Welcomed as "Game-Changing"', BBC News, 6 March 2024, https://www.bbc.com/news/entertainment-arts-68488760.

69 Niall Ferguson, *Empire: How Britain Made the Modern World* (London: Penguin Books, 2004).

3. Tackling Mass Migration

1 Story provided by a migration-linked charity. A pseudonym has been used in order to protect his identity.
2 'Service for Life', Human Rights Watch, 16 April 2009, https://www.hrw.org/report/2009/04/16/service-life/state-repression-and-indefinite-conscription-eritrea.
3 Jehanne Henry, '"They Were Shouting 'Kill Them'"', Human Rights Watch, 17 November 2019, https://www.hrw.org/report/2019/11/18/they-were-shouting-kill-them/sudans-violent-crackdown-protesters-khartoum.
4 Roald Høvring, '10 Things You Should Know about the Deadliest Migration Route', NRC, 20 March 2024, https://www.nrc.no/feature/2024/10-things-you-should-know-about-the-Central-Mediterranean-migration-route.
5 UNHCR, 'Arrivals to Europe from Libya – 2021 in Review', 21 April 2022, https://data.unhcr.org/en/documents/details/92165.
6 'Small Boat Activity in the English Channel', GOV.UK, 8 February 2025, https://www.gov.uk/government/publications/migrants-detected-crossing-the-english-channel-in-small-boats (data set: https://assets.publishing.service.gov.uk/media/67af4620e270ceae39f9e21e/14_Feb_2025_Small_boats_-_time_series.ods).
7 Samuel Kofi Tetteh Baah et al., 'Updating the International Poverty Line with the 2017 PPPs', World Bank Blogs, 2 May 2022, https://blogs.worldbank.org/en/opendata/updating-international-poverty-line-2017-ppps.
8 'World Bank Country and Lending Groups', World Bank, https://datahelpdesk.worldbank.org/knowledgebase/articles/906519-world-bank-country-and-lending-groups.
9 International Organization for Migration, *World Migration Report 2024* (UN, 2024).
10 'Global Trends 2023', UNHCR, 13 June 2024, https://www.unhcr.org/global-trends-report-2023.

11. According to UNHCR, between 2013 and 2023 the number of asylum seekers worldwide increased from 1.2 to 6.9 million. Sources: 'UNHCR Global Trends 2013', UNHCR, 20 June 2014, https://www.unhcr.org/ph/wp-content/uploads/sites/28/2017/03/GlobalTrends2013.pdf; 'Global Trends 2023'.
12. 'Channel Migrants: More than 1,000 People Cross in Single Day', BBC News, 10 October 2022, https://www.bbc.com/news/uk-england-kent-63201048.
13. Bob Dale and Jones Simon, 'Channel Migrants: Home Office Figures in 2024 Show 36,816 Crossed', BBC News, 1 January 2025, https://www.bbc.com/news/articles/c5y45dmg2pjo.
14. 'Smuggling of Migrants', Migration Data Portal, 21 May 2024, https://www.migrationdataportal.org/themes/smuggling-migrants.
15. International Organization for Migration, *World Migration Report 2024*.
16. Lucile Smith and Ben Steele, 'Greek Coastguard Threw Migrants Overboard to Their Deaths, Witnesses Say', BBC, 17 June 2024, https://www.bbc.co.uk/news/articles/c0vv717yvpeo.
17. Helena Smith, 'Shocking Images of Drowned Syrian Boy Show Tragic Plight of Refugees', *Guardian*, 2 September 2015, https://www.theguardian.com/world/2015/sep/02/shocking-image-of-drowned-syrian-boy-shows-tragic-plight-of-refugees.
18. Jessica Elgot, 'Family of Syrian Boy Washed up on Beach Were Trying to Reach Canada', *Guardian*, 3 September 2015, https://www.theguardian.com/world/2015/sep/03/refugee-crisis-syrian-boy-washed-up-on-beach-turkey-trying-to-reach-canada.
19. 'Annual Report and Accounts 2023 to 2024', UK Home Office, 2024, https://assets.publishing.service.gov.uk/media/66b249b40808eaf43b50de07/2023-24_Home_Office_Annual_Report_and_Accounts.pdf.
20. 'Trump Promises "Largest Deportation Operation in American History" If Elected', ABC News, 18 December 2023, https://www.abc.net.au/news/2023-12-18/donald-trump-promises-largest-deportation-operation/103241936.
21. Marie-Claire Sodergren, 'The True Value of a Paycheck: Understanding PPP-Adjusted Income Statistics', ILOSTAT, 6 August 2024, https://ilostat.ilo.org/blog/the-true-value-of-a-paycheck-understanding-ppp-adjusted-income-statistics/.

22 'The Sustainable Development Goals Report 2024', UN, 2024, https://unstats.un.org/sdgs/report/2024/The-Sustainable-Development-Goals-Report-2024.pdf.
23 Author's private conversations with finance minister counterparts.
24 'China–Africa Joint Statement on Deepening Cooperation within the Framework of the Global Development Initiative', China International Development Cooperation Agency, 6 September 2024, http://en.cidca.gov.cn/2024-09/06/c_1019586.htm.
25 'France Begins Withdrawing Its Troops from Niger', France 24, 10 October 2023, https://www.france24.com/en/africa/20231010-france-begins-withdrawing-its-troops-from-niger.
26 Sam Mednick, 'Niger's Junta Asks for Help from Russian Group Wagner as It Faces Military Intervention Threat', AP News, 6 August 2023, https://apnews.com/article/wagner-russia-coup-niger-military-force-e0e1108b58a9e955af465a3efe6605c0.
27 Grigor Atanesian, 'Russia in Africa: How Disinformation Operations Target the Continent', BBC News, 1 February 2023, https://www.bbc.com/news/world-africa-64451376.
28 Anaelle Jonah, '"Time to Move on": France Faces Gradual Decline of Influence in Africa', France 24, 2 January 2025, https://www.france24.com/en/africa/20250102-france-faces-gradual-decline-of-influence-in-africa.
29 Details of David Maxwell Fyfe's life and career are taken from David Patrick Maxwell Fyfe, *Political Adventure: The Memoirs of the Earl of Kilmuir*, 1st ed. (London: Weidenfeld and Nicolson, 1964).
30 Maxwell Fyfe, *Political Adventure: The Memoirs of the Earl of Kilmuir*, 1st ed. (London: Weidenfeld and Nicolson, 1964).
31 Maxwell Fyfe.
32 Maxwell Fyfe.
33 David Scott FitzGerald, 'Never Again?', in *Refuge Beyond Reach*, 1st ed. (Oxford: Oxford University Press, 2019), 21–40, https://doi.org/10.1093/oso/9780190874155.003.0002.
34 Melanie Glower, 'Article 31 of the Refugee Convention', House of Commons Library, 15 July 2021, https://researchbriefings.files.parliament.uk/documents/CBP-9281/CBP-9281.pdf.
35 'HIV Statistics, Globally and by WHO Region, 2024', WHO, 22 July 2024,

https://cdn.who.int/media/docs/default-source/hq-hiv-hepatitis-and-stis-library/j0482-who-ias-hiv-statistics_aw-1_final_ys.pdf?sfvrsn=61d39578_3.

36 'G8 Leaders Agree $50bn Aid Boost', BBC News, 8 July 2005, http://news.bbc.co.uk/1/hi/business/4662297.stm.

37 Technically speaking, the target was for 0.7% of Gross National Income (GNI); for ease of understanding, GDP is used instead.

38 'DFID Results Estimates 2015–2020: Sector Report', UK Department for International Development, 27 August 2020, https://assets.publishing.service.gov.uk/media/5f8d8aea8fa8f56ad340d1da/dfid-results-estimates-sector--report-2015-2020-update-16oct20.pdf.

39 Ian Mitchell, Beata Cichocka and Edward Wickstead, 'Commitment to Development Index 2023', Center for Global Development, 13 September 2023, https://www.cgdev.org/publication/commitment-development-index-2023.

40 'Net ODA', OECD, https://www.oecd.org/en/data/indicators/net-oda.html.

41 Paul Collier, *Left Behind: A New Economics for Neglected Places* (London: Allen Lane, 2024).

42 See 'Gross Domestic Product 2012–2020', Central Department of Statistics and Ministry of Planning and National Development. Republic of Somaliland, 28 January 2025, https://www.somalilandcsd.org/wp-content/uploads/2021/08/Final-Somaliland-GDP-2020-Report-1.pdf and 'GDP per Capita (Current US$) – Somalia', World Bank, 2025, https://data.worldbank.org/indicator/NY.GDP.PCAP.CD?locations=SO.

43 'Our History', British International Investment, https://www.bii.co.uk/en/about/our-history/.

44 'International Development in a Contested World: Ending Extreme Poverty and Tackling Climate Change. A White Paper on International Development', GOV.UK, November 2023, https://www.gov.uk/government/publications/international-development-in-a-contested-world-ending-extreme-poverty-and-tackling-climate-change/international-development-in-a-contested-world-ending-extreme-poverty-and-tackling-climate-change-a-white-paper-on-international-development.

45 Matt Dathan, 'Don't Repeat "Woeful" Tory Overspend on Asylum, Labour Told', *The Times*, 29 August 2024, https://www.thetimes.com/uk/politics/article/labour-risks-repeating-home-office-asylum-budget-mistakes-25j30djwp.

46 In the 2025–26 financial year, a change of 1p to the basic tax rate is £6.5 billion. Source: 'Direct Effects of Illustrative Tax Changes Bulletin (January 2025)'.

4. Climate and Energy Leader

1 Details of James Lovelock's life and career sourced from the following interviews: 'James Lovelock, National Life Stories: An Oral History of British Science', interview by Paul Merchant, 8 April 2010, British Library, https://web.archive.org/web/20220407191522/https://sounds.bl.uk/related-content/TRANSCRIPTS/021T-C1379X0015XX-0000A1.pdf. and 'James Lovelock, Measuring the Atmosphere', interview by Christopher Sykes, 2001, Web of Stories, https://www.webofstories.com/play/james.lovelock/14.
2 Bo G. Malmström, *Nobel Lectures: Including Presentation Speeches and Laureates' Biographies* (London et al.: World Scientific, 1997).
3 'James Lovelock, National Life Stories', British Library.
4 Martin Childs, 'Joe Farman: Scientist Who First Uncovered the Hole in the Ozone Layer', *Independent*, 20 May 2013, https://www.independent.co.uk/news/obituaries/joe-farman-scientist-who-first-uncovered-the-hole-in-the-ozone-layer-8624438.html.
5 Childs.
6 'International Day for the Preservation of the Ozone Layer', United Nations, n.d., https://www.un.org/en/observances/ozone-day.
7 'Scientific Assessment of Ozone Depletion 2022, GAW Report No. 278', World Meteorological Organization (WMO), October 2022, https://ozone.unep.org/sites/default/files/2023-02/Scientific-Assessment-of-Ozone-Depletion-2022.pdf.
8 World Meteorological Organization, 'Scientific Assessment of Ozone Depletion 2022', WMO, October 2022, https://ozone.unep.org/system/files/documents/Scientific-Assessment-of-Ozone-Depletion-2022.pdf.
9 'Countries Agree to Curb Powerful Greenhouse Gases in Largest Climate Breakthrough since Paris', UN Environment Programme, 15 October 2016, https://www.unep.org/news-and-stories/press-release/countries-agree-curb-powerful-greenhouse-gases-largest-climate.

10 Ben Cooke, 'Hottest World Temperature Record Broken for Second Day in Row', *The Times*, 24 July 2024, https://www.thetimes.com/world/europe/article/hottest-day-on-record-as-global-surface-air-temperature-rises-d9s8v9h6d.

11 James Ashworth, 'For the First Time, Global Temperatures above 1.5°C Limit for an Entire Year', Natural History Museum, 9 July 2024, https://www.nhm.ac.uk/discover/news/2024/july/for-first-time-global-temperatures-above-limit-for-entire-year.html.

12 Zeke Hausfather, 'Analysis: When Might the World Exceed 1.5C and 2C of Global Warming?', Carbon Brief, 4 December 2020, https://www.carbonbrief.org/analysis-when-might-the-world-exceed-1-5c-and-2c-of-global-warming/.

13 'Paris Agreement', United Nations Framework Convention on Climate Change (UNFCCC), 2016, https://unfccc.int/sites/default/files/resource/parisagreement_publication.pdf.

14 'New Record Daily Global Average Temperature Reached in July 2024', Copernicus, 25 July 2024, https://climate.copernicus.eu/new-record-daily-global-average-temperature-reached-july-2024.

15 'Climate Change: Global Sea Level', NOAA Climate.Gov, 22 August 2023, http://www.climate.gov/news-features/understanding-climate/climate-change-global-sea-level.

16 Lyndsey Fox et al., 'Quantifying the Effect of Anthropogenic Climate Change on Calcifying Plankton', *Scientific Reports* 10, no. 1 (31 January 2020): 1620, https://doi.org/10.1038/s41598-020-58501-w.

17 'Emissions Gap Report 2023: Broken Record – Temperatures Hit New Highs, yet World Fails to Cut Emissions (Again)', United Nations Environment Programme, November 2023, https://doi.org/10.59117/20.500.11822/43922.

18 United Nations Environment Programme.

19 Intergovernmental Panel on Climate Change (IPCC), 'Chapter 5: Global Carbon and Other Biogeochemical Cycles and Feedbacks', in *Climate Change 2021 – The Physical Science Basis: Working Group I Contribution to the Sixth Assessment Report of the Intergovernmental Panel on Climate Change*, 1st ed. (Cambridge University Press, 2023), https://doi.org/10.1017/9781009157896.

20 'Africa Energy Outlook 2022', IEA, 2022, https://www.iea.org/reports/africa-energy-outlook-2022.

21 'Ministerial Declaration on the Great Green Wall', UNCCD, https://www.unccd.int/news-stories/press-releases/ministerial-declaration-great-green-wall.

22 Andrew Harding, 'Madagascar on the Brink of Climate Change-Induced Famine', BBC News, 24 August 2021, https://www.bbc.com/news/world-africa-58303792.

23 Rachel Savage and Nyasha Chingono, '"Levels Are Dropping": Drought Saps Zambia and Zimbabwe of Hydropower', *Guardian*, 11 November 2024, https://www.theguardian.com/global-development/2024/nov/11/levels-are-dropping-drought-saps-zambia-and-zimbabwe-of-hydropower.

24 Nyasha Chingono, 'Nearly 68 Million Suffering from Drought in Southern Africa, Says Regional Bloc', Reuters, 17 August 2024, https://www.reuters.com/world/africa/nearly-68-million-suffering-drought-southern-africa-says-regional-bloc-2024-08-17/.

25 David Souter et al., 'Status of Coral Reefs of the World: 2020', Global Coral Reef Monitoring Network and International Coral Reef Initiative, 5 October 2021, https://doi.org/10.59387/WOTJ9184.

26 Damian Carrington, 'Greenland Losing 30m Tonnes of Ice an Hour, Study Reveals', *Guardian*, 17 January 2024, https://www.theguardian.com/environment/2024/jan/17/greenland-losing-30m-tonnes-of-ice-an-hour-study-reveals.

27 Mark Lynas, Benjamin Z. Houlton and Simon Perry, 'Greater than 99% Consensus on Human Caused Climate Change in the Peer-Reviewed Scientific Literature', *Environmental Research Letters* 16, no. 11 (October 2021): 114005, https://doi.org/10.1088/1748-9326/ac2966.

28 IPCC, 'Chapter 3', in *Global Warming of 1.5°C: IPCC Special Report on Impacts of Global Warming of 1.5°C above Pre-Industrial Levels in Context of Strengthening Response to Climate Change, Sustainable Development, and Efforts to Eradicate Poverty*, 1st ed. (Cambridge University Press, 2022), https://doi.org/10.1017/9781009157940.

29 'Trump Picks Oil-Industry CEO Chris Wright as Energy Secretary Nominee', *Reuters*, 18 November 2024, https://www.reuters.com/world/us/trump-picks-oil-industry-ceo-chris-wright-energy-secretary-2024-11-16/.

30 'Coal 2024', IEA, December 2024, https://www.iea.org/reports/coal-2024.

NOTES TO PAGES 110–13

31 Attracta Mooney et al., 'Russia Urges Donald Trump to Remain in Paris Agreement at Upside-down COP29', *Financial Times*, 15 November 2024, https://www.ft.com/content/d8fd9c52-c12b-4909-9d31-6ef0c81250c9.
32 Mooney et al.
33 Matt Oliver, 'Britain Paying Highest Electricity Prices in the World', *Daily Telegraph*, 26 September 2024, https://www.telegraph.co.uk/business/2024/09/26/britain-burdened-most-expensive-electricity-prices-in-world/.
34 'Cabinet Office Annual Report and Accounts 2021–22', GOV.UK, 9 February 2023, https://www.gov.uk/government/publications/cabinet-office-annual-report-and-accounts-2021-22/cabinet-office-annual-report-and-accounts-2021-22-html.
35 'A Speech by HRH the Prince of Wales at the Countryside in 1970 Conference, Steering Committee for Wales, Cardiff', 19 February 1970, https://www.royal.uk/clarencehouse/speech/speech-hrh-prince-wales-countryside-1970-conference-steering-committee-wales-cardiff.
36 Jeremy Plester, 'King Charles's "Dotty" Environmental Views Are Now Mainstream', *Guardian*, 22 September 2022, https://www.theguardian.com/news/2022/sep/22/king-charles-dotty-environmental-views-are-now-mainstream.
37 'Speech to the Royal Society (Climate Change)', Margaret Thatcher Foundation, 27 September 1988, https://www.margaretthatcher.org/document/107346.
38 'Speech to United Nations General Assembly (Global Environment)', Margaret Thatcher Foundation, 8 November 1989, https://www.margaretthatcher.org/document/107817.
39 'Speech Opening Hadley Centre for Climate Prediction and Research', Margaret Thatcher Foundation, 21 May 1990, https://www.margaretthatcher.org/document/108102.
40 'Earth Summit', *Hansard*, 15 June 1992, https://hansard.parliament.uk/commons/1992-06-15/debates/9f0c6a35-237c-425c-a648-25cee1c5cf1c/EarthSummit.
41 Tony Blair, 'Tony Blair: A Bold, Progressive Agenda for Climate Change', Tony Blair Institute for Global Change, 16 February 2020, https://institute.global/insights/climate-and-energy/tony-blair-bold-progressive-agenda-climate-change.

42 Roger Hildingsson and Åsa Knaggård, 'The Swedish Carbon Tax: A Resilient Success', in *Successful Public Policy in the Nordic Countries: Cases, Lessons, Challenges*, ed. Caroline de la Porte et al. (Oxford University Press, 2022), 0, https://doi.org/10.1093/oso/9780192856296.003.0012.

43 Nerijus Adomaitis, 'In Norway, Nearly All New Cars Sold in 2024 Were Fully Electric', Reuters, 2 January 2025, https://www.reuters.com/business/autos-transportation/norway-nearly-all-new-cars-sold-2024-were-fully-electric-2025-01-02/.

44 'Electricity Production', Norwegian Energy, 16 May 2024, https://energifaktanorge.no/en/norsk-energiforsyning/kraftproduksjon/.

45 Colin P. Morice et al., 'An Updated Assessment of Near-Surface Temperature Change from 1850: The HadCRUT5 Data Set', *Journal of Geophysical Research: Atmospheres* 126, no. 3 (16 February 2021): e2019JD032361, https://doi.org/10.1029/2019JD032361.

46 'UK First Major Economy to Halve Emissions', GOV.UK, https://www.gov.uk/government/news/uk-first-major-economy-to-halve-emissions.

47 Jan Burck et al., 'Climate Change Performance Index 2025', 20 November 2024, https://ccpi.org/download/climate-change-performance-index-2025/.

48 The author acknowledges the Global Carbon Project, which is responsible for the Global Carbon Budget, and thanks the national fossil carbon emissions modelling group for producing and making available their model output.

49 'Greenhouse Gas Emissions from Energy Data Explorer – Data Tools', IEA, 2 August 2024, https://www.iea.org/data-and-statistics/data-tools/greenhouse-gas-emissions-from-energy-data-explorer.

50 Simon Hare, 'Ratcliffe-on-Soar: Final Fuel Delivery Is End of the Line for Coal', BBC News, 1 July 2024, https://www.bbc.com/news/articles/c886qd2g80xo.

51 Jonathan Chadwick, 'UK Wind Power Hits Record High as It Provides 70% of Electricity', *Mail Online*, 17 December 2024, https://www.dailymail.co.uk/sciencetech/article-14200757/UK-wind-power-hits-record-high-provides-70-Britains-electricity-promising-data-reveals.html.

52 Forrest Crellin, Nora Buli and Nina Chestney, 'Gas Price Shock Set to Add to Europe's Industrial Pain', Reuters, 6 December 2024, https://

www.reuters.com/business/energy/gas-price-shock-set-add-europes-industrial-pain-2024-12-06/.
53 Patrick Whitelaw et al., 'Shale Gas Reserve Evaluation by Laboratory Pyrolysis and Gas Holding Capacity Consistent with Field Data', *Nature Communications* 10, no. 1 (20 August 2019): 3659, https://doi.org/10.1038/s41467-019-11653-4.
54 'International energy price comparison statistics', UK Department for Energy Security and Net Zero, 28 November 2024, https://www.gov.uk/government/collections/international-energy-price-comparisons.
55 'Issue Deep Dive: UK/Climate', Donor Tracker, https://donortracker.org/donor_profiles/united-kingdom/climate.
56 Mike Wardle, Simon Mills and Michael Mainelli, 'The Global Green Finance Index 13', Long Finance, 23 April 2024, https://www.longfinance.net/media/documents/GGFI_13_Report_2024.04.23_v1.0.pdf.
57 Ellen McHale, 'What Wildlife Lives in Kew Gardens?', Royal Botanical Gardens, 12 March 2020, https://www.kew.org/read-and-watch/wildlife-kew-gardens.
58 'Our Collections', Royal Botanical Gardens, n.d., https://www.kew.org/science/collections-and-resources/collections.
59 Nicholas H. Stern, ed., *The Economics of Climate Change: The Stern Review* (Cambridge: Cambridge University Press, 2014), https://doi.org/10.1017/CBO9780511817434.
60 'Clean Energy Innovation', IEA, July 2020, https://www.iea.org/reports/clean-energy-innovation.
61 SEIA / Wood Mackenzie, 'Solar Market Insight Report 2023 Year in Review', SEIA, 5 March 2024, https://seia.org/research-resources/solar-market-insight-report-2023-year-review/.

5. Free Trade Advocate

1 The story of Masataka Okuma is largely based on the following sources: Hugh Cortazzi, ed., *Britain & Japan: Biographical Portraits: Vol. VI*, Brill eBook Titles 2010 (Folkestone: Global Oriental Ltd, 2007), https://doi.org/10.1163/ej.9781905246335.1-448; Hitoshi Suzuki, *Japanese Investment and British Trade Unionism: Thatcher and Nissan Revisited in the Wake*

of Brexit, New Directions in East Asian History (Singapore: Springer Singapore, 2020), https://doi.org/10.1007/978-981-15-9058-0.
2. Chris Rhodes, 'The Motor Industry: Statistics and Policy', House of Commons Library, 16 December 2019, https://researchbriefings.files.parliament.uk/documents/SN00611/SN00611.pdf.
3. Charles Smith, 'Mr. Smith Goes to Tokyo', *Number 1 Shimbun*, August 2018, https://www.fccj.or.jp/sites/default/files/2021-03/08_August_2018_standard.pdf.
4. Paul Lewis, 'The Latest Battle of Poitiers', *The New York Times*, 14 January 1983, https://www.nytimes.com/1983/01/14/business/the-latest-battle-of-poitiers.html.
5. NissanUK, 'Nissan Sunderland Plant 25th Anniversary Celebration Video', YouTube, 8 September 2011, https://www.youtube.com/watch?v=JyLbfia6zfY.
6. 'Records Tumble at Nissan Sunderland Plant in 25th Anniversary Year', Nissan, 4 January 2012, https://europe.nissannews.com/en-GB/releases/records-tumble-at-nissan-sunderland-plant-in-25th-anniversary-year.
7. 'Written Evidence from Nissan Motors UK (BEV0045)', House of Commons Business, Energy and Industrial Strategy Committee, 26 April 2023, https://committees.parliament.uk/writtenevidence/118626/pdf/.
8. 'December 2023 UK Car Manufacturing', SMMT Media Centre, 24 January 2024, https://media.smmt.co.uk/december-2023-uk-car-manufacturing/.
9. 'Business Investment in the UK', ONS, 23 December 2024, https://www.ons.gov.uk/economy/grossdomesticproductgdp/bulletins/businessinvestment/julytoseptember2024revisedresults.
10. Figures adjusted for reporting lag by only counting those documented by GTA before 31 December during each corresponding year.
11. John McCormick, 'Trump Calls Tariffs the "Most Beautiful Word"', *Wall Street Journal*, 16 October 2024, https://www.wsj.com/livecoverage/harris-trump-election-10-16-2024/card/trump-calls-tariffs-the-most-beautiful-word--YMVPAupw4EjBRp6yobOy.
12. Jim Tankersley and Mark Landler, 'Trump's Love for Tariffs Began in Japan's '80s Boom', *The New York Times*, 15 May 2019, https://www.nytimes.com/2019/05/15/us/politics/china-trade-donald-trump.html.
13. 'World Economic League Table 2025', CEBR.

14 'GTA Database', Global Trade Alert, 2024, https://www.old.globaltradealert.org/data_extraction.
15 'Global Trade Outlook and Statistics', WTO, April 2024, https://www.wto.org/english/res_e/booksp_e/trade_outlook24_e.pdf.
16 Abdi Latif Dahir, 'Africa's Vaccine Drive Is Threatened by India's Supply Halt', *The New York Times*, 24 April 2021, https://www.nytimes.com/2021/04/24/world/africa/africa-india-vaccine-threat.html.
17 Meredith M. Paker, 'Industrial, Regional, and Gender Divides in British Unemployment between the Wars', *European Review of Economic History* 28, no. 4 (8 November 2024): 457–516, https://doi.org/10.1093/ereh/heae007.
18 National Bureau of Economic Research, 'Unemployment Rate for United States [M0892AUSM156SNBR]', retrieved from FRED, Federal Reserve Bank of St. Louis, 17 August 2012, https://fred.stlouisfed.org/series/M0892AUSM156SNBR.
19 Dan P. Silverman, 'Fantasy and Reality in Nazi Work-Creation Programs, 1933–1936', *The Journal of Modern History* 65, No. 1 (March 1993): 113–51.
20 R. J. Overy, 'Unemployment in the Third Reich', in *War and Economy in the Third Reich*, online edition (Oxford University Press, 1994), https://doi.org/10.1093/acprof:oso/9780198202905.001.0001.
21 'Poverty Headcount Ratio', World Bank, 2023, https://data.worldbank.org/indicator/SI.POV.DDAY.
22 Economist Impact, 'Trade in Transition: Navigating the Tides of Uncertainty – Global Report', The Economist Group, 2024, https://impact.economist.com/projects/trade-in-transition/pdfs/Trade_in_Transition_Global_Report_2024.pdf.
23 'Exports of Goods and Services (Current US$)', World Bank, 2025, https://data.worldbank.org/indicator/NE.EXP.GNFS.CD.
24 'Economic Report on Africa 2024: Investing in a Just and Sustainable Transition in Africa', UNECA, 2024.
25 Barbara D'Andrea et al., 'Thirty Years of Trade Growth and Poverty Reduction', WTO, 24 April 2024, https://www.wto.org/english/blogs_e/data_blog_e/blog_dta_24apr24_e.htm.
26 'FDI Stocks', OECD, https://www.oecd.org/en/data/indicators/fdi-stocks.html.
27 'UK Foreign Direct Investment, Trends and Analysis – Office for National Statistics', ONS, 3 August 2020, https://www.ons.gov.uk/economy/

nationalaccounts/balanceofpayments/articles/ukforeigndirectinvestmenttrendsandanalysis/august2020.

28 For example, the UK's share of FDI projects in the following report is similar to pre-Brexit: Julie Teigland, Hanne Jesca Bax and Marc Lhermitte, 'EY Attractiveness Survey', EY, June 2024, https://www.ey.com/content/dam/ey-unified-site/ey-com/en-gl/campaigns/foreign-direct-investment-surveys/documents/ey-attractiveness-survey-06-2024-v3.pdf.

29 Niall Ferguson, *Empire: How Britain Made the Modern World* (London: Penguin Books, 2004).

30 The following institutions were included in the count for each country: LMAA (UK), LCIA (UK), GAFTA (UK), ICC (France), SIAC (Singapore), HKIAC (Hong Kong, China), SCC (Sweden). Reported GAFTA cases are from 1 October 2022 to 30 September 2023.

31 'International Data Insights Report 2nd Edition 2024', The Law Society of England and Wales, 10 September 2024, https://www.lawsociety.org.uk/topics/research/international-data-insights-2024.

32 Dominic Webb and Matthew Ward, 'Statistics on UK Trade with the EU', House of Commons Library, 23 August 2024, https://researchbriefings.files.parliament.uk/documents/CBP-7851/CBP-7851.pdf.

33 Calculation by author using the following sources: 'Gross Domestic Product at market prices: Current price: Seasonally adjusted £m', ONS, 13 February 2025, https://www.ons.gov.uk/economy/grossdomesticproductgdp/timeseries/ybha/pn2; 'Trade and investment core statistics book', Department for Business & Trade, 4 April 2025, https://www.gov.uk/government/statistics/trade-and-investment-core-statistics-book/trade-and-investment-core-statistics-book.

34 Calculations by author using the following sources: 'U.S. International Trade in Goods and Services, January 2025', U.S. Census Bureau and U.S. Bureau of Economic Analysis, 6 March 2025, https://www.census.gov/foreign-trade/Press-Release/ft900/ft900_2501.pdf; 'Gross Domestic Product (Third Estimate), Corporate Profits, and GDP by Industry, 4th Quarter and Year 2024', U.S. Bureau of Economic Analysis, 27 March 2025, https://www.bea.gov/sites/default/files/2025-03/gdp4q24-3rd.pdf.

35 Calculations by author using the same sources as note 34.

36 'Goods and Services (BPM6): Exports and Imports of Goods and Services, Annual', UNCTAD, 30 August 2024, https://unctadstat.unctad.org/datacentre/dataviewer/US.GoodsAndServicesBpm6.

37 Author's calculations based on statistics from WTO Stats, available at: https://stats.wto.org/.

38 'UK-Japan Digital Partnership (December 2022)', GOV.UK, 23 January 2025, https://www.gov.uk/government/publications/uk-japan-digital-partnership/uk-japan-digital-partnership.

39 'The Bletchley Declaration by Countries Attending the AI Safety Summit, 1-2 November 2023', GOV.UK, 1 November 2023, https://www.gov.uk/government/publications/ai-safety-summit-2023-the-bletchley-declaration/the-bletchley-declaration-by-countries-attending-the-ai-safety-summit-1-2-november-2023.

6. Pandemic Prevention

1 The story of Martin Landray and the RECOVERY trial is based on the following sources: James Gallagher, 'Covid: The London Bus Trip That Saved Maybe a Million Lives', BBC News, 25 March 2021, https://www.bbc.com/news/health-56508369; 'Recovery Trial', *Inside Health*, BBC Sounds, 23 March 2021, https://www.bbc.co.uk/sounds/play/m000tccg; Dylan Scott, 'How the UK Found the First Effective Covid-19 Treatment – and Saved a Million Lives', Vox, 26 April 2021, https://www.vox.com/22397833/dexamethasone-coronavirus-uk-recovery-trial.

2 'Streptomycin Treatment of Pulmonary Tuberculosis: A Medical Research Council Investigation', *British Medical Journal* 2, no. 4582 (30 October 1948): 769–82, https://doi.org/10.1136/bmj.2.4582.769.

3 Arun Bhatt, 'Evolution of Clinical Research: A History Before and Beyond James Lind', *Perspectives in Clinical Research* 1, no. 1 (2010): 6–10.

4 The RECOVERY Collaborative Group, 'Dexamethasone in Hospitalized Patients with Covid-19', *New England Journal of Medicine* 384, no. 8 (24 February 2021): 693–704, https://doi.org/10.1056/NEJMoa2021436.

5 'Report on Covid-19 in Critical Care', ICNARC, 1 May 2020, https://web.archive.org/web/20200507113944/https://www.icnarc.org/DataServices/Attachments/Download/f48efee2-d38b-ea11-9125-00505601089b.

NOTES TO PAGES 142–43

6   The RECOVERY Collaborative Group, 'Effect of Hydroxychloroquine in Hospitalized Patients with Covid-19', *New England Journal of Medicine* 383, no. 21 (18 November 2020): 2030–40, https://doi.org/10.1056/NEJMoa2022926.
7   'Coronavirus (Covid-19) Update: FDA Revokes Emergency Use Authorization for Chloroquine and Hydroxychloroquine', FDA, 15 June 2020, https://www.fda.gov/news-events/press-announcements/coronavirus-covid-19-update-fda-revokes-emergency-use-authorization-chloroquine-and.
8   10 Downing Street, 'Coronavirus Press Conference (16 June 2020)', YouTube, 16 June 2020, https://www.youtube.com/watch?v=x9gdDvZW3v0.
9   NHS England, 'Covid Treatment Developed in the NHS Saves a Million Lives', NHS England, 23 March 2021, https://www.england.nhs.uk/2021/03/covid-treatment-developed-in-the-nhs-saves-a-million-lives/.
10 'Tocilizumab Reduces Deaths in Patients Hospitalised with Covid-19', RECOVERY Trial, 11 February 2021, https://www.recoverytrial.net/news/tocilizumab-reduces-deaths-in-patients-hospitalised-with-covid-19.
11 'RECOVERY Trial Finds Regeneron's Monoclonal Antibody Combination Reduces Deaths for Hospitalised Covid-19 Patients Who Have Not Mounted Their Own Immune Response', RECOVERY Trial, 16 June 2021, https://www.recoverytrial.net/news/recovery-trial-finds-regeneron2019s-monoclonal-antibody-combination-reduces-deaths-for-hospitalised-covid-19-patients-who-have-not-mounted-their-own-immune-response-1.
12 Ezekiel J. Emanuel, Cathy Zhang and Amaya Diana, 'Where Is America's Groundbreaking Covid-19 Research?', *The New York Times*, 1 September 2020, https://www.nytimes.com/2020/09/01/opinion/coronavirus-clinical-research.html.
13 The story of Sarah Gilbert and the development of the Covid vaccine is based on the following sources: 'Sarah Gilbert on Developing a Vaccine for Covid-19', *The Life Scientific*, BBC Sounds, 15 September 2020, https://www.bbc.co.uk/sounds/play/m000mj18; Robin McKie, 'Life Savers: The Amazing Story of the Oxford/AstraZeneca Covid Vaccine', *Observer*, 14 February 2021, https://www.theguardian.com/world/2021/feb/14/life-savers-story-oxford-astrazeneca-coronavirus-vaccine-scientists; Elisabeth Mahase, 'How the Oxford-AstraZeneca Covid-19 Vaccine Was Made', *BMJ*, 12 January 2021, n86, https://doi.org/10.1136/bmj.n86.

14 Robin McKie, 'The Vaccine Miracle: How Scientists Waged the Battle against Covid-19', *Observer*, 6 December 2020, https://www.theguardian.com/world/2020/dec/06/the-vaccine-miracle-how-scientists-waged-the-battle-against-covid-19.

15 'AstraZeneca and Oxford University Announce Landmark Agreement for Covid-19 Vaccine', AstraZeneca, 30 April 2020, https://www.astrazeneca.com/media-centre/press-releases/2020/astrazeneca-and-oxford-university-announce-landmark-agreement-for-covid-19-vaccine.html.

16 Josh Holder, 'Tracking Coronavirus Vaccinations Around the World [Archived 1 July 2021]', The New York Times, 30 June 2021, https://web.archive.org/web/20210701020636/https://www.nytimes.com/interactive/2021/world/covid-vaccinations-tracker.html.

17 'Report of the Joint Allocation Taskforce (JAT) on the Distribution of COVAX Facility Secured Vaccines', WHO, 6 July 2021, https://www.who.int/docs/default-source/coronaviruse/covax-05-jat-report_final.pdf.

18 'Oxford Vaccine Saved Most Lives in Its First Year of Rollout', 15 July 2022, https://www.ox.ac.uk/news/2022-07-15-oxford-vaccine-saved-most-lives-its-first-year-rollout.

19 'Key Outcomes One World Protected – COVAX AMC Summit', Gavi, 2 March 2022, https://siidata.org/wp-content/uploads/2022/04/COVAX-AMC-Donors-Table.pdf.

20 'WHO Covid-19 Dashboard: Number of Covid-19 Deaths Reported to WHO (Cumulative Total)', WHO Data, 5 January 2025, https://data.who.int/dashboards/covid19/deaths.

21 Priya Joi, '10 Infectious Diseases That Could Be the next Pandemic', Gavi, 7 May 2020, https://www.gavi.org/vaccineswork/10-infectious-diseases-could-be-next-pandemic.

22 The Rt Hon the Baroness Hallett DBE, 'Module 1: The Resilience and Preparedness of the United Kingdom', UK Covid-19 Inquiry, 18 July 2024, https://covid19.public-inquiry.uk/wp-content/uploads/2024/07/18095012/UK-Covid-19-Inquiry-Module-1-Full-Report.pdf.

23 Mohsen Naghavi et al., 'Global Burden of Bacterial Antimicrobial Resistance 1990–2021: A Systematic Analysis with Forecasts to 2050', *Lancet* 404, no. 10459 (28 September 2024): 1199–1226, https://doi.org/10.1016/S0140-6736(24)01867-1.

NOTES TO PAGES 148–51

24 Cancer accounts for approximately 10 million deaths a year. See for example Freddie Bray et al., 'Global Cancer Statistics 2022: GLOBOCAN Estimates of Incidence and Mortality Worldwide for 36 Cancers in 185 Countries', *CA: A Cancer Journal for Clinicians* 74, no. 3 (May 2024): 229–63, https://doi.org/10.3322/caac.21834.
25 Ian Johnston and Oliver Barnes, 'Vaccine Stocks Hit by Robert Kennedy Jr Nomination', *Financial Times*, 15 November 2024, https://www.ft.com/content/401e8947-bd02-4ac8-9fb2-eab01977eb4c.
26 'Foreign Secretary Congratulates Sierra Leone on Eliminating Ebola', GOV.UK, 7 November 2015, https://www.gov.uk/government/news/foreign-secretary-congratulates-sierra-leone-on-eliminating-ebola.
27 Claire Graham, 'RFA *Argus*: The Hospital Ship That Boasts a Belfast "Home"', BBC News, 29 September 2015, https://www.bbc.com/news/uk-northern-ireland-34391922.
28 Sarah Boseley, 'Pauline Cafferkey: Dedicated Nurse and Reluctant Ebola Hero', *Lancet* 388, no. 10043 (30 July 2016): 455, https://doi.org/10.1016/S0140-6736(16)30369-5.
29 Calculation by author based on information published on the Nobel Prize's website, available at: https://www.nobelprize.org/. A laureate was counted if they were a person (not organisation), were affiliated with a UK institution or resident in the UK and were born abroad. Peace and Literature categories were not included.
30 'UK-Educated Economists Scoop Nobel for Imperial Legacy Research', *Times Higher Education*, 14 October 2024, https://www.timeshighereducation.com/news/uk-educated-economists-scoop-nobel-imperial-legacy-research.
31 See https://www.scimagojr.com/help.php for details.
32 'Our Role in Beating Cancer Globally', Cancer Research UK, 28 June 2019, https://www.cancerresearchuk.org/global-role.
33 BHF Press Office, 'The BHF Joins Forces with International Research Funders to Improve Global Heart Health', British Heart Foundation, 22 June 2021, https://www.bhf.org.uk/what-we-do/news-from-the-bhf/news-archive/2021/june/international-funders-work-hand-in-hand-to-improve-global-heart-health.
34 'History of the Sanger Institute', Wellcome Sanger Institute, https://www.sanger.ac.uk/about/history-of-the-sanger-institute/.
35 Randeep Ramesh, 'Jeremy Hunt Launches Genomics Body to Oversee

Healthcare Revolution', *Guardian*, 4 July 2013, https://www.theguardian.com/politics/2013/jul/05/health-jeremy-hunt.

36 Aaron Klug, 'The Discovery of the DNA Double Helix', *Journal of Molecular Biology* 335, no. 1 (2 January 2004): 3–26, https://doi.org/10.1016/j.jmb.2003.11.015.

37 James M. Heather and Benjamin Chain, 'The Sequence of Sequencers: The History of Sequencing DNA', *Genomics* 107, no. 1 (January 2016): 1–8, https://doi.org/10.1016/j.ygeno.2015.11.003.

38 Marc A. Shampo, Robert A. Kyle and David P. Steensma, 'Ian Wilmut—Pioneer of Cloning', *Mayo Clinic Proceedings* 88, no. 5 (1 May 2013): e41, https://doi.org/10.1016/j.mayocp.2012.01.028.

39 Martin H. Johnson, 'Robert Edwards: The Path to IVF', *Reproductive Biomedicine Online* 23, no. 2 (August 2011): 245–62, https://doi.org/10.1016/j.rbmo.2011.04.010.

40 'UK to Create World-First "early Warning System" for Pandemics', GOV.UK, 5 November 2024, https://www.gov.uk/government/news/uk-to-create-world-first-early-warning-system-for-pandemics.

41 'Curriculum Vitae: Dr Tedros Adhanom Ghebreyesus', 2017, https://www.who.int/docs/default-source/who-leadership-team/cv-tedros-dg-candidate-2017.pdf.

42 'Smallpox', WHO, https://www.who.int/health-topics/smallpox.

43 Theodore H. Tulchinsky, 'John Snow, Cholera, the Broad Street Pump; Waterborne Diseases Then and Now', *Case Studies in Public Health*, 2018, 77–99, https://doi.org/10.1016/B978-0-12-804571-8.00017-2.

44 Robert Gaynes, 'The Discovery of Penicillin—New Insights After More Than 75 Years of Clinical Use', *Emerging Infectious Diseases* 23, no. 5 (May 2017): 849–53, https://doi.org/10.3201/eid2305.161556.

45 Maria Elisa Di Cicco, Vincenzo Ragazzo and Tiago Jacinto, 'Mortality in Relation to Smoking: The British Doctors Study', *Breathe* 12, no. 3 (September 2016): 275–76, https://doi.org/10.1183/20734735.013416.

46 Kate S Lim and Anuradha Mishra, 'Sir Harold Ridley as the Pioneer of Intraocular Lenses: His Inspiration Drawn from World War II Pilots', *Cureus* 16, no. 9 (n.d.): e68722, https://doi.org/10.7759/cureus.68722.

47 S. Campbell, 'A Short History of Sonography in Obstetrics and Gynaecology', *Facts, Views & Vision in ObGyn* 5, no. 3 (2013): 213–29.

48 John Jackson, 'Father of the Modern Hip Replacement: Professor Sir John Charnley (1911–82)', *Journal of Medical Biography* 19, no. 4 (November 2011): 151–56, https://doi.org/10.1258/jmb.2011.011021.

49 Remah Moustafa Kamel, 'Assisted Reproductive Technology after the Birth of Louise Brown', *Journal of Reproduction & Infertility* 14, no. 3 (2013): 96–109.

50 Helen Burchell and Katy Prickett, 'Pioneering Surgeons Recall First Triple Transplant Operation', BBC News, 17 December 2016, https://www.bbc.com/news/uk-england-cambridgeshire-38250640.

51 'Gene Therapy Offers a Potential Cure to Children Born without an Immune System', Great Ormond Street Hospital for Children, 11 May 2021, https://www.gosh.nhs.uk/news/gene-therapy-offers-a-potential-cure-to-children-born-without-an-immune-system/.

52 Roger Highfield, 'World's First Commercial Bionic Hand', *Daily Telegraph*, 10 June 2008, https://www.telegraph.co.uk/news/science/science-news/3344056/Worlds-first-commercial-bionic-hand.html.

53 Michel Garenne and Enéas Gakusi, 'Health Transitions in Sub-Saharan Africa: Overview of Mortality Trends in Children under 5 Years Old (1950–2000)', *Bulletin of the World Health Organization* 84, no. 6 (June 2006): 470–78, https://doi.org/10.2471/blt.05.029231.

54 UN IGME, 'Levels and Trends in Child Mortality 2023', UNICEF, 12 March 2024, https://data.unicef.org/resources/levels-and-trends-in-child-mortality-2024/.

55 'Health Systems Strengthening for Global Health Security and Universal Health Coverage', FCDO Position Paper (Foreign, Commonwealth & Development Office, December 2021), https://assets.publishing.service.gov.uk/media/61b093eae90e0704423dc07c/Health-Systems-Strengthening-Position-Paper.pdf.

56 'Health Partnership Scheme: Impact Report 2011–2019', Tropical Health & Education Trust, August 2019, https://www.thet.org/wp-content/uploads/2017/09/20443_HPS_Impact_Report-2019-8.pdf.

57 'DAC5: Aid (ODA) by Sector and Provider', OECD, 16 January 2024, https://data-explorer.oecd.org/.

58 'Growth Equity in European Healthtech', MTIP / dealroom.co, June 2024, https://dealroom.co/uploaded/2024/06/Dealroom-Growth-Equity-Healthtech-MTIP_2024.pdf.

59 'Companies Ranked by Market Cap', CompaniesMarketCap.com, n.d., https://companiesmarketcap.com.
60 'Company History', Oxford Nanopore Technologies, https://nanoporetech.com/about/history.
61 Madhumita Murgia, 'Pandemic Puts Oxford Nanopore "on the Map"', *Financial Times*, 8 November 2021, https://www.ft.com/content/605ab02f-3f17-4c34-9671-c33b9d181222.
62 'PwC Life Sciences Future 50', PwC, October 2023, https://www.pwc.co.uk/industries/assets/life-sciences-future50.pdf.
63 'Cambridge Cluster Insights', Cambridge Ahead, https://www.cambridgeahead.co.uk/cambridge-cluster-insights/.
64 'World University Rankings by Subject 2025: Life Sciences', *Times Higher Education*, 15 January 2025, https://www.timeshighereducation.com/world-university-rankings/2025/subject-ranking/life-sciences.
65 'Political Declaration of the High-Level Meeting on Antimicrobial Resistance', UN, 9 September 2024, https://www.un.org/pga/wp-content/uploads/sites/108/2024/09/FINAL-Text-AMR-to-PGA.pdf.
66 Mustafa Suleyman, *The Coming Wave* (New York: Crown, 2023).
67 For example, in 2022, the IMF estimated the economic loss to be £13.8 trillion through 2024. See here: 'A Disrupted Global Recovery', IMF, 25 January 2022, https://www.imf.org/en/Blogs/Articles/2022/01/25/blog-a-disrupted-global-recovery.
68 'Healthcare and Life Sciences', UK Government, https://www.great.gov.uk/international/investment/sectors/healthcare-and-life-sciences/.

7. Human Rights Voice

1 'Retract Iran Remark, Husband Tells Boris Johnson', BBC News, 7 November 2017, https://www.bbc.com/news/uk-politics-41896225.
2 'Death Sentences and Executions 2023', Amnesty International, 29 May 2024, https://www.amnesty.org/en/documents/act50/7952/2024/en/.
3 'Journalists Imprisoned between 1992 and 2023', Committee to Protect Journalists, https://cpj.org/data/.
4 'World Watch List 2025', Open Doors, 2025, https://www.opendoors.org/2025-advocacyreport.

5 Huma Haider, 'The Persecution of Christians in the Middle East.', K4D Helpdesk Report (Institute of Development Studies, 16 February 2017), https://assets.publishing.service.gov.uk/media/59786a0040f0b65dcb00000a/042-Persecution-of-Christians-in-the-Middle-East.pdf.
6 Jeremy Hunt, 'We Must Not Allow a Misguided Political Correctness to Stop Us from Helping Persecuted Christians', *Daily Telegraph*, 26 December 2018, https://www.telegraph.co.uk/news/2018/12/26/must-not-allow-misguided-political-correctness-stop-us-helping/.
7 Elise A. Mitchell, 'British Slave Trade in the Atlantic', in *Oxford Research Encyclopedia of African History* (Oxford University Press, 2024), https://doi.org/10.1093/acrefore/9780190277734.013.893.
8 Amnesty International, ed., *Amnesty International, 1961–1976: A Chronology* (London: Amnesty International Publications, 1976).
9 Hugh O'Shaughnessy, 'Peter Benenson', *Independent*, 28 February 2005, https://www.independent.co.uk/news/obituaries/peter-benenson-13233.html.
10 Peter Benenson, 'The Forgotten Prisoners', *The Observer*, 28 May 1961, https://www.theguardian.com/uk/1961/may/28/fromthearchive.theguardian.
11 NATO, '"The Atlantic Charter" – Declaration of Principles Issued by the President of the United States and the Prime Minister of the United Kingdom', NATO, 14 August 1941, http://www.nato.int/cps/en/natohq/official_texts_16912.htm.
12 Samuel White, 'The UK's Compliance with the ICCPR and ECHR: A Tale of Two Treaties', in *International Courts versus Non-Compliance Mechanisms: Comparative Advantages in Strengthening Treaty Implementation*, ed. Christina Voigt and Caroline Foster, 1st ed. (Cambridge University Press, 2024), https://doi.org/10.1017/9781009373913.
13 Shashank P. Kumar and Cecily Rose, 'A Study of Lawyers Appearing before the International Court of Justice, 1999–2012', *European Journal of International Law* 25, no. 3 (1 August 2014): 893–917, https://doi.org/10.1093/ejil/chu057.
14 Permanent Mission of the Federal Republic of Germany to the United Nations of New York, 'Sixth Committee – Agenda Item 85: The Scope and Application of the Principle of Universal Jurisdiction. Statement by the Federal Republic of Germany, 12 October 2022', https://www.un.org/

en/ga/sixth/77/pdfs/statements/universal_jurisdiction/12mtg_germany. pdf.
15 Richard Spencer, 'Sweden to Put Iranian "Mass Executioner" on Trial', *The Times*, 9 August 2021, https://www.thetimes.com/world/article/sweden-to-put-iranian-mass-executioner-on-trial-zsnlhng0h.
16 'Danish Human Rights', Denmark.dk, https://denmark.dk/society-and-business/human-rights.
17 Ministère de l'Europe et des Affaires étrangères, 'Abolition of the Death Penalty', Ministry for Europe and Foreign Affairs, https://www.diplomatie.gouv.fr/en/french-foreign-policy/human-rights/abolition-of-the-death-penalty/.
18 'Drafting of the Universal Declaration of Human Rights', United Nations Dag Hammarskjöld Library, 31 January 2025, https://research.un.org/en/undhr/draftingcommittee.
19 Martin Chulov, 'Deposed Saudi Crown Prince Confined to Palace', *Guardian*, 29 June 2017, https://www.theguardian.com/world/2017/jun/29/deposed-saudi-crown-prince-mohammed-bin-nayef-confined-to-palace.
20 Hersham Alghannam, 'Influence Abroad: Saudi Arabia Replaces Salafism in Its Soft Power Outreach', Carnegie Endowment for International Peace, 23 December 2024, https://carnegieendowment.org/research/2024/12/influence-abroad-saudi-arabia-replaces-salafism-in-its-soft-power-outreach?lang=en.
21 '"Tell Your Boss": Recording Said to Link Jamal Khashoggi's Killing to Crown Prince', *Daily Telegraph*, 13 November 2018, https://www.telegraph.co.uk/news/2018/11/13/tell-boss-recording-said-linkjamal-khashoggis-killing-crown/.

8. The Next Silicon Valley

1 The story of Demis Hassabis and DeepMind is mostly based on the following sources: David Rowan, 'DeepMind: Inside Google's Super-Brain', *Wired*, 22 June 2015, https://www.wired.com/story/deepmind/; 'Demis Hassabis: DeepMind – AI, Superintelligence & the Future of Humanity', Lex Fridman Podcast #299', 1 July 2022, https://www.youtube.com/watch?v=Gfr50f6ZBvo; Azeem Azhar, 'Azeem's Picks: Demis Hassabis on

DeepMind's Journey from Games to Fundamental Science', *Harvard Business Review*, 5 May 2023, https://hbr.org/podcast/2023/05/azeems-picks-demis-hassabis-on-deepminds-journey-from-games-to-fundamental-science; 'Demis Hassabis', *Profile*, BBC Sounds, 5 December 2020, https://www.bbc.co.uk/sounds/play/m000q3nq; Academy of Achievement, 'Demis Hassabis', 29 May 2018, https://www.youtube.com/watch?v=1X7Koxx4qJE.

2   'Re-Invading Space: Bullfrog Competition Winners', *Amiga Power*, August 1992, https://amr.abime.net/issue_16_pages.

3   Matthew Syed, 'Demis Hassabis Interview: The Kid from the Comp Who Founded DeepMind and Cracked a Mighty Riddle of Science', *The Times*, 5 December 2020, https://www.thetimes.com/article/demis-hassabis-interview-the-kid-from-the-comp-who-founded-deepmind-and-cracked-a-mighty-riddle-of-science-g3v3z9b80.

4   'Google Buys UK Artificial Intelligence Start-up DeepMind', BBC News, 27 January 2014, https://www.bbc.com/news/technology-25908379.

5   Alistair Connell et al., 'Implementation of a Digitally Enabled Care Pathway (Part 1): Impact on Clinical Outcomes and Associated Health Care Costs', *Journal of Medical Internet Research* 21, no. 7 (15 July 2019): e13147, https://doi.org/10.2196/13147.

6   David Cox, 'DeepMind Wants to Use Its AI to Cure Neglected Diseases', *Wired*, 23 June 2021, https://www.wired.com/story/deepmind-alphafold-protein-diseases/.

7   Georgina Rannard, 'Google DeepMind Co-Founder Demis Hassabis Shares Nobel Chemistry Prize', BBC News, 9 October 2024, https://www.bbc.com/news/articles/czrm0p2mxvyo.

8   Frank Land, 'The Story of LEO – the World's First Business Computer', University of Warwick, 14 April 2022, https://warwick.ac.uk/services/library/mrc/archives_online/digital/leo/story/.

9   Jack Howlett, 'Computing at Harwell', Chiltern Computing, 1979, http://www.chilton-computing.org.uk/acl/literature/reports/p009.htm.

10 Simon Lavington, *A History of Manchester Computers* (Manchester: NCC Publications, 1975).

11 Simon Lavington, 'An Appreciation of Dina St Johnston (1930–2007) Founder of the UK's First Software House', *Computer Journal* 52, no. 3 (1 May 2009): 378–87, https://doi.org/10.1093/comjnl/bxn019.

12 Tim Berners-Lee, 'Information Management: A Proposal', w3.org, March 1989, https://www.w3.org/History/1989/proposal.html.
13 Calculation by author based on the following sources: 'eCommerce Market Size by Country [Updated 2024]', MobiLoud, 26 September 2024, https://www.mobiloud.com/blog/ecommerce-market-size-by-country; World Bank, 'Population, Total', The World Bank, 2025, https://data.worldbank.org/indicator/SP.POP.TOTL.
14 'UK Tech Sector Achieves Best Year Ever as Success Feeds Cities Outside London', GOV.UK, 20 December 2021, https://www.gov.uk/government/news/uk-tech-sector-achieves-best-year-ever-as-success-feeds-cities-outside-london.
15 'UK Tech Sector Retains #1 Spot in Europe and #3 in World as Sector Resilience Brings Continued Growth', GOV.UK, 21 December 2022, https://www.gov.uk/government/news/uk-tech-sector-retains-1-spot-in-europe-and-3-in-world-as-sector-resilience-brings-continued-growth.
16 Alex Hamilton, 'European Tech in 2023', Dealroom.co, 29 December 2023, https://dealroom.co/blog/european-tech-in-2023.
17 Data file: https://drive.google.com/file/d/1ROmCVORVe_HNSQ_GmF9_AQmcVcXLzSRJ/view?usp=sharing.
18 Editorial, 'Artificial Intelligence: Intelligent Planning', *The Times*, 13 January 2025, https://www.thetimes.com/comment/the-times-view/article/the-times-view-on-artificial-intelligence-intelligent-planning-9d2f3qh65.
19 *Global Innovation Index 2024: Innovation in the Face of Uncertainty* (World Intellectual Property Organization, 2024), https://doi.org/10.34667/TIND.50062.
20 Margaret Pugh O'Mara, *The Code: Silicon Valley and the Remaking of America* (Penguin Publishing Group, 2019).
21 'DIU Announces Strategic Allocation of 2024 Budget', 20 June 2024, https://www.diu.mil/latest/diu-announces-strategic-allocation-of-2024-budget-and-plan-to-scale.
22 'UK Should Have Fastest Broadband Network in Europe by 2015', GOV.UK, 4 September 2012, https://www.gov.uk/government/news/uk-should-have-fastest-broadband-network-in-europe-by-2015.
23 'The European Broadband Scorecard 2015 – Update', Ofcom, 4 March 2016, https://www.ofcom.org.uk/siteassets/resources/documents/research-

and-data/broadband-research/scorecard/2016/european-broadband-scorecard-2015-update.pdf?v=334808.
24 'FTTH/B Market Panorama in Europe', FTTH Council Europe, September 2023, https://www.ftthcouncil.eu/resources/all-publications-and-assets/2043/european-ftth-b-market-panorama-2024.
25 'Prime Minister Sets out Blueprint to Turbocharge AI', GOV.UK, 13 January 2025, https://www.gov.uk/government/news/prime-minister-sets-out-blueprint-to-turbocharge-ai.
26 William Wright and James Thornhill, 'Comparing the Asset Allocation of Global Pension Systems', New Financial, September 2024, https://www.newfinancial.org/reports/comparing-the-asset-allocation-of-global-pension-systems.
27 Connor MacDonald, 'Unleashing Capital', Policy Exchange, 8 November 2022, https://policyexchange.org.uk/wp-content/uploads/2022/11/Unleashing-Capital.pdf.
28 'Mansion House 2023', GOV.UK, 11 July 2023, https://www.gov.uk/government/collections/mansion-house-2023.
29 'Chancellor's Mansion House Reforms to Boost Typical Pension by over £1,000 a Year', GOV.UK, https://www.gov.uk/government/news/chancellors-mansion-house-reforms-to-boost-typical-pension-by-over-1000-a-year.
30 'Companies Ranked by Market Cap', CompaniesMarketCap.com, n.d., https://companiesmarketcap.com.
31 'Artificial Intelligence', ETO Research Almanac, 6 January 2025, https://almanac.eto.tech/topics/ai/#research-organizations.
32 Suleyman, *The Coming Wave*.
33 'International Scientific Report on the Safety of Advanced AI – Interim Report', UK Government, May 2024, https://assets.publishing.service.gov.uk/media/6716673b96def6d27a4c9b24/international_scientific_report_on_the_safety_of_advanced_ai_interim_report.pdf.
34 Thomas Pope and Cassia Rowland, 'Public Service Productivity', Institute for Government, 18 April 2024, https://www.instituteforgovernment.org.uk/explainer/public-service-productivity.
35 'UK Public Sector Productivity Goes from Bad to Worse, ONS Data Shows', Reuters, 3 May 2024, https://www.reuters.com/world/uk/uk-public-sector-productivity-goes-bad-worse-ons-data-shows-2024-05-03/.

36 See my full speech on the topic here (note: at the time the estimate was a 0.5% increase in productivity growth; this was later revised to 1%): 'Chancellor Jeremy Hunt's Speech at the Centre for Policy Studies', GOV.UK, 12 June 2023, https://www.gov.uk/government/speeches/chancellor-jeremy-hunts-speech-at-the-centre-for-policy-studies.

37 'UK Public Sector Workers Get Above-Inflation Pay Rises, Worth 9 Billion Pounds', Reuters, 29 July 2024, sec. United Kingdom, https://www.reuters.com/world/uk/uk-public-sector-workers-get-above-inflation-pay-rises-worth-9-billion-pounds-2024-07-29/.

38 Louise Murphy, 'A U-Shaped Legacy', Resolution Foundation, 23 March 2024, https://www.resolutionfoundation.org/app/uploads/2024/03/U-shaped-legacy.pdf.

39 'Economic and Fiscal Outlook', Office for Budget Responsibility, October 2024, https://obr.uk/docs/dlm_uploads/OBR_Economic_and_fiscal_outlook_Oct_2024.pdf.

40 Estimation by author based on data from the UK Office for National Statistics and the US Bureau of Economic Analysis.

9. A Global Vocation

1 Elizabeth L. Rhoads, 'Citizenship Denied, Deferred and Assumed: A Legal History of Racialized Citizenship in Myanmar', *Citizenship Studies* 27, no. 1 (2 January 2023): 38–58, https://doi.org/10.1080/13621025.2022.2137468.

2 Wa Lone et al., 'Massacre in Myanmar: One Grave for 10 Rohingya Men', Reuters, 8 February 2018, https://www.reuters.com/investigates/special-report/myanmar-rakhine-events/.

3 Shoon Naing and Thu Thu Aung, 'Black Hoods, Kneeling, No Sleep – Reuters Reporter Details Myanmar Custody', Reuters, 24 July 2018, https://www.reuters.com/article/world/black-hoods-kneeling-no-sleep-reuters-reporter-details-myanmar-custody-idUSKBN1KE1PD/.

4 Shoon Naing and Antoni Slodkowski, 'Myanmar Policeman Describes "Trap" to Arrest Reuters Reporter', Reuters, 20 April 2018, https://www.reuters.com/article/technology/myanmar-policeman-describes-trap-to-arrest-reuters-reporter-idUSL3N1RW4RX/.

5 Thu Thu Aung and Antoni Slodkowski, 'Myanmar Policeman Who Detailed Reuters Reporters' Entrapment Freed from Jail', Reuters, 15 February 2019, https://www.reuters.com/article/world/myanmar-policeman-who-detailed-reuters-reporters-entrapment-freed-from-jail-idUSKCN1PQ3GN/.
6 Jamie Fullerton and Jacob Goldberg, 'Reuters Reporters Jailed for Seven Years in Myanmar', *Guardian*, 3 September 2018, https://www.theguardian.com/world/2018/sep/03/myanmar-reuters-journalists-sentenced-to-seven-years-in-prison-rohingya.
7 '"The Prison Papers" Unveil in-Depth Reports on Incarcerated Journalists and Their Plight for Press Freedom', RSF, 12 September 2024, https://rsf.org/en/prison-papers-unveil-depth-reports-incarcerated-journalists-and-their-plight-press-freedom.
8 'Burma: Chronology of Aung San Suu Kyi's Detention', Human Rights Watch, 13 November 2010, https://www.hrw.org/news/2010/11/13/burma-chronology-aung-san-suu-kyis-detention.
9 Oliver Smith, 'Welcome to the World's Weirdest Capital City', *Daily Telegraph*, 14 May 2019, https://www.telegraph.co.uk/travel/destinations/asia/myanmar/articles/naypyidaw-myanmar-ghost-city/.
10 Simon Lewis and Shoon Naing, 'Two Reuters Reporters Freed in Myanmar after More than 500 Days in Jail', Reuters, 7 May 2019, https://www.reuters.com/article/world/two-reuters-reporters-freed-in-myanmar-after-more-than-500-days-in-jail-idUSKCN1SD057/.
11 Szu Ping Chan, 'Britain Topples Germany to Become Europe's Top Investment Spot', *Daily Telegraph*, 20 January 2025, https://www.telegraph.co.uk/business/2025/01/20/britain-topples-germany-to-become-europes-top-investment/.
12 'World Economic League Table 2025', CEBR.
13 'World Happiness Report 2025: People Are Much Kinder Than We Expect, Research Shows', World Happiness Report, 20 March 2025, https://worldhappiness.report/news/world-happiness-report-2025-people-are-much-kinder-than-we-expect-research-shows/.

IMAGE CREDITS

Author with President Trump, credit: author (p. 17)
Brigadier Richards, credit: RN photographer (p. 27)
Author with President Zelensky, credit: Ukrainian Presidential Press Service (p. 46)
Author with Oleg Gordievksy, credit: UK government photographer (p. 51)
Author with Wang Yi, credit: FCDO photographer (p. 54)
British Prosecuting Counsel at Nuremberg, credit: piemags/ww2archive / Alamy Stock Photo (p. 94)
James Lovelock, credit: Kathy deWitt / Alamy Stock Photo (p. 105)
Margaret Thatcher, credit: PA Images / Alamy Stock Photo (p. 123)
Author with Rishi Sunak, credit: Simon Walker / No. 10 Downing Street (p. 126)
Sir Martin Landray, credit: Graham Bagley/Oxford Population Health (p. 140)
Dame Sarah Gilbert, credit: PA Images / Alamy Stock Photo (p. 144)
Author with Nazanin Zaghari-Ratcliffe, credit: author (p. 166)
Sir Demis Hassabis, Photo: Google (p. 182)
Sir Tim Berners-Lee, credit: WENN Rights Ltd / Alamy Stock Photo (p. 187)
Wa Lone, credit: Associated Press / Alamy Stock Photo (p. 209)
Author with Aung San Suu Kyi, credit: Associated Press / Alamy Stock Photo (p. 212)
Author with Dr Henry Kissinger, credit: FCDO photographer (p. 225)

INDEX

abolition, of enslavement 168–169
Afghanistan 40–41, 74, 89
   British soldiers killed 30
   US withdrawal from 35–36
AI (Artificial Intelligence) 69, 180–185, 190–191, 194, 198–199, 203
   Chinese 63, 197
   French strength in 196
   safe use of 199
AI Safety Summit, 2023 137, 198
AIDS 97–98
Al Saud, Mohammed bin Salman 172–173
Aldrich, Michael 187
Alphabet corp. 191
AlphaFold 184
AlphaGo 183
AltaVista 192
Amazon 191
Ames, Aldrich 34
Amnesty International 170
antibiotics 147, 156
Apple corp. 191
Armed Forces, British
   in Afghanistan 30
   in Iraq 30, 40–41
   nuclear capability 39, 44–45, 117–118
   professionalism of 40–41
   Royal Air Force 40, 43
   Royal Navy 40, 42, 149, 169
   in Sierra Leone 26–30, 149–150
   size of 42
   Special Forces 29–30, 40
   technology needs 40, 43–44
Ashoori, Anoosheh 162, 167
Assad, Bashir al- 15–16
AstraZeneca 145–146, 154
Atlantic Charter 170
Attlee, Clement 227
AUKUS 43
Aung San Suu Kyi 77, 210–214
Australia 21, 51, 59, 69, 115, 137, 196, 216, 217
autocracy
   China 63
   versus democracy 61–63, 67, 80, 161, 224
   rise of 60–61
Autonomy corp. 195
Autumn Statement of 2022 10, 179
Autumn Statement of 2023 125

Babbage, Charles 185
'Baby' computer 185
Baker, David 184
Bangladesh 130, 213
BBC 60, 64–65, 77–78, 186, 231
Beijing University 197
Bell Labs 190
Belt and Road Initiative 90
Benenson, Peter 169–170
Benn, Hilary 97
Berlin, Isaiah 168
Berlin Wall, fall of 33–34, 65
Berners-Lee, Tim 186
Berry, Jake 11
Bevin, Ernest 206
Biden, Joe 31, 46, 62, 128
   discussion with Xi Jinping 60–61
   tariffs under 128
   withdrawal from Afghanistan 35
Bill of Rights 81
bin Laden, Osama 173
biodiversity 108, 115, 119
Blair, Tony 97, 113
Bletchley Park 169, 185
blood diamonds 26
Bolton, John 15–16
Bowler, James 7–8
Boyle, Danny 186
Brady, Graham 11
Braverman, Suella 74
Brexit 12–13, 18, 23, 33, 112, 125, 131, 134–136, 205, 215
British Antarctic Survey 106
'British disease' 122
British Heart Foundation 150
British Leyland 121–122

British Medical Association (BMA) 200
Brown, Gordon 113, 179
Brown, Louise 153
budgets 5–6, 9–12, 177–180, 200
Burkina Faso 109
Burt, Alistair 160
Bush, George W. 97

Cafferkey, Pauline 149
Cambridge University 150, 180–182, 190
Cameron, David 49, 71, 113, 152, 171, 194, 214
Canada 69, 137, 196, 216, 217
Cancer Research UK 150
Central African Republic 89
Centre for Economics and Business Research (CEBR) 63, 127–128, 217
Chad 109
Charles III, king 112, 119
Charnley, John 153
Charter of the International Military Tribunal 93
Chevening scholarships 73
child soldiers 25
China 63, 156–157
   AI innovation 197
   autocracy in 63
   Belt and Road Initiative 90
   British relations with 60–61
   clean energy 110, 128
   and climate change 110
   coexistence with 67
   defence spending 39–40

INDEX

demographic challenges 62
dialogue with 23
diplomacy in Asia 214
dissidents in 57–58, 81
dual circulation strategy 128
economic strengths 62–63
economy versus US
    economy 62–63, 69
executions in 167
exports 130, 135
foreign investment in 61–62
human rights 60–61, 172
Hunt negotiations with 53–60
influence in developing
    countries 91, 173–174, 215
lending 63, 90
New Cold War 67
origin of COVID 139, 141, 156
soft power 80
support for Russia 36–37
Taiwan. *see* Taiwan
tariff effects on 129
technological power 138, 188, 197
total global trade 137
Chinese Urgent Action Working
    Group 57
chlorofluorocarbons (CFCs) 103–107
Christians, persecution of 167–168
Chugg, Dan 214
Churchill, Winston 93, 170
Clarke, Ken 5
Clifford, Matt 194
climate change 19, 69, 91, 106–110, 116, 203

Climate Change Act 2008 113
Climate Change Performance
    Index 115
Climate Research Unit (CRU) 114
Clinton, Bill 71, 73–74
Clinton, Hillary 128
cloning 152
Clooney, Amal 213–214
Cockfield, Arthur, Baron
    Cockfield 133
Coffey, Thérèse 10
Cold War 33–34, 66–67, 81
Collis, Simon 173
Colossus 185
Comprehensive and Progressive
    Agreement for Trans-Pacific
    Partnership (CPTPP) 137
Convention Against Torture
    Initiative 171
COP26 111
Copernicus Climate Change
    Service 107
Corn Laws 132
corruption scores 71
COVID-19 pandemic 90, 128, 129
    death toll 146, 157
    economic cost of 157
    lockdown 139
    research in UK 139–143
    vaccine development 144–147
Crick, Francis 152
Crimea, Russian invasion of 22, 35
Cuban missile crisis 67

Darzi, Ara, Baron Darzi of
    Denham 156, 214

Davie, Tim 64–65, 78, 231
Davies, Sally 156
DeepMind 181–184, 195, 198
DeepSeek 197
defence spending. *see* spending, defence
Defense Advanced Research Projects Agency (DARPA) 49, 191
Defense Innovation Unit (DIU) 49, 191
democracy
  benefits of 224–225
  contrast with autocracy. *see* autocracy
  current events 20
  defence of 81, 100
  dependence on US 216
  disenchantment with 64
  journalism in 76
  'magic' of 51
  Myanmar 210–211
  number of countries 65–66
  preservation of 51
  South Korea 65
  UK defence of 66–67
  weakness 70
Democratic Republic of Congo 89
Denmark 114, 115, 171, 221
Department of Defense (DOD) 191
dexamethasone 142–143
Djibouti 91, 109
Doll, Richard 153

Ebola epidemic 148–150
  death rate 149
  successful intervention against 150
education. *see* universities
electric cars 110, 125, 126
Elixir Studios 181
Elizabeth II, queen 79
Elliott-Automation 186
Enigma code machine 185
Enterprise Investment Scheme (EIS) 193–194, 196
Eritrea 83–84, 86, 109
Estonia 200
  British support for 42
Ethiopia 37, 83, 89, 109
European Convention on Human Rights (ECHR) 91, 95–96, 170
European Economic Convention (EEC) 122, 124–125
European Union
  regulation of AI 199
  single market 133
  tariffs under 126, 128
  total global trade 134–137
Extinction Rebellion (XR) 114

Facebook 181, 194
Falun Gong 57
Farman, Joe 106
Farrar, Jeremy 139
Ferguson, Niall 132
FIFA 76–77
Finland 221
Fleming, Alexander 153
Fleming Centre 156

INDEX

Fordham, Simon 29
Foreign Affairs Committee 160
Forum on China–Africa
    Cooperation 90
Fox, Charles James 169
France 69
    abolition of the death
        penalty 171
    aid for Ebola in Guinea 149
    anti-immigration 88
    and climate movement 114
    defence spending 32, 39–40
    as donor of aid 98
    embassies 67
    influence in Africa 90
    nuclear power use 117
    pandemic 142
    protectionist policies 123
    recent challenges 20
    relationship with UK 69
    technology investments 196–197
Franklin, Rosalind 152
freedom, artistic 79
Freedom House (think tank) 65
Freeland, Chrystia 15, 174
French, Rita 175
Fukuyama, Francis 34

Gaza 78, 90
General Agreement on Tariffs and
    Trade (GATT) 132
General Data Protection
    Regulation (GDPR) 128
genetics 69, 144, 151–153
Geneva Conventions 169
Genomics England 151–152

Georgia, Russian invasion of 22,
    35
Germany 35, 51, 69, 76, 88, 127,
    188, 217
    COVID-19 vaccine 145–146
    defence spending 32, 39
    as donor of aid 98
    and human rights 171
    protectionist policies 129
    robotics 197
Ghebreyesus, Tedros
    Adhanom 152
Gilbert, Sarah 143–145
glaciers, reduction of 109
Gleneagles summit 97
Global Clean Power Alliance 118
Global Green Finance Index 118
Global Justice Now 114
Global Warming Policy
    Foundation 114
globalisation 128–130, 147, 156
Goering, Hermann 93–94
'golden triangle' 182, 190
Google 182, 191–195
Gorbachev, Mikhail 33, 175
Gordievsky, Oleg 33–34, 38
Gore, Al 119
Great Reform Act 81
Greenland 109
Gurr, Doug 119

Hadley Centre for Climate Science
    and Services 113, 114
Hague, William 65, 221
Hall, Tony 78
Hammond, Philip 7, 162

Harris, Kamala 64
Harry, Duke of Sussex 79
Harwell CADET computer 186
Hassabis, Demis 180–185, 198
Health and Social Care Select Committee 3
Heaney, Steve 28
Hedges, Matthew 174
Helm, Dieter 118
Henry Jackson Society 39
Hewlett Packard 195
Hezbollah 162
Hill, Austin Bradford 153
Hitler, Adolph 129
Holocaust 95
Hong Kong 68
  democracy in 55–56, 60
Horby, Peter 141
Hotcourses co. 192
Houthi movement 174
human genome project 151
human rights 157–166
concept of 170
disability rights 171
executions 167
public pressure 169
religious persecution 167–168, 208
same-sex marriage 171
UK as advocate for 167–168, 171–174, 214–216
women's rights 172, 175
Human Rights Act 96
Hunt, Charlie 4, 179
Hunt, Jeremy
  as Chancellor 3–17, 41–42, 118, 125, 177–180, 202, 206
  in China 55–57
  as Culture Secretary 76, 186, 192–193
  as entrepreneur 192
  experience in government 18–19
  as Foreign Secretary 14–16, 31–32, 49, 74, 99, 159–167, 174, 205–207, 211–214
  as Health Secretary 58, 148–149, 151, 155, 161
  meeting with Volodomyr Zelensky 46–47
  as MP 97
Hunt, Lucia 1–7, 178–179
hydroxychloroquine 142

immigration. *see also* migration, mass
  anti-immigration riots 86
  asylum 95
  climate change 108
  and foreign aid 90, 98
  foreign policy 99–100
  hostility towards 88
  laws 91
  legal framework 101–102
  levels 101
  resistance to 87–88
  strategies to limit 89
India 130
  defence spending 39
  exports 130
  neutrality in Ukraine war 37
  protectionist policies 128
  purchasing power 89
  Russian oil and gas 36

INDEX

Inflation Reduction Act 128
Inn Din massacre 208
Intel 194
Intelligence services, British 40
International Conference on Military Trials 93
International Court of Justice 171, 212
International Covenant on Civil and Political Rights 170
International Criminal Court 170–171
International Development Select Committee 97
International Monetary Fund (IMF) 21, 62, 118
International Panel on Climate Change (IPCC) 110
internet freedom scores 71, 217
Iran 81, 159–165, 172, 173, 175, 215
Ireland 73, 104
ISIS 171
Israel 16, 48, 167, 215
   cyber security 197
   technology development 191–192

J. Lyons and Co. 185
Jackson, Robert 92, 94
Japan 51, 69, 74, 121–123, 126, 137, 216
   as donor of aid 98
   robotics 197
   spending on COVID 146
   UK–Japan Digital Partnership 137
Javid, Sajid 2, 7
Jenner, Edward 153
Jenner Institute 143
Jenrick, Robert 7
Jews
   migration laws to protect 95
   persecution of 168
Johnson, Boris 3, 46, 113, 160, 166, 221
Jordan 74
journalism, British 76–78
journalists, threats to 167–174
Jumper, John 184
Just Stop Oil 114

Kabbah, Ahmad Tejan 30
Kallay, Foday 28
Kamajor militia 28
Kelly, John 17
Kennedy, Robert F. Jr. 148
Kenya 86, 97, 99
Kew Gardens 119
Khartoum massacre 84
Khashoggi, Jamal, murder of 172–173
Kissinger, Henry 22–23, 225
Kwarteng, Kwasi 8
Kyaw Soe Oo 207–210, 213
Kyoto Protocol 113

Lammy, David 118
Landray, Martin 139–143
Lassa fever 147
Lawson, Nigel 114, 179
Le Pen, Marine 88
Lebanon 65, 78, 162
Legg, Shane 181

283

LGBTQ+ 92, 185
Li, Keqiang 58
Li, Wenzu 57, 59
Lind, James 140
Lionhead Studios 181
Litvinenko, Alexander 35
Liu, Xiaobo 59
Liu, Yandong 58–59
Liverpool School of Tropical Medicine 152
Llewellyn, Edward, Baron Llewellyn of Steep 214
Lockheed Martin 40, 190–191
Lombardelli, Clare 8
Lomé peace agreement 26
London 2012 Summer Olympics 186
London School of Economics 119
London School of Hygiene and Tropical Medicine (LSHTM) 152
Lovelace, Ada 185
Lovelock, James 101–106, 110–111, 114
Lynch, Mike 195
Lyons, Nicholas 196
Lyons Electronic Office (LEO) 185

Ma, Jack 62
McCallum, Ken 64
McDonald, Simon 206
McKinsey 194
McLeod, Kristen 125
Macron, Emmanuel 46, 88
Madagascar 109
Magna Carta 81, 169

Major, John 113
Malawi 89
Mali 89, 109
Mandela, Nelson 163, 175, 210
Mansion House reforms 196
Marburg virus 147
Marchenko, Serhiy 47
Margolyes, Miriam 6
Marshall Plan 99
Mauritania 109
Maxwell Fyfe, David 91–95
May, Theresa 3, 14–16, 111, 113, 205, 221
measles 147
Medicines and Healthcare products Regulatory Agency (MHRA) 145
Merkel, Angela 206
MERS 144, 147
Meta 191
Microsoft 191
migration, mass 70, 101–102. *see also* immigration
  dangers of 84–86
  statistics 86–87
Mill, John Stuart 168
Min Aung Hlaing 210
Ministry of Defence (MOD) 162
Moavero Milanesi, Enzo 111
Molina, Mario 104–106
Montreal Protocol 106–107
Mordaunt, Penny 162
Morrish family 161
most favoured nation status 132
Mounstephen, Philip 168
Mpox 147

INDEX

Murdoch, Rupert 76
music, British 78
Musk, Elon 188, 200–201
Muslims, persecution of 168, 208
Myanmar 175, 207

NASA 103, 106, 107, 191
National Health Service (NHS) 3, 141–142, 149, 152–155, 200
National Institute for Health and Care Research 141
Natural Environment Research Council 104
Natural History Museum 108, 119
Nazi party 51, 92–94, 185
Netanyahu, Benjamin 191–192
Netherlands, the 20, 115, 221
  as donor of aid 98
Niger 90, 109
Nigeria 99, 109
Nissan corporation, in the UK 121–126
Nobel Prizes 150, 152, 184, 210
North Atlantic Treaty Organization (NATO) 14–15, 32–33, 42–45, 49, 206, 227
  change to 31
  as peace-making organisation 38–39
  preservation of 49
  response to Ukraine 36
  spending as percentage of GDP 45–50
  strengthening of 51
  UK armed forces in 218
North Korea 42, 167, 172

Norway 114, 221
  as donor of aid 98
Nouri, Hamid 171
Nuremberg trials 93–94
Nvidia 191

Obama, Barack 31
Okuma, Masataka 121–122, 124
Operation Barras 29
Operation Gritrock 149
Operation Palliser 26–28, 32
Osborne, George 7, 179, 193
Oxford AstraZeneca vaccine 145–146
Oxford University 71, 74, 100, 143, 146, 150, 154, 182, 190, 210
Oxford Vaccine Group 144
ozone layer 104–106

Paris Agreement 107, 110–111, 114
Partygate scandal 12
Pathfinder Platoon 28
pension funds, British 196
People to People's Dialogue 58
persecution, religious 167–168, 208
Pfizer-BioNTech mRNA vaccine 145–146
Pollard, Andrew 144
power, soft 71, 74, 80–81, 201–202, 216, 218
press, free 73, 167, 174, 221
productivity 131, 134–138, 150, 194, 200–201, 228
Putin, Vladimir 32–36, 68

Qwen 197

285

Raine, June 145
Randomised Evaluation of COVID-19 Therapy (RECOVERY) Trial 142–143
randomised trials 140–141
Ratcliffe, Richard 159–161, 165
Reeves, Rachel 5, 194
Refugee Convention 95–96
refugees 83–86, 95–96, 101–102, 213. *see also* immigration
Regeneron 143
Reuters 208, 213
Revolutionary Guard, Iran (IRGC) 163
Rhodes scholarship 73
Ricardo, David 127, 131
Richards, David 26–28
Ridley, Harold 153
Rift Valley fever 147
Robertson, Peter 39
Robinson, Christina 1, 161
Rohingya 208, 213
Roosevelt, Eleanor 171
Roosevelt, Franklin Delano 170
Rowland, F. Sherwood 104
Royal Free Hospital 149, 183
Royal Irish Regiment 28–29
Rudd, Amber 74
Rudd, Kevin 70
rule of law 37, 65, 68, 93–94, 94, 217
Rumsfeld, Donald 31
Russia
  anti-French propaganda in Africa 90
  bribery 77
  defence spending 39
  dialogue with 23
  diplomats expelled 35
  energy reserves 138
  fake news 64–65
  influence in developing countries 91
  invasion of Crimea and Georgia 22, 35
  invasion of Ukraine 12, 18, 22, 36, 40, 46, 49–50, 68, 130
  Montreal Protocol 106
  opposition leaders 81
  and Paris agreement 110
  power block 37
  sanctions against 36
  threat of nuclear weapons 45
  wildfires in 107

St Johnston, Dina 186
St Mary's Hospital, London 156
Sakharov, Andrei 176
Salafism 173
Sanger, Frederick 152
Sankoh, Foday 28
SARS-CoV-2 virus. *see* COVID-19 pandemic
Saudi Arabia 110
  and Paris agreement 110
  relationship with UK 172–174
  women's rights in 175
Schmidt, Eric 191
Scholar, Tom 7
security, laboratory 156–157
Seed Enterprise Investment Scheme (SEIS) 194, 196
Senegal 109

INDEX

Serum Institute 129
Shah of Iran 162, 164
Shamkhani, Ali 163
Shapps, Grant 118
Sharma, Alok 113
Shawcross, Hartley 93
Shockley, William 190
Sierra Leone 149, 175
   civil war 25–26, 41
   death penalty abolition 175
   and Paris agreement 110
   UK work against Ebola 149–150
Silicon Valley 48–49, 101,
   180–182, 185, 190, 193, 199
Silva, Rohan 193
Singapore 74, 130, 156, 193
Sino-British Joint Declaration 60
Skripal, Sergei 35
small modular reactors
   (SMRs) 117
Smith, Adam 131, 138
Smoot–Hawley Tariff Act 129
smuggling, human 87–89, 95, 99
Snow, John 153
Society for the Abolition of the
   Slave Trade 168
solar energy 119
South Africa 37, 99
   democracy in 63–64
South Korea 51, 137, 193
   democracy 65, 69
   robotics 197
spending, defence 14, 19, 22,
   31–33, 38–41, 44–48, 49–51,
   67, 98, 139, 190–191, 198–203
Sputnik 1 190

Stalin, Josef 206
Stanford Industrial Park 190
Starmer, Keir 22, 45, 96, 113
Stern, Nick 119
Stock, Kathleen 74
Streams (app) 183
Sudan 83–84, 86, 109, 175
Suffragettes 81, 169
Suleyman, Mustafa 181, 198
Sunak, Rishi 2, 12, 45–46, 113,
   126, 198
Sunderland Nissan plant 124–126
Supreme Leader of Iran 163
Sweden 114, 171, 221
Switzerland 137, 186, 221, 224
Syria 15–16, 89, 162, 175

Tahbaz, Morad 162, 167
Taiwan 137, 193
   biosafety 156–157
   defence spending 48
   democracy in 68
   flashpoint with China 68
tariffs. *see* trade, free
Tatmadaw 208, 210, 212
technology
   and Brexit 134, 136–137
   and climate change 110–111
   dependence on China 69, 128
   energy needs 117
   investment in 196
   military 42–43
   as opportunity 14, 19–20, 48,
   138, 178–180, 199–202, 207,
   224–225, 228
   Silicon Valley. *see* Silicon Valley

technology (*cont.*)
  trade agreements for 137–138
  UK tech sector 79, 185, 187–199, 202–203, 216–217
  vaccines. *see* vaccines
temperature, global 107–108
Terman, Fred 190
Tesla 191
Texas 119
Thatcher, Margaret 33, 112, 119–124, 131, 175
  on climate change 112–113
  against protectionism 133
Thiel, Peter 181
Thunberg, Greta 114
Tibet 68
Tigray War 37
Tocilizumab 143
Tora, Summia 74
Tracey, Irene 190
trade, free 123, 126–128, 131–138
Trump, Donald J. 14–18, 45, 66, 110, 148, 216
  anti-globalisation 64, 128
  anti-immigration 88
  COVID-19 pandemic 142
  isolationism 31–32, 37, 70
  and NATO spending 45, 50
  opinion on Brexit 18
  pull out from Iran deal 163
  and Saudi Arabia 173
  tariffs under 62, 127, 129, 134–137
  unpredictability of 68
  view on China 61–62, 127
  and Vladimir Putin 35

withdrawal from Paris Agreement 110
withdrawal of US from WHO 148, 156–157
Truss, Liz 1–4, 8, 10–11, 166
Tsinghua University 197
Tsuchiya, Toshiaki 124
Turing, Alan 185–186
Tyndall Centre for Climate Change Research 114

Uchida, Makoto 125–126
UK–Japan Digital Partnership 137
Ukraine 175
  British military aid for 40–41, 46–48
  neutral countries in war 90
  Russian invasion of 12, 18, 22, 31–32, 34–37, 43–45, 49–50, 67–68, 81, 116, 118, 148, 175
  supply chain risks of 128, 130
UN Conference on Environment and Development 113
UN Environment Programme 107
UN Framework Convention on Climate Change 113
UN High Council on Refugees (UNHCR) 84
UN Human Development Index 220–221
UN Human Rights Council 175
UN Security Council 221
UN War Crimes Commission 92
UN World Food Programme 99
'unicorn' tech companies 187–188
United Arab Emirates (UAE) 172, 174

INDEX

United Kingdom
  aid for Ebola in Sierra Leone 149
  climate change performance index 114–115
  defence spending. *see* spending, defence
  democracy in 71
  dispute arbitration 133–134
  economy 217–218
  emissions 217
  energy reserves 122
  financial services sector 197–198
  foreign investment in 131
  free trade. *see* trade, free
  freedom of media 217
  funding sources 199
  as human rights advocate 55–61, 92, 96, 159–167, 168, 170–175, 205–216, 207, 221
  locally supplied oil and gas 117
  low corruption 217
  over-centralisation of 70
  productivity. *see* productivity
  reduction in use of coal 116
  total global trade 137
  welfare system 201
United Nations 28
United States Armed Forces
  in Afghanistan 30–31
  in Iraq 30–31
United States of America 196, 217
  aid for Ebola in Liberia 149
  economy 62
  funding for NATO 32–33
  and human rights 171
  isolationism 31–32, 224
  low-cost energy in 116
  polarisation in 70
  support for democracy 21, 216
  technology companies 197
  trade deficits 127
Universal Declaration of Human Rights 171
universities
  academic freedom 76
  Chinese 63, 197
  financial situation of 74, 199, 201–202
  health research 155–156
  influence of 61, 71–72, 150–151, 216–217
  international students 71, 73–74, 75
  partnership with industry 184–185
  ranking of 14, 22, 76, 101, 150, 182, 197, 217–218
  and tech startups 187–190
  technological advancement 188, 197–198
University College London (UCL) 150, 181, 183
USAID, dismantling of 98

vaccines 98, 124, 128
  COVID-19 14, 90, 129, 142, 145–148
  research in UK 155–156
Vance, J.D. 32
Vaughan Programming Services 186
Victoria Falls 109
Vietnam 139, 167

Wa Lone 207–210, 213–214
Wagner Group 90
Waldegrave, William 221
Wang, Qiaoling 57
Wang, Quanzhang 57–60
Wang, Yi 53, 55–56
Wang, Yu 57
Watson, James 152
Wellcome Sanger Institute 146, 151
Wellcome Trust 139, 150
West Side Boys militia 28–30
White Helmets 15–16
Whitty, Chris 144
Wilberforce, William 168–169
Wilkins, Maurice 152
William, Prince of Wales 79
Williamson, Gavin 162
women's rights 172, 175. *see also* Suffragettes
Woodward, Barbara 56–57
World Bank 62, 86, 118
World Happiness Report 220–221
World Health Organization (WHO) 146–149, 152, 155
World Patient Safety Day 155
World Trade Organization (WTO) 130, 132, 137
World Values Survey 64
World War I 36, 68
World War II 31, 66, 92, 132, 185
World Wide Web, invention of 186–187

Xi, Jinping 58, 60–61, 90, 197
Xinjiang 68, 175
Xu, Yan 57

Yahoo 192
Yazidis, persecution of 168
Yemen 83, 162, 174

Zaghari-Ratcliffe, Nazanin 159–167
Zambezi river 109
Zambia 109
Zarif, Javad 163
Zelensky, Volodomyr 46–47
Zhang, Yongzhen 144
Zimbabwe 109
Zuckerberg, Mark 194